# GRAHAM KERR'S SMART COOKING

# GRAHAM KERR'S SMART COOKING

## Graham Kerr

DOUBLEDAY
New York  London  Toronto  Sydney  Auckland

PUBLISHED BY DOUBLEDAY
a division of Bantam Doubleday Dell Publishing Group, Inc.
666 Fifth Avenue, New York, New York 10103

DOUBLEDAY and the portrayal of an anchor with a dolphin
are registered trademarks of Doubleday,
a division of Bantam Doubleday Dell Publishing Group, Inc.

■

LIBRARY OF CONGRESS CATALOGING IN PUBLICATION DATA
Kerr, Graham.
Graham Kerr's smart cooking / Graham Kerr. – 1st ed.
     p.    cm.
   Includes index.
   1. Cookery. 2. Low-cholesterol diet–Recipes. 3. Low-fat diet–Recipes.
   I. Title. II. Title: Smart cooking.
TX714.K48  1991
641.5'63 – dc20      91-21525 CIP

ISBN 0-385-42074-9
Copyright © by Graham Kerr

■

NUTRIENT CALCULATION:  Nutrient calculation was performed using
the Minnesota Nutrition Data System (NDS) software developed by the
Nutrition Coordinating Center, University of Minnesota, Minneapolis, MN.
Food Database version 3A; Nutrition Database version 18.

PHOTOGRAPHY:  Allyson Gofton and Alan Gillard – Auckland, New Zealand

GRAPHIC DESIGN:  Connie Lunde – Seattle, Washington

ILLUSTRATION:  Sandy Silverthorne – Eugene, Oregon

ART DIRECTOR:  Carol Malcolm-Russo, Doubleday

# Acknowledgments

Natural bookbirth isn't done alone - it is a team effort and I want to record my thanks, appreciation and affection for everyone who has contributed so much:

Robert Prince and Cynthia Morse, my food associates; Christine Rylko and Brenda Bryant for computer analysis and overall systems management; John McLean for his "eagle eye"; Allyson Gofton for photographic foodstyling; Alan Gillard for photography; Sandy Silverthorne for the whimsical drawings; Connie Lunde for laying out each and every page; John McEwen for tenacity; Natalie Hall, my wonderful secretary; Judith Kern, wielder of the mighty editorial pencil at Doubleday; every one of our special friends at KING TV in Seattle, who tasted every dish. To my much loved son, Andy, for making my time go further and my beloved wife, lifelong friend and producer, Treena, to whom I now dedicate this book. Eat and be well!

Graham Kerr
September 1991

# Table of Contents

# Introduction

*T*his book is about celebration and about being truly happy because we care enough to make some changes in the way we eat.

I'm a food man from way back. My parents were hoteliers; my earliest friends were chefs and waiters. My business was, and is, to please. For 26 years I did this by thinking of food only as it contributed to our sensual pleasure. "After all," I reasoned, "if it doesn't look, smell, taste, and feel fantastic, it won't bring them back for a second visit."

For years I made "good business" by applying this principle of sensual enhancement. *The senses were everything, the only thing!* From time to time I did get one or two letters pleading, "don't you use a little too much butter and cream?" My serious answer to that was, "Madam, you could get run over by a bus and just think what you would have missed!"

And then came the jolt. My wife, Treena, suddenly had serious heart problems. She hadn't been run over by a bus but she had been buttered and creamed by the way we had been eating!

I began to develop a whole new approach to food. I became preoccupied with what food *did* to us rather than how it looked and satisfied.

I was obsessed with using *less* fat, *less* sugar, *less* alcohol, *less* salt, *less* artificial color and flavor, *less* processing, *less* restructuring. More whole grains, fresh fruits and vegetables ... all biodynamically organic! What had been smooth and succulent became grainy; what had been soft and velvety became thin. Inviting aromas disappeared. Colors faded to earthtones, the less to encourage a lust attack! So overwhelming was the evidence of risk that science outsmarted the senses and, as Julia Child puts it, "food became medicine."

This couldn't continue; my entire family observed that "food used to be so much fun but now all the joy of eating has gone." Having successfully removed everything that looked even remotely risky, I was faced with creating at least a partial return of the sensual enhancement. It was either fix it up or eat alone!

I took time to make these changes so that what we ate would delight and not destroy. My first task was to consider the senses and their individual roles in our enjoyment of food.

We enjoy food with our senses: sight, smell, taste, touch, and even sound. No wonder food preferences are so hard to change! I broke *taste* down into six basic groups: salt, sweet, sour, bitter, picante (spicehot), and mouthroundfulness - the sensation of fat/smooth.

I saw that salt, sweet, and fat/smooth could be hard to change because each seemed to say "Please Sir, I *demand* some more," whereas sour, bitter, and spicehot appeared to be self-limiting and less risky for most people.

we want more!!

The big question was, could I minimize the intrinsic desire for salt, sweet, and fat by maximizing the sour, bitter, and spicehot categories and enhancing those flavors with warm aromas, vivid colors, and varied textures?

In short, could I create a sensual smoke-screen that would allow me to remove the excessive use of salt, sugar, and fat without a loss of *overall* enjoyment? This was a terrific challenge!

I eventually shortened this idea to the one word *MINIMAX*. By combining the abbreviations *MINI* and *MAX* I was able to say that healthy alternative styles of cooking need both risk reduction and flavor enhancement, and that this should always be considered one integrated activity to - "minimize risk, maximize flavor."

minimax

I applied the *MINIMAX* concept to the moderate-to-high risk recipes of my past and gradually developed a kind of framework that allowed me total freedom to create *within* its limitations.

**My goals were as follows:**

■ To serve smaller portions of a wider variety of fresh foods, and to achieve this by increasing aromas, colors, and textures to offset taste and volume changes.

■ To reduce refined carbohydrates and to increase complex carbohydrates; that is, to eat fewer refined flour and sugar products, especially filled bakery items, and more fruit, vegetables, whole grains, peas, beans, and lentils.

■ To eat less meat, fish, and poultry (no more than a total of 6 ounces per day) and more peas, beans, lentils, whole grains, low-fat dairy products, seeds, and pastas.

■ To use less oil/fat in salads and sauces, especially for pastas, and to eat only small amounts of polyunsaturated margarines on breads and muffins.

■ To use fewer whole eggs (3-4 egg yolks a week for healthy folk) and less saturated fat from all animal protein and from tropical oils (palm, coconut etc).

■ To moderate the use of alcohol by substituting fruit juices or new de-alcoholized wines and by adding soda to ordinary table wines.

■ To decrease the use of sodium by eating fewer packaged and prepared foods that are high in sodium, by removing salt from the table, and by increasing the use of citrus juices, fresh herbs, and spices, which I call "bright notes."

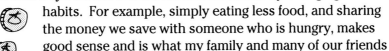

■ To read nutrition labels and ingredient lists on food packages and to look for those that use less fat, saturated fat, cholesterol, and sodium.

■ To allow the proper atmosphere for digestion by eating fewer "fast food" meals and enjoying more time with friends and family at the table.

■ To find ways we can benefit the less fortunate by changing our eating habits. For example, simply eating less food, and sharing the money we save with someone who is hungry, makes good sense and is what my family and many of our friends have done for years. Our own non-profit, educational corporation can provide you with information on how to begin the process yourself. If interested, please contact Creative Lifestyle International, P.O. Box 504, Tacoma, Washington 98401.

All of these goals have been applied to every single recipe in this book, and each *apparent* restriction has forced me to think differently about how and even why I cook.

By examining ideas, techniques, and recipes, one can get the measure of how they taste and look, and rework them to retain what is "good" while applying *MINIMAX* standards to reduce their potential risk.

The occasional Fettucini Alfredo or chocolate cake isn't going to cause an immediate disaster, but a semi-regular diet of these high-risk foods has a cumulative effect. You will not learn to enjoy the aromas, colors, and textures of healthy foods, and could face a serious health risk.

Food *is* fun. It gives pleasure to the senses. By placing limits on that pleasure, one invites rebellion. We tend to do ourselves damage just to declare ourselves *free!* What I discovered within my own family is that a clear understanding of the issues brings about not only acquiescence but an extraordinary enthusiasm and desire to pass on the benefits to others. This is why it is important to me that you think of these *MINIMAX* suggestions as issues and ideas, *not* absolutes. Each idea is an option, an alternative, a choice that you can make only when you understand why so that you can explain your decision to yourself and to others.

Our whole family chose to understand *before* we changed and, as a result, the changes have meant lower food costs, smaller portions, fresher food, weight loss, and consistent energy. We've also grown to enjoy the clean, crisp tastes that rely more on aroma, color, and texture than fats, salts, and sugars. In fact, we now prefer them to our *velvet memories!*

The most important first step in any decision is to know our own special circumstances - those you inherit in your physical makeup from your parents, and those you acquire from the way you were brought up to eat.

Your doctor will be able to assess your present exposure to inherited risk and, by inquiring about your parents and siblings, will form a reasonably accurate profile accompanied by some sensible recommendations. However, only you will know about your *traditional* eating habits.

Have your doctor give you a thorough physical exam. Discuss your family health problems and ask him questions about appropriate measures to adopt. Show him this book and ask which of the *MINIMAX* numbers that accompany each recipe should be your maximum level ... for example, how many fat grams to consume each day? What percentage of calories from fat?

Write a list of *all* your favorite comfort foods, the ones that bring to mind some warm memories of the past. From this list you will see where your "traditions" may need some modification!

The problem with permanent change is that we replace the known with the unknown. This is especially hard if we really like a soft, creamy wine sauce and don't like the sound of non-fat yogurt and cornstarch taking its place! Please hold on to your culture and especially your sense and style of hospitality as *principles*, but break the mold into which these wonderful attributes are often poured.

Every *comfort food* recipe has its emotional attachments. You might list yours and try to separate the tradition from the ingredients. A perfect example is the Swiss Fondue, where the idea of stirring the pot with friends is great but the recipe is loaded with fat. Please *keep* the tradition, but innovate with the ingredients.

I've done this dozens of times in this book.

## AROMA

*I*t is the aroma that fills the space between the plate and your head. In this *apparent* emptiness wafts most of the real art of cooking. Just hold your nose and eat and you'll see how vital aromas are!

Volatile oils, esters, and essences are the perfumes of the plate and come from many sources but none so concentrated and complex as from herbs and spices. As with any "perfume," these special aromas will fade in time, and this is especially so when some herbs are dried and some spices

are ground.  If it is possible for you to grow
your own herbs, then please, *please* do it!
The second best alternative is to purchase
fresh herbs from your produce department.
If you buy them dried, put the purchase
date on the cap.  Keep them in a closed cupboard and check them for
aroma after six months.  If they seem to have lost their essential pun-
gency, you had better *replace* them rather than risk spoiling a relatively
expensive recipe with a few cents worth of "chaff."

Spices work the same way.  If pre-ground they too will rapidly
deteriorate.  This is why pepper is freshly ground by waiters in
restaurants where the food matters.  I use a small high speed
electric "chopping mill" to powder my spices when I need
them.  This works very well for the *Garam masala*
" warming spices" that are added to Indian dishes just
before serving (page 111) and the popular *creole*
seasonings that add warmth and depth (page 50).
Essentially these little "mills" work like the old pestle
and mortar but in a fraction of the time, and they are
well worth the investment.

## DE-ALCOHOLIZED WINES

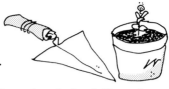

$\mathcal{D}$e-alcoholized wine is made the way wine is usually made, after which
the alcohol is removed.

Until recently, the alcohol was extracted by heating the wine and
evaporating the alcohol; however, this changed the way
the wines tasted, in part because it changed their
aroma.  Now there is a new invention, rather like the
desalinization system that removes salt from seawater.
This reverse osmosis "pump" removes all the odorless
water and alcohol.  The water is then replaced and the
characteristic flavors of the grapes remain substantially the same.

De-alcoholized wine is *different* from wines with
alcohol.  The warm bite that alcohol brings, together
with its ability to age a wine, makes it a unique and
living thing that I enjoyed from my youth through my gourmet days.
I admire and celebrate the skills of competent wine makers and have
no wish to denigrate their ability or to ban their products; however,
I do want to find creative alternatives for those who are at risk.

I use good de-alcoholized wines, especially those bottled in the Napa Valley of Northern California, because I won't cook with a wine that I wouldn't drink with pleasure, other than those specially concentrated and seasoned for recipe use. De-alcoholized wine provides aroma, color, and is, in my opinion, indispensable. I am asked often, "what if I haven't got a de-alcoholized wine? Can I use a regular white or red?" My answer is always the same, "De-alcoholized wines are *my* personal choice. Please make your own decision. Good wines with alcohol will work just as well, and in any event, within a few minutes most of the alcohol will evaporate!"

## MEAT IN THE MINOR KEY

*A* great deal of risk and added expense comes from the amount of meat we eat. Meat comes complete with both saturated fat and cholesterol, and while it is an excellent source of protein, we simply do not have to consume it in such pioneer portions!

In the "old days" I would suggest 2 pounds of raw meat for a four portion casserole (8 ounces per head). I first reduced this to 6 ounces, then to 4 ounces, and every now and then down to 2. This puts "meat in the minor key." Obviously there is an immediate visual change. Where meat was the center of attraction, it now becomes either the co-star or the understudy.

In order to fill the plate, other foods will become the stars; foods that have shape, size, texture, and the natural bulk to satisfy visually as well as to provide energy. This, of course, will mean more vegetables, more beans, whole grains, and pasta, all of which need to be beautifully cooked.

## FRESH AND BEST IN SEASON

*W*herever you live, the chances are that vegetables and fruits also grow. When they reach prime season in your area, they are not only less expensive but they taste great! Whenever you add good *fresh* fruit and good *fresh* vegetables to your menu, you add good health and good taste at lower cost.

The following list includes all the popular vegetables in their proper major season. All vegetables are in 3 1/2 ounce (100 gram) portions and are fresh prior to being cooked. Please use the chart as a guide to your selection.

# Vegetable Chart

| VEGETABLE | CALORIES | PROTEIN | COOKING METHODS & TIME IN MINUTES |
|---|---|---|---|
| **SPRING** | | | |
| Artichokes | 41 | 2.16 | Steam – 30, Pressure – 10 |
| Asparagus | 26 | 2.74 | Steam – 10, Pressure – 2 |
| Beet Greens | 16 | 0.89 | Steam – 20, Bag Boil – 20 |
| Chard | 16 | 1.54 | Steam – 20, Bag Boil – 20 |
| Collards | 16 | 1.28 | Steam – 20, Bag Boil – 20 |
| Corn | 82 | 3.05 | Steam – 8, Pressure – 5, Bag Boil – 10 |
| Cress *(Water)* | 9 | 1.84 | Salads |
| Dandelion Greens | 14 | 1.10 | Steam – 3 |
| Endive | 17 | 1.25 | Salads |
| Kale | 15 | 1.21 | Steam – 25, Pressure – 3 |
| Lettuce | 16 | 1.62 | Salads |
| Lima Beans *(Fresh)* | 101 | 6.13 | Steam – 3, Pressure – 25, Bag Boil – 30 |
| Mustard Greens | 18 | 1.00 | Steam – 3 |
| Peas | 40 | 3.14 | Steam – 12, Pressure – 14, Bag Boil – 35 |
| Radishes | 17 | 0.60 | Salads |
| Spinach | 22 | 2.42 | Steam – 8, Bag Boil – 10, Salads |
| Turnip Greens | 15 | 0.85 | Steam – 20 |
| **SUMMER** | | | |
| Beans *(Green)* | 25 | 1.29 | Steam – 15, Pressure – 3, Bag Boil – 18 |
| Beans *(Yellow Wax)* | 25 | 1.29 | Steam – 3, Pressure – 3, Bag Boil – 18 |
| Beets | 30 | 1.02 | Bake – 45, Pressure – 14 |
| Celery | 14 | 0.46 | Steam – 20, Pressure – 3, Casserole – 60 |
| Cabbage | 20 | 0.92 | Steam – 8, Pressure – 8, Salads |
| Cabbage *(Chinese)* | 12 | 1.53 | Steam – 3, Pressure – 6 |
| Cucumber | 13 | 0.54 | Salads |
| Eggplant | 26 | 0.78 | Bag Boil – 15, Casserole – 45 |
| Kohlrabi | 29 | 1.80 | Steam – 20, Pressure – 6 |
| Okra | 41 | 2.29 | Steam – 15 |
| Pea Pods | 40 | 3.14 | Steam – 5, Pressure – 2, Bag Boil – 7 |
| Pepper *(Green)* | 17 | 0.60 | Steam – 5, Casserole – 30, Salads |
| Squash *(Summer)* | 17 | 0.77 | Steam – 5, Pressure – 5 |
| **AUTUMN** | | | |
| Broccoli | 28 | 3.10 | Steam – 10, Pressure – 2 |
| Brussels Sprouts | 45 | 3.86 | Steam – 10, Pressure – 3, Bag Boil – 12 |
| Cauliflower | 18 | 1.56 | Steam – 30, Pressure – 5, Bag Boil – 20 |
| Parsnips | 83 | 1.35 | Bag Boil – 27, Bake – 60 |
| Squash *(Winter)* | 33 | 0.76 | Bake – 75, Pressure – 10 |
| Sweet Potato | 80 | 1.34 | Bake – 60, Pressure – 10 |
| **WINTER** | | | |
| Artichokes *(Jerusalem)* | 91 | 1.81 | Steam – 25, Bake – 45, Bag Boil – 30 |
| Rutabaga | 32 | 1.02 | Steam – 5, Pressure – 5, Bake – 60 |
| Squash *(Winter)* | 33 | 0.76 | Pressure – 10, Bake – 75 |
| Sweet Potato | 80 | 1.34 | Pressure – 10, Bake – 60 |
| Turnip | 17 | 0.67 | Steam – 20, Pressure – 5, Bake – 60 |

| VEGETABLE | CALORIES | PROTEIN | COOKING METHODS & TIME IN MINUTES |
|---|---|---|---|
| **ALL YEAR** | | | |
| Bean Sprouts | 10 | 1.19 | Steam – 3, Bag Boil – 5, Salads |
| Carrots | 41 | 1.00 | Steam – 20, Pressure *(Whole)* – 6, Pressure *(Sliced)* – 3 |
| Garlic | 149 | 6.36 | Seasoning |
| Green Onions | 25 | 1.74 | Steam – 5, Salads |
| Leek | 11 | 0.80 | Steam – 15, Pressure – 5, Bake – 45 |
| Mushroom | 19 | 1.50 | Raw in Salads |
| Onion | 24 | 0.76 | Steam – 6, Pressure – 6, Bag Boil – 20, Bake – 60 |
| Potatoes | 104 | 2.18 | Steam – 10, Pressure – 25, Bake – 90 |

## READING LABELS

*A*lmost every processed or packaged food has a label that carries nutritional information. The problem is that few people know how to apply the information to their lives.

The first thing you should learn to assess is the fat content. When you read the label make note of three numbers: the fat in grams, the total calories, and the portion size.

Be sure that their portion is your portion! If they list a 3 ounce serving of ice cream and you eat two thirds of a cup, that's 6 ounces and you must double *their* figures. Three ounces is a *single* scoop! If the calories for 3 ounces are 150 and you eat two scoops (6 ounces), the result is 2 x 150 = 300 calories.

Each one gram of fat is nine calories, therefore, multiply the number of fat grams in the portion you have chosen by nine. This will give you the number of calories from fat. Divide the fat calories by the total calories and you will have the percentage of calories from fat. For example, in the above serving of ice cream, if the fat listed is 8 grams, then:

$$8 \times 9 = 72 \text{ calories} \qquad \frac{72}{100} = .48 \text{ or } 48\% \text{ calories from fat}$$

The American Heart Association has suggested that no more than 30 percent of our calories should come from fat and that *less* than one third of those should come from saturated fats. This 30 percent is for a healthy individual and is not recommended for someone with known risks.

Only your personal physician will know what your percentage should be, and you really *must* discover how your system works and the needs of your family.

Keeping track of saturated fats isn't so easy. On many ice cream labels the amount of saturated fat isn't shown. You may write to the producer or inquire with a registered dietitian, since each brand will vary.

You will note that I have listed percentages for every recipe. You need to know that the average percentage in this book is 24 percent. If you exceed 30 percent on one dish it's not the end of the world, *providing* you compensate with very low fat food for the rest of the day.

## EAT UP YOUR OXYGEN

*It* would certainly be remiss of me if I did not add a brief word about exercise. The fact is that if you are going to make changes, you will be eating less and this will cause you to lose weight, but what weight? For the most part, your body is comprised of water, lean muscle, fats, and bone. When you reduce carbohydrates the body needs less water and you can drop as much as five pounds in one day from water alone. Of course, the moment you eat any carbohydrates, the body conveniently holds up the water works and bingo ... you gain back your "weight loss" overnight!

In the *MINIMAX* concept our consumption of fat goes down, and refined carbohydrates (sugars, cakes, cookies) are replaced by more complex carbohydrates (whole grains, legumes). So there isn't much water loss.

move it and *lose* it ...

If you simply ate less fat and overall calories and lay quite still in bed, your body would draw upon both lean muscle and fat for energy. If you move around actively you build your muscles, and their action appears to massage the fat that infiltrates them. In this squeezed state the fat is more available as fuel and is used for energy. You now firm up by building muscle and lose weight *eventually* from useless, unsightly fat.

While this obvious benefit is taking place, you have another, quieter victory in progress. As you exert yourself, you breathe deeper and more rapidly and your heart beats faster. Your blood is circulated through the lungs, where it picks up extra oxygen and carries this off to both muscles and your brain. The brain "eats" over 4 liters of oxygen each day. If it has insufficient oxygen it feels "tired." If it gets "enough," the chances are that you will feel better, which, in turn, gets you moving faster, and that burns more calories ... from fat!

All this, however, depends upon your decision to apply the *MINIMAX* principles to your life and not only to *eat less* but to *move more* on a committed basis, come rain or shine.

Now ... on to the centerfold recipes ... Have fun and a good digestion!

Graham Kerr
Kirkland, Washington

# BAGUETTE OF MUSHROOMS

"$\mathcal{N}$othing could be finer than to be in Carolina ...?!" Well ... we've found it! Fresh, wild mushrooms (chanterelles) in a very special sauce. We also tried this with regular button mushrooms and it comes out equal with Carolina ... our daughter, Tessa, happens to live there, so we know!

The unusually cut French bread stick (baguette) is made to look like a hollow tree trunk, filled to overflowing with wild mushrooms. I cut it diagonally for a main course and straight across for a starter. The main course needs a beautiful fresh salad with lots of herbs and edible flowers (see Helpful Hints).

## Nutritional Profile

| PER SERVING | CLASSIC | MINIMAX |
|---|---|---|
| Calories | 497 | 324 |
| Fat (gm) | 36 | 8 |
| Calories From Fat | 66% | 21% |
| Cholesterol (mg) | 112 | 14 |
| Sodium (mg) | 1103 | 752 |
| Fiber (gm) | 3 | 4 |

■ *Classic Compared – Chanterelles and Smoked Ham in Cream*

## Time Estimate

| | | | | | | | | | |
|---|---|---|---|---|---|---|---|---|---|
| Hands On | | | | | | | | | |
| Unsupervised | | | | | | | | | |

Minutes  10  20  30  40  50  60  70  80  90

## Cost Estimate

| | | | |
|---|---|---|---|
| Low | Medium | Medium High | Celebration |

*Serves 4*

## INGREDIENTS

4 teaspoons extra light olive oil with a dash of sesame oil (20 ml)

3 shallots, finely chopped

2 tablespoons loosely packed fresh thyme leaves (30 ml)

¼ teaspoon freshly grated nutmeg (1.25 ml)

⅛ teaspoon freshly ground black pepper (.6 ml)

½ cup de-alcoholized chardonnay wine (118 ml)

2 tablespoons de-alcoholized chardonnay wine (30 ml) mixed with 2 tablespoons cornstarch (30 ml)

½ cup evaporated skim milk (118 ml)

1¼ cups chicken stock (295 ml) (recipe page 210)

½ cup strained yogurt (118 ml) (recipe page 210)

2 ounces Canadian bacon (57 gm), sliced thin

1 pound chanterelle mushrooms (450 gm) (if not in season, use regular button mushrooms, wiped clean and trimmed)

2 ounces smoked turkey breast (57 gm), cut in small strips

⅛ teaspoon cayenne pepper (.6 ml)

1 tablespoon fresh chopped parsley (15 ml)

4 sprigs fresh thyme

1 (12 inch) French baguette (28 cm) (French bread "stick")

## THE FILLING

■ In a small saucepan, heat 1 teaspoon (5 ml) of the olive oil. Add the shallots, 1 tablespoon (15 ml) of the thyme, nutmeg and freshly ground pepper. Cook until the shallots are translucent.

■ Pour in the de-alcoholized wine and boil until reduced by half. Add the cornstarch paste, bring to a boil and stir until thickened. Remove from the heat and add the evaporated milk and ¼ cup (59 ml) of the chicken stock.

■ Put the pan into a bowl of ice water in order to cool it quickly, or just stand there and wait for it! When cooled, add the yogurt and stir in the remaining tablespoon (15 ml) of the thyme. Strained yogurt can break up into little flecks if it is added to hot liquids. For this reason, do please cool the sauce so that the whitening effect can take place and the sauce will look smooth and glossy.

■ Heat the remaining olive oil in a low sided stewpot. Add the Canadian bacon, mixing it lightly with the oil.

■ Separate the mushroom caps from the stems and slice the stems. Drop the stems into the stewpot and saute for five minutes. Now add the caps and stir gently.

■ Add a little of the remaining chicken stock to kick up some steam, then add the rest, stirring lightly. Cover and simmer for 5 minutes. Remove from the heat.

■ Pour the cooking liquid from the stewpot through a fine mesh strainer into the yogurt sauce. Mix thoroughly. Pour the yogurt sauce back into the mushrooms and stir together. Add the turkey and cayenne. Mix in the parsley.

■ To Serve: Cut the baguette into 1 inch (2.5 cm) slices and remove most of the soft center, leaving only a thin layer of dough on the bottom, forming a shallow bread "cup". Put the bread slices on an ovenproof plate and toast in the oven until golden brown. Pour ½ cup (118 ml) of the chanterelle cream over the bread and garnish with a sprig of thyme.

## Helpful Hints and Observations

"WILD" SALAD - One of the truly great advances in modern food is the re-discovery of the herb salad. Choice leaves should include sorrel, arugula (rocket), lemon balm, bowles mint and raddichio. You can scatter in white garlic, chive blossoms, small pansies, ... the list is almost endless and the result is literally fantastic! You may even experiment with the fruited vinegars, such as raspberry, mixed with a little oil and fresh lemon juice and sprinkled in at the last moment.

## Unusual Ingredients

CHANTERELLE MUSHROOMS - This is one of the best known and best liked wild species of the almost 40,000 different varieties of mushrooms in the world. Nestled in the nooks and crannies of forests around the globe, their caps look like frilly, orange, oriental parasols, but unless you have a trained mushroom hunter with you, I wouldn't recommend gathering wild mushrooms on your own. Several species are poisonous. Either hunt the delicious chanterelle down in your local food market or simply rush ahead and make the recipe with button mushrooms.

BAGUETTES - Long, thin, delicious loaves of white bread. Follow your nose to a bakery to enjoy the classic baguette. In France, you will often see them strapped to the back of bicycles as people peddle home with the evening groceries. This mode of transport is not strictly necessary, but, on the other hand, it's great aerobic exercise!

# HUMMUS

$\mathcal{D}$ips can be great fun: they help people to over-come initial shyness at social gatherings by giving them something to do with their hands. I've adapted the famous Middle Eastern Hummus for you so that it falls within our Minimax boundaries.

For serving, look out for classic Middle Eastern bowls and platters. They are very colorful and make great conversation pieces. Set the jicama and pita bread slices out on dishes surrounding the dip. It's a good idea to split the dip into two bowls for parties of six or more.

## Nutritional Profile

| PER SERVING | CLASSIC | MINIMAX |
|---|---|---|
| Calories | 391 | 206 |
| Fat (gm) | 33 | 3 |
| Calories From Fat | 76% | 14% |
| Cholesterol (mg) | 21 | 0 |
| Sodium (mg) | 596 | 191 |
| Fiber (gm) | 2 | 7 |

■  *Classic Compared – Avocado Dip*

## Time Estimate

| Hands On | | | | | | | | | |
|---|---|---|---|---|---|---|---|---|---|
| Unsupervised | | | | | | | | | |
| *Minutes* | 10 | 20 | 30 | 40 | 50 | 60 | 70 | 80 | 90 |

## Cost Estimate

| Low | Medium | Medium High | Celebration |
|---|---|---|---|
| | | | |

*Serves 8*

## INGREDIENTS

1 jicama (about 2 pounds (900 gm) maximum)

¼ cup freshly squeezed lime juice (59 ml)

2 (15 ounce) cans garbanzo beans (425 gm)

6 tablespoons sesame tahini (90 ml)

¾ cup water (177 ml)

4 garlic cloves, peeled and chopped

2 tablespoons fresh chopped parsley (30 ml)

5 tablespoons freshly squeezed lemon juice (75 ml)

¼ teaspoon cayenne pepper (1.25 ml)

1 teaspoon finely chopped fresh cilantro, or
to taste (5 ml)

Pita Bread, whole wheat, cut in wedges

## FIRST PREPARE

■  Cut thin slices of jicama in wedge shapes and marinate overnight in the lime juice.

## NOW COOK

■  Drain the garbanzo beans and puree them in a food processor.

■  While it's still in the can, thoroughly stir the tahini, in order to obtain a consistent mixture of solids and cream.  Scoop the tahini into the processor with the garbanzos.  Pour in the water.

■  Add the garlic, parsley, lemon juice and cayenne.

■  Continue processing until you have a creamy, smooth texture.

■  Add cilantro and more cayenne to taste.

■  Serve the Hummus with the marinated jicama and pita bread triangles for dipping.

## Helpful Hints and Observations

TAHINI - Be sure to shake the can vigorously and then stir the contents well because the solids tend to settle.  If you don't use the whole can, store the leftovers in a sealed glass jar under refrigeration.

GARBANZOS - The canned beans are quite good for this dip but are usually much too soft for use either in a salad or as garnishes for chicken dishes.  Please try the following method of cooking garbanzo beans from scratch.

DRIED LEGUMES FROM SCRATCH - Wash the garbanzo beans, then soak them overnight in 3 to 4 times as much water as beans.  Remove any that float — these may be moldy.  Pour off the water and rinse well.  Recover with fresh water and bring the beans to a slow boil.  Garbanzo beans are quite hard.  You might need to simmer them for as long as 3 hours until they're tender.

If you forget to soak your beans overnight, there is a short cut.  Put the beans in a large pot and cover with cold water.  Bring to a boil and simmer for 2 minutes, then remove from the heat. Let them stand, tightly covered, for 1 hour.  Now cook as suggested.

## Unusual Ingredients

JICAMA - A tuber with great "relatives":  from the morning glory family, a cousin of sweet potatoes.  Grown in Central America, jicama is now readily available in supermarket produce aisles.  It has a texture and taste similar to water chestnuts, for which (in a pinch) it can be used as a substitute!  Try it sliced raw in your salads for a delightful, sweet, crunchy sensation.

TAHINI - This "sesame butter" is made from finely ground, hulled sesame seeds and oil.  Sesame seeds have been used for centuries as a protein source in many countries, particularly in the Middle East and Africa.  Tahini's uses won't stop with this recipe.  Try it as a spread on crackers, or an ingredient in salad dressings, sauces, and casseroles.

GARBANZO BEANS - You might know these beans by another name, chick-peas, or even by their latin name, arietinum, which means "like a ram" (because of their irregular circular shape).  The beans can be red, black, or tan — tan being the color grown most often.  This versatile legume is a good source of calcium, phosphorus and potassium.  Try them in your chili recipes or salads.

# SHRIMP ROLLS 690

*This is an excellent example of "East meets West":
the blending of previously distinct cultures to come
up with unique ideas. One of the masters of this
craft is Jeremiah Tower, the chef/owner of several
popular San Francisco restaurants, including "690"
on Van Ness Avenue, where this is served. It needed
very little change to make it a great Minimax dish!*

*The idea is to serve these filled rice paper
packages as either a first course or a hot weather
main dish. They are literally bursting with aromas,
colors and textures.*

## Nutritional Profile

| PER SERVING | CLASSIC | MINIMAX |
|---|---|---|
| Calories | 473 | 152 |
| Fat (gm) | 34 | 6 |
| Calories From Fat | 65% | 37% |
| Cholesterol (mg) | 75 | 63 |
| Sodium (mg) | 757 | 341 |
| Fiber (gm) | 8 | 2 |

■ *Classic Compared – Shrimp Rolls*

## Time Estimate

Hands On
Unsupervised

Minutes    10   20   30   40   50   60   70   80   90

## Cost Estimate

Low       Medium      Medium High    Celebration

*Serves 4*

## INGREDIENTS

8 ounces fish stock (227 gm) (recipe page 210)

1 teaspoon freshly grated ginger root (5 ml)

2 tablespoons 4 inch (10 cm) lemon grass strands (30 ml)

1 cup cooked small shrimp meat (236 ml), coarsely chopped

½ teaspoon chili powder (2.5 ml)

⅓ cup strained yogurt (78 ml) (recipe page 210)

Salt and freshly ground pepper to taste

4 (8 to 9 inch) dried rice papers (20 to 23 cm)

1 teaspoon turmeric (5 ml)

1 cup water (236 ml)

1 small cucumber, peeled, seeded and cut into matchsticks

2 cabbage leaves, cut into fine strips

12 mint leaves, cut into fine strips

1 tablespoon low-salt soy sauce (15 ml)

4 tablespoons fresh lime juice (60 ml)

3 tablespoons extra light olive oil with a dash of sesame oil (45 ml)

¼ teaspoon sesame oil (1.25 ml)

1 tablespoon fresh cilantro (15 ml)

1 small red bell pepper, halved lengthwise, cored and seeded

1 small green bell pepper, halved lengthwise, cored and seeded

1 jalapeño pepper, halved lengthwise, cored and seeded

## NOW COOK

■ Mix the shrimp with the strained yogurt and the chili powder and season to taste with the salt and pepper.

■ Preheat the broiler. Lay the peppers, skin side up, on a flat broiling pan, and place the pan 3 to 4 inches (8-10 cm) below the heat source. Broil until the skins are charred and black. Slip them directly into a heavy-weight plastic storage bag and let them cool. Rub off the charred skins and cut into fine dice.

■ In a small saucepan, bring the fish stock, grated ginger and lemon grass to a boil and reduce by half. Strain the stock into a measuring cup. Whisk in 3 tablespoons (45 ml) of the lime juice, the soy sauce and oils.

■ In a bowl, combine the warm water and the remaining lime juice. If you prefer a colorful set of rice papers, add turmeric to the bowl of warm water! Submerge the rice papers one at a time, until they start to soften - about 15 seconds. Remove to a damp napkin and cover with another damp napkin. Repeat until all the papers are done. Keep them covered until ready to use - they dry out rapidly!

■ Fill each paper with shrimp mixture, cucumber, cabbage and mint. Roll up loosely and place on individual plates.

■ Just before serving, stir the roasted peppers and cilantro into the sauce.

■ Pour a spoonful of sauce over each roll and serve.

## Unusual Ingredients

RICE PAPER - Please don't let the presence of rice papers deter you from cooking this dish. It's simply a very thin, Southeast Asian pastry wrapper, that you've probably eaten many times as "spring rolls." Indeed, rice paper is as ordinary in Thai cooking as a sesame seed hamburger bun in American cuisine. It will be easy to pick up at your local Thai market. You can find one easily by checking the telephone yellow pages. When you go to the market, you'll see that rice paper is sold dried, in 1 pound (450 gm) packages. You'll have enough sheets to experiment with many different fillings - you're only as limited as your imagination!

LEMON GRASS - See Unusual Ingredients, page 67.

TURMERIC - A bright yellow spice that is native to Southern Asia. It is in the ginger family, technically a rhizome. A rhizome is actually an underground stem that gives rise to new roots and above-ground shoots. Turmeric is found dried and in powdered form and is used in curries, curry powder and natural dyes.

# BLACK BEAN SOUP

This is one of Brazil's favorite foods. It is often served with side dishes of many kinds of boiled meats. Perhaps they use the leftover bones to make meat stocks to use in place of the often recommended water.

My recipe is simply a soup (no side dishes). But it does help to serve it from a tureen, preferably rustic in appearance ... the tureen adds to the mystique! Then add the dollop of the yogurt-cilantro mixture at the table.

## Nutritional Profile

| PER SERVING | CLASSIC | MINIMAX |
|---|---|---|
| Calories | 591 | 480 |
| Fat (gm) | 29 | 15 |
| Calories From Fat | 44% | 29% |
| Cholesterol (mg) | 19 | 36 |
| Sodium (mg) | 708 | 63 |
| Fiber (gm) | 19 | 16 |

■ *Classic Compared – Black Bean Soup*

## Time Estimate

Hands On
Unsupervised

| Minutes | 10 | 20 | 30 | 40 | 50 | 60 | 70 | 80 | 90 |

## Cost Estimate

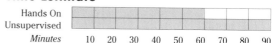

Low　　　Medium　　Medium High　　Celebration

*Serves 6*

## INGREDIENTS

1 pound black turtle beans (450 gm)

2 large ham hocks, stripped of all visible fat

4 teaspoons extra light olive oil with a dash of sesame oil (20 ml)

2 large yellow onions, peeled and diced

4 garlic cloves, peeled and chopped

3 quarts water (or good beef stock) (3 L)

½ teaspoon freshly ground black pepper (2.5 ml)

Pinch of cayenne pepper

4 teaspoons ground cumin seed (20 ml)

4 sprigs of oregano

3 bay leaves

1 medium red bell pepper, seeded and diced

3 tablespoons fresh chopped parsley (45 ml)

1 tablespoon brown sugar (15 ml)

1 tablespoon freshly squeezed lemon juice (15 ml)

2 teaspoons orange zest (10 ml)

1 cup strained yogurt (236 ml) (recipe page 210) mixed with 1 teaspoon fresh chopped cilantro (5 ml)

## FIRST PREPARE

■ The night before making this splendid soup, place the black beans in a bowl of water and let them soak overnight.

■ Blanch the ham hocks by putting them in a medium saucepan with enough cold water to cover and bring to the boil. Pour off the water and rinse out the pan.

## NOW COOK

■ In a 10 inch (25 cm) diameter Dutch oven, or high-sided casserole pot, heat 1 tablespoon of the olive oil and saute the onions and garlic.

■ Rinse and drain the black beans thoroughly. Pour them into the pot and place the ham hocks in the center. This allows the bean flavor to be evenly "en-hocked!"

■ Cover with the water or stock, add the freshly ground black pepper and stir in the cayenne, 1 tablespoon of the cumin seed, the oregano and bay leaves. Bring to a boil and simmer for 1½ hours. Now remove the ham hocks and bay leaves, setting the ham hocks aside in a medium sized bowl and discarding the bay leaves.

■ Remove 1½ cups (354 ml) of beans from the soup, along with 1½ cups (354 ml) of the cooking liquid and puree these in a food processor. Pour this mixture through a sieve, into a large bowl. With a wooden spoon, push the beans through the sieve. Pour the puree back into the pot and discard the residue in the sieve.

■ Chop approximately 1½ cups (354 ml) of the lean ham hock meat into very small chunks and toss them back into the soup.

■ In a hot, small saucepan stir the remaining olive oil with the red pepper, parsley, the remaining cumin seed and the brown sugar. Mix in the lemon juice and orange zest and stir into the hot soup. What a fabulous aroma!

■ Take the soup to the table with the yogurt-cilantro mixture on the side.

### Helpful Hints and Observations

STOCK VS. WATER - You can use fresh water or stock. There is enough flavor to make it on the water but given the choice, I'll always go for the depth of flavor that comes from a good beef stock.

HAM HOCKS - Do please watch out for their size. These are very heavily fatted in some cases and you need to strip away every vestige of visible fat before the long cooking process.

### Unusual Ingredients

BLACK BEANS - Also called "turtle beans", they add a rich, almost purple, color to many dishes. As an added bonus, their taste is as deep and hearty as their color. Black beans contain substantial amounts of potassium and phosphorus. They are a good source of calcium and contain iron, as well.

CUMIN - These zesty seeds come from a very dainty plant with small rose colored or white flowers. Their earthy spiciness is an essential part of curry-spice mixtures. Please don't leave their taste out of this recipe!

BAY LEAVES - A smallish, oblong-shaped leaf with a sharp tip, culled from a medium-sized evergreen tree. I use bay leaves in many dishes: simmered in stocks, casseroles, soups, et al, they add a quality that is complicated to describe; somewhat pungent, sweet and bitter at the same time. The Romans didn't find it difficult to describe their feelings about bay leaf. The word, "bay," is from "laudre" to praise, and bay leaf wreaths were used to crown victorious leaders!

# FAVA BEAN SOUP PROCACCINI

*This* is the recipe that took away the dreaded "Broken Spoon Award!" Back in 1970, Weight Watchers gave me this "badge of dishonor" because of my liberal use of ... well ... everything! I created this dish for Nina Procaccini, who is head of recipe research for Weight Watchers, to demonstrate my new style of cooking. Fava beans are one of her favorite ingredients, and now, I hope, they will become one of your's!

    This is the kind of soup that should be served from a tureen at the table. You could probably get a beautiful one at a great price in an antique shop. It's a good investment because you'll want to serve soup often as part of your Minimax lifestyle.

## Nutritional Profile

| PER SERVING | CLASSIC | MINIMAX |
|---|---|---|
| Calories | 381 | 153 |
| Fat (gm) | 22 | 2 |
| Calories From Fat | 52% | 10% |
| Cholesterol (mg) | 48 | .01 |
| Sodium (mg) | 421 | 81 |
| Fiber (gm) | 8 | 8 |

■ *Classic Compared – Soup au Pistou*

## Time Estimate

| | | | | | | | | | |
|---|---|---|---|---|---|---|---|---|---|
| Hands On | | | | | | | | | |
| Unsupervised | | | | | | | | | |
| *Minutes* | 10 | 20 | 30 | 40 | 50 | 60 | 70 | 80 | 90 |

## Cost Estimate

| Low | Medium | Medium High | Celebration |
|---|---|---|---|

*Serves 6*

## INGREDIENTS

1 teaspoon extra light olive oil with a dash of sesame oil (5 ml)

8 ounces sweet onions (I prefer Walla Walla) (227 gm), peeled and cut in ½ inch (1.5 cm) cubes

2 large garlic cloves, peeled and thinly sliced

½ cup thinly sliced bulb fennel (118 ml)

1 (6 ounce) can no-salt tomato paste (170 gm)

1 quart water (1 L)

1 (19 ounce) can fava beans (539 gm)

½ cup arugula (118 ml)

½ cup mustard greens (118 ml)

1 pound Roma tomatoes (500 gm), peeled and sieved (see Helpful Hints)

Black pepper to taste

BOUQUET GARNI

6 whole cloves

12 black peppercorns

2 bay leaves, crushed

1 sprig of rosemary, crushed

## NOW COOK

■ Heat the olive oil in a large soup pot over medium heat. Fry the onions and garlic until soft. Add half the fennel, the tomato paste and the water. Stir and bring to a boil.

■ Drop in the bouquet garni and fava beans. Cook for 30 minutes.

■ Drop arugula and mustard greens in boiling water and blanch for 30 seconds. Plunge immediately into cold water to refresh. Set aside.

■ Slice the arugula and mustard greens and add them to the soup. At the last minute, add the remaining fennel and the fresh tomato puree. Season with pepper to taste.

■ Remember to remove the bouquet garni before serving the soup ... it could get nasty if a wide mouthed, talkative guest swallowed it!

## Helpful Hints and Observations

TO PEEL TOMATOES - Drop them into a pot of boiling water for a minute or two. The skin will split and start to peel back. Remove from the water. The skin will come off easily.

SWEATING THE VEGETABLES - In practically all my soups, sauces, stocks and casseroles, I use a standard technique that I think will do you a great deal of good. It's called "sweating": a process where the vegetables cook in a small amount of olive oil, never more than 1 tablespoon (15 ml). Sweating raises the temperature of the vegetables enough to release their aromatic and flavorful volatile oils.

TO MAKE A BOUQUET GARNI - The method might depend on the ingredients: some can simply be held together with kitchen string, others can be wrapped in muslin (cheesecloth) and tied with string. I used a wire mesh tea ball for this one.

OIL - I use several different oils, mostly light in flavor because I look to other foods and seasonings to provide aromatic combinations. I do, however, add a touch of toasted sesame seed oil to my oil. This provides just enough nutty finish to release my fond memories of clarified butter! By the way, a "touch" is ¹⁄₁₆th part (1 ounce to 1 pint) (30 ml to 473 ml).

## Unusual Ingredients

FAVA BEANS - A big bean with big, meaty taste and texture. You might also know them as broad beans. They are available fresh in their pods, canned and dried. If you use dried beans, you have to soak them overnight, bring them to a boil, and then simmer for an hour or until tender. To save time, I've called for the precooked, canned beans in this recipe.

ARUGULA - Pronounced, a-ROO-ga-la. The name seems dependent on your nationality: arugula in the United States and Italy; rocket in Britain; roquette in France. Arugula is a dark salad green with an unexpectedly nutty, peppery taste. If you can't find it at the supermarket, it is easily grown from seed. Although I've used it in soup for this recipe, don't miss using arugula as an addition to your fresh salads.

FENNEL BULB - From tip to root, all of the fennel plant can be utilized in your kitchen. The dried seeds are an aromatic addition to baked breads; the leaves are wonderful stuffed inside a grilled fish; and in this recipe, the root, or bulb, chopped like an onion. Similar to arugula, it's an easy grower in the garden.

# SEATTLE CLAM CHOWDER

*N*ew England clam chowders are velvet experiences - very dense, very white, very creamy. This was the standard we set out to match! I hope you like this creative alternative. It is very crisp, fawn colored, and almost Asian in its sweet and sour style.

Seattle is, after all, a Pacific rim gateway city; how better to celebrate its relationships?

For serving I like very colorful, chunky soup bowls, set on larger plates, with crisp, oven-warmed French bread. Serve a salad on the side and this is a meal in itself.

## Nutritional Profile

| PER SERVING | CLASSIC | MINIMAX |
|---|---|---|
| Calories | 430 | 281 |
| Fat (gm) | 20 | 4 |
| Calories From Fat | 43% | 12% |
| Cholesterol (mg) | 60 | 34 |
| Sodium (mg) | 784 | 354 |
| Fiber (gm) | 6 | 5 |

■ *Classic Compared – Clam Chowder*

## Time Estimate

| | | | | | | | | | |
|---|---|---|---|---|---|---|---|---|---|
| Hands On | | | | | | | | | |
| Unsupervised | | | | | | | | | |

Minutes 10 20 30 40 50 60 70 80 90

## Cost Estimate

| Low | Medium | Medium High | Celebration |
|---|---|---|---|

*Serves 6*

## INGREDIENTS

1 teaspoon extra light olive oil with a dash of sesame oil (5 ml)

1 cup diced onion (236 ml)

3 tablespoons fresh thyme (45 ml)

3 bay leaves

1 cup de-alcoholized white wine (236 ml)

3 cups fish stock (708 ml) (recipe page 210)

6 pounds clams (2.7 kg) (yields 10 ounces clam meat (284 gm), de-shelled)

3 cups raw, peeled and diced potatoes (708 ml)

1½ cups raw chopped leeks (354 ml)

2 cups fresh corn kernels (472 ml) (3 fresh ears)

3 tablespoons cornstarch (45 ml) mixed with 6 tablespoons water (90 ml)

1 cup strained yogurt (236 ml) (recipe page 210)

4 ounces Canadian bacon (113 gm) (5 thin slices), diced

¼ teaspoon freshly ground black pepper (1.25 ml)

2 tablespoons fresh chopped parsley (30 ml)

## NOW COOK

■ Heat the olive oil in a high-sided casserole and saute the onions, thyme and bay leaves until the onions are translucent.

■ Stir in the de-alcoholized white wine and a third of the fish stock. This becomes your steaming base. Keep it very hot, creating a fierce boil.

■ Drop in the clams, making sure the steaming base is kept at a boil. Cover and steam for 3 minutes.

■ Using pot holders, lift the casserole, holding the lid tightly in place. Give a vertical shake, which will distribute the steaming base evenly throughout the clams.

■ Place the casserole back on the burner and steam for another 3 minutes. Uncover and the clams will be wide open. Discard any that remain firmly closed.

■ Pour the clams and steaming base into a strainer or colander set over a large bowl. The steaming base and clam juice should drain through the strainer into the bowl.

■ Wash out the casserole, and return it to the hot burner. Add the remaining fish stock. Pour the clam juice and steaming base through a strainer, lined with muslin (this removes any sand particles from the juice) and add it to the stock. Now boil for 10 minutes to concentrate. (You should have

about 5 cups (1.2 L) total, after boiling.) Strain once more, unless you are very confident!

■ Shuck the clams and chop them in half, if extra large. Place them in a bowl and set aside.

■ Add the diced potatoes to the clam concentrate. Simmer for 5 minutes. Stir in the leeks and simmer 5 more minutes. Add three quarters of the corn and cook for another 5 minutes.

■ Remove 1 cup (236 ml) of the broth from the chowder and place it in a small bowl. Stir in the cornstarch paste. Add the yogurt to the warm thickened broth and stir thoroughly (see Helpful Hints). Pour back into the casserole, bring to a boil and stir until thickened.

■ Add the Canadian bacon, clams, and the remaining corn and cook for 5 minutes. Season with the freshly ground pepper and parsley.

### Helpful Hints and Observations

ADDING NON-FAT YOGURT - Please note the way I have had to add the non-fat yogurt. I remove the hot stock from the heat and thicken it before adding the cold yogurt in order to stop it breaking into little tiny lumps. Another easy way is to add the cornstarch to the yogurt and then add the stock, returning the thin cream to the heat to thicken ... your choice!

### Unusual Ingredients

CLAMS - These marine mollusks are marketed in basically three forms: in the shell, shucked and canned. For this recipe, I recommend buying them in the shell. Make sure they are alive, with their valves tightly closed. Refrigerated at 40°F (4°C) they should stay alive for several days. Shucked clams are the whole meat. They should be plump, free of broken shells, with a clear liquor. Clams are also available canned, whole or minced, in brine or clam liquor. These are not much good for this recipe.

CANADIAN BACON - Different from regular bacon? You bet. The Canadian type is made from a section of boneless pork loin encircled in a very thin layer of fat, thereby making it a borderline Minimax choice. I use the least possible to just let its flavor be known.

LEEKS - These add wonderful taste without burdensome calories, fats or sodium. They're a splendid addition to the produce aisle: like giant green onions with snow white bulbs and flat green leaves. Buy the ones that appear crisp and unblemished. The only caveat: give them a good rinsing with cool water. Leeks can hide soil that literally goes along for the ride.

# THAI SOUP *(Tom Yum Gai)*

This is a good example of the classic Asian
Hot and Sour Soup: a thin, broth-styled liquid, chock
full of aromatic seasonings that jostle each other for
equal billing. It winds up not too spicy, not too sour,
not too rich, but just right! When it's right, it's a great
test of the cook's general ability to prepare great
Asian food.

I often serve this as a "revival" first course. Let's
face it, I can't imagine a taste bud that couldn't be
made to sit up and beg for more. Include all the bits
and pieces with the caution that you should not try to
chew the galangal, lemon grass or Kaffir lime leaves.
They are strictly there to let you know that it's full of
the most authentic flavors.

## Nutritional Profile

| PER SERVING | CLASSIC | MINIMAX |
|---|---|---|
| Calories | 288 | 135 |
| Fat (gm) | 17 | 5 |
| Calories From Fat | 54% | 35% |
| Cholesterol (mg) | 40 | 34 |
| Sodium (mg) | 1569 | 154 |
| Fiber (gm) | .1 | 1 |

■ *Classic Compared – Cream of Chicken*

## Time Estimate

| | | | | | | | | | |
|---|---|---|---|---|---|---|---|---|---|
| Hands On | | | | | | | | | |
| Unsupervised | | | | | | | | | |
| *Minutes* | 10 | 20 | 30 | 40 | 50 | 60 | 70 | 80 | 90 |

## Cost Estimate

| | | | |
|---|---|---|---|
| Low | Medium | Medium High | Celebration |

*Serves 4*

## INGREDIENTS

CHICKEN STOCK

1 tablespoon extra light olive oil with a dash of sesame oil (15 ml)

1 medium onion, peeled and coarsely chopped

1 stalk celery, coarsely chopped

2 large carrots, coarsely chopped

1 small bunch of fresh thyme

3 whole cloves

5 whole black peppercorns

2 bay leaves

1 whole chicken, about 3½ pounds (1.6 kg)

7 cups water (1.7 L)

SOUP

4 cups prepared chicken stock (944 ml)

1 lemon grass stalk, crushed and cut in 1 inch (2.5 cm) sections

3 Kaffir lime leaves*

2 slices galangal*

1 teaspoon roasted chili paste* (hot, hot, hot!) (5 ml)

2 tablespoons fish sauce (30 ml)*

1½ tablespoons fresh lemon juice (23 ml)

1 green onion, sliced on the diagonal

1 cup fresh mushrooms (236 ml), quartered

1 tablespoon fresh cilantro leaves (15 ml)

2 cups diced thigh and leg meat from the stock chicken (472 ml)

*\* Available at Asian markets*

## FIRST PREPARE THE STOCK

■ This is a phenomenal chicken stock, quite different from any you've ever eaten. In a large stock pot, over high heat, pour in the olive oil, add the celery, onion, carrots, thyme, cloves, peppercorns and bay leaves and cook for 2 minutes to release the flavors. Drop the chicken in on top. Pour 1 cup of the water over all and cover. Let the chicken steam, with it's sinews cracking and exploding with flavor, 15 to 20 minutes. Add the remaining 6 cups (1.4 L) of water, cover and simmer gently for 30 minutes. Strain the chicken stock. Skin and de-bone the cooked chicken.

## NOW COOK THE SOUP

■ Pour the strained chicken stock into a large saucepan. Do not pour in any of the sediments that have settled to the bottom. Add the lemon grass, Kaffir lime leaves and galangal. Bring to a boil, put the lid on and boil for 5 minutes.

■ Stir in 1 teaspoon (5 ml) of chili paste - no more, this is hot stuff. Continue stirring in the fish sauce, lemon juice, green onion, mushrooms, cilantro and cooked chicken meat. That's it! Inhale deeply and savor the aromas!

## Helpful Hints and Observations

"STEAM BURSTING" - The method described for preparing the stock is one of the most important I will ever give you. It takes even tough old birds and helps to make them tender and it creates the most wonderful basic chicken stock.

FREEZING STOCK - It helps to over-produce good stocks so that you can freeze them either in ice cube form for use in making small sauces or in sealable plastic bags for 1 to 2 pint (500 to 900 ml) quantities, for soups, stews, etc. I always label mine clearly, date them and use them within six months of freezing.

BASHING THE AROMATICS - When using small, whole pieces of food like lemon grass, crushing helps to break up the fiber and extract more of the flavor.

STOCK POT - It really pays to invest in a good-sized stock pot. Over the years I have found that thin-walled (and thin-bottomed) pans just don't last. Better by far is the heavy-based aluminum pan that is completely sealed by some permanent non-stick glaze, such as the SCANPAN 2001+. It should be easy to clean inside and out and for the average home cook needn't hold more than 6 quarts (5.7 liters).

## Unusual Ingredients

KAFFIR LIME LEAVES - Kaffir lime leaves and the rinds of its pear-shaped fruits are used in Southeast Asia for cooking. Highly aromatic, with a strong floral fragrance, they add peaks to Thai cooking.

FISH SAUCE - Fish sauce is added to nearly every dish in Southeast Asian cooking. It is made by packing fish, usually anchovies, mackerel, or both in wooden barrels or ceramic crocks. The fish is then covered with brine and allowed to ferment in the tropical sun for months. The resulting brown liquid is drained off and used for dipping and seasoning.

GALANGAL - Galangal resembles ginger root in appearance and is botanically in the same family. It is a rhizome, or an underground stem. It is a pale yellow color with zebra-like stripes.

# RED SNAPPER YUCATAN

The famous anthropologist-explorer, William
Bartram, visited the Seminole Indians in 1791 and
was served red snapper steamed with fresh oranges.
I picked up on this classic regional idea, developed
by the Mexican people in the Yucatan Peninsula and
consider it to be one of the great dishes of the world.

In the classic version, the fish is usually served
whole but I have used the more readily available
fillets.  Steamed rice is an ideal accompaniment and
if you like fresh spinach, then cook it quickly and
serve it in the whole leaf form, while it is still bright
green - just squeeze it lightly to remove the excess
liquid before putting it on the plate.

## Nutritional Profile

| PER SERVING | CLASSIC | MINIMAX |
|---|---|---|
| Calories | 513 | 273 |
| Fat (gm) | 22 | 8 |
| Calories From Fat | 38% | 27% |
| Cholesterol (mg) | 204 | 116 |
| Sodium (mg) | 1318 | 720 |
| Fiber (gm) | 4 | 1 |

■ *Classic Compared – Baked Red Snapper*

## Time Estimate

Hands On
Unsupervised

| Minutes | 10 | 20 | 30 | 40 | 50 | 60 | 70 | 80 | 90 |
|---|---|---|---|---|---|---|---|---|---|

## Cost Estimate

| Low | Medium | Medium High | Celebration |
|---|---|---|---|

*Serves 4*

## INGREDIENTS

1 tablespoon extra light olive oil with a dash of sesame oil (15 ml)

½ cup finely sliced onion (118 ml)

½ cup sliced red bell pepper (118 ml)

½ cup pimento stuffed olives (118 ml), sliced

2 teaspoons (10 ml) + ½ tablespoon (8 ml) fresh chopped cilantro

4 tablespoons freshly squeezed orange juice (60 ml)

2 tablespoons freshly squeezed lemon juice (30 ml)

4 (6 ounce) red snapper fillets (170 gm each)

¼ teaspoon freshly ground salt (1.25 ml)

⅛ teaspoon freshly ground black pepper (.6 ml)

1 teaspoon arrowroot (5 ml) mixed with ¼ cup freshly squeezed orange juice (59 ml)

## NOW COOK

■ Preheat the oven to 400°F (205°C).

■ In a large ovenproof skillet, heat the oil and fry the onion until soft. Add the pepper, olives, 2 teaspoons (10 ml) of the cilantro, 3 tablespoons (45 ml) of the orange juice and the lemon juice and cook for 2-3 minutes.

■ Brush the fish fillets with the remaining orange juice, season with the salt and pepper and add to the skillet. Arrange an oven rack in the top third of the oven and bake for 12 minutes.

■ Transfer the cooked fish to a serving platter, reserving the juice and vegetables in the skillet. Remove the skillet from the oven, stir in the arrowroot paste, return to the stove top on low heat and stir until thickened.

■ Sprinkle the sauce with the remaining cilantro, pour over the fish and serve.

# SALMON CHINA MOON

$\mathcal{B}$arbara Troop, one of my favorite cookbook writers and owner/chef of the "China Moon" restaurant in San Francisco, suggested this simple yet elegant salmon dish for our collaboration. It took only very minor changes to meet the Minimax nutrition profile.

This dish is very elegant, especially if it's served on one of those glossy black plates. The sauce is brushed on the fish but can also be strained into small pots for dipping.

## Nutritional Profile

| PER SERVING | CLASSIC | MINIMAX |
|---|---|---|
| Calories | 386 | 403 |
| Fat (gm) | 18 | 10 |
| Calories From Fat | 43% | 22% |
| Cholesterol (mg) | 86 | 55 |
| Sodium (mg) | 209 | 143 |
| Fiber (gm) | 1 | 2 |

■ *Classic Compared – Spicy Salmon*

## Time Estimate

| | | | | | | | | |
|---|---|---|---|---|---|---|---|---|
| Hands On | | | | | | | | |
| Unsupervised | | | | | | | | |

| *Minutes* | 10 | 20 | 30 | 40 | 50 | 60 | 70 | 80 | 90 |

## Cost Estimate

| | | | |
|---|---|---|---|
| Low | Medium | Medium High | Celebration |

*Serves 4*

## INGREDIENTS

4 (5-6 ounce) fresh salmon steaks (142-170 gm each), cut ¾ inch (2 cm) thick

2 cups water (472 ml)

1 cup uncooked long grain white rice (236 ml)

¼ red bell pepper, thinly sliced 1½-inches (4 cm) long

4 green onions, green part only, finely sliced

1 teaspoon extra light olive oil with a dash of sesame oil (5 ml)

2 garlic cloves, peeled and finely minced

2 tablespoons finely sliced threads of fresh ginger root (30 ml)

1 tablespoon fermented black beans (15 ml)

1 teaspoon dried red chili flakes (5 ml)

1 tablespoon rice vinegar (15 ml)

½ cup de-alcoholized white wine (118 ml)

## FIRST PREPARE

■ Remove the salmon's free bones (see Helpful Hints).

## NOW COOK

■ Put the water in a medium saucepan, bring to a boil, add the rice and simmer 15 minutes. The rice should have a firm texture, without sticking together. Add the peppers and half of the sliced green onions.

■ In a large saute pan, heat the olive oil and saute the minced garlic, half the ginger, the beans and red chili flakes, stirring to blend, for 5 minutes. Add the rice vinegar and half of the de-alcoholized white wine.

■ On an ovenproof plate or a Pyrex pie pan, at least 1 inch (2.5 cm) smaller in diameter than your steamer, lay out the fish steaks next to one another, arranged back-to-belly for a pretty fit. Sprinkle with the remaining green onions and ginger, then pour the black bean mixture evenly on top. Use only a bare sprinkling if the ginger is the stronger, thick-skinned variety. You can be more liberal with the subtle, young type. Lightly press the scallion with the broad side of a knife to release its juices, then distribute evenly over the fish.

■ Pour water into your steamer pot to a depth of 4 inches (10 cm) and bring to a full boil. Put the plate of prepared salmon in the steamer, cover tightly, and steam over medium-high heat for 8 minutes. While steaming, do not lift the lid to peek at the fish, lest you dissipate the heat.

When properly steamed, the fish will still look moist and red, but will not be fleshy or raw.

■ Remove the plate from the steamer. Pour the steaming liquid through a strainer into a small saucepan. Stir in the remaining de-alcoholized white wine.

■ Serve the hot fish immediately. You can also serve this dish at room temperature: just remove the salmon from the steamer when it is about 1 minute underdone and let it cook to completion from its own inner heat.

■ Just before serving, remove the rib and backbones and pull off the skin in a neat ribbon with the aid of a small knife. Discard most of the green onion, leaving a few nuggets on top for color, or garnish the salmon with one of the prettier whole green onion stalks. Serve the fish in the steamer basket, or transfer it carefully to heated serving plates with a spatula.

■ Spoon the rice into small, individual molds and flip onto each serving plate. Glaze the salmon and rice with the salmon's steaming liquid. Leftovers keep 1-2 days in the refrigerator and are very good cold. The salmon juices gel into a delicious aspic.

## Helpful Hints and Observations

TO BONE SALMON STEAKS - Before you steam the salmon, remove the "free" bones. They fan out on either side of the back bones in a "V" shape. Press down either side of the bone ends as this will make them protrude. Using a pair of fine needle nosed pliers, pull out the bones and discard. After the fish is cooked, strip off the outer skin and carefully remove the rib and backbones.

## Unusual Ingredients

FERMENTED BLACK BEANS - According to some historians, fermented, salted, black soybeans are the oldest recorded soyfood in history! A very popular Chinese seasoning in the modern age, you'll find fermented black beans packaged in heavy plastic bags. They might be labeled Chinese black beans, salted beans, fermented black beans or even ginger black beans. They're made by cooking small, black soybeans until soft, mixing them with a mold, and then covering them with a brining solution for six months. A few shreds of ginger or maybe orange peel can be added in the final soaking stage. Stored in an airtight container at room temperature, away from light, heat and moisture, they will keep indefinitely. If you are concerned about sodium, before using them, rinse the beans under cold running water to remove the salt.

# SALMON PISEGNA

*This dish was created for one of my "nutritional heroes." Chef David Pisegna was a very highly regarded Executive Chef at a luxury hotel when he decided to make a remarkable career change to become Executive Chef at a hospital! Now Chef Pisegna creates nutritious and delicious food for hospital patients. Don't we all wish we could check into his hospital when we are in need of treatment and recuperation? I created this dish for him, using his favorite ingredients: the famous Copper River Sockeye Salmon and asparagus.*

*I suggest serving this poached salmon cold, adorned with the creamy asparagus sauce. Steamed carrots and squash would add a splash of bright color contrast.*

## Nutritional Profile

| PER SERVING | CLASSIC | MINIMAX |
|---|---|---|
| Calories | 608 | 435 |
| Fat (gm) | 35 | 18 |
| Calories From Fat | 52% | 37% |
| Cholesterol (mg) | 225 | 99 |
| Sodium (mg) | 110 | 505 |
| Fiber (gm) | .03 | 2 |

■ *Classic Compared – Salmon with Mayonnaise Sauce*

## Time Estimate

| | | | | | | | | | |
|---|---|---|---|---|---|---|---|---|---|
Hands On / Unsupervised

Minutes: 10 20 30 40 50 60 70 80 90

## Cost Estimate

| Low | Medium | Medium High | Celebration |
|---|---|---|---|

*Serves 6*

## INGREDIENTS

1 tablespoon extra light olive oil with a dash of sesame oil (15 ml)

1 large onion, coarsely chopped

½ cup celery leaves (118 ml), chopped

4 sprigs fresh thyme

12 whole cloves

2 bay leaves

3 sprigs fresh tarragon

3 sprigs fresh dill

1 teaspoon freshly ground salt (5 ml)

8 cups water (1.8 L)

1 whole (4 pound) salmon (1.8 kg), head and tail removed

¼ cup balsamic vinegar (59 ml)

ASPARAGUS SAUCE

1½ pounds asparagus (680 gm)

8 tablespoons strained yogurt (120 ml) (recipe page 210)

1 tablespoon fresh tarragon, finely chopped (15 ml)

Freshly ground white pepper

## NOW COOK

■ Heat the oil in a fish poacher. Add the onion, celery, thyme, cloves, bay leaves, tarragon and dill and cook for about 2 minutes to release the volatile oils. Add the water, bring to a boil, cover and simmer for 15 minutes.

■ Sprinkle the salmon with the salt, put it in the fish poacher, add the vinegar and cover. The fish should poach for 4 minutes per pound. This 4 pound (1.8 kg) salmon should poach for 16 minutes.

■ After the salmon is cooked, let it cool in the poaching liquid. When completely cool, remove the skin and bones using a relatively simple technique (see Helpful Hints).

■ The Sauce: Cut off the tough stem ends of the asparagus and discard. Cut off the very tips and keep separated. In 2 separate pans, steam the asparagus tips and stems until just tender. The reason to keep them separate is that the tips need just about 4 minutes and the stems about 10 minutes.

■ Put the cooked stems in a food processor or blender and puree. You should have about 4 tablespoons (60 ml) of asparagus puree.

■ In a small bowl, mix the puree with the yogurt, tarragon and white pepper to taste. Fold in the tips. The sauce is now ready to adorn your salmon.

## Helpful Hints and Observations

BONELESS AND BEAUTIFUL - To de-bone your salmon and keep one side whole for a lovely presentation, use the following simple technique:

Carefully remove the salmon to a cutting board just large enough to hold it. First remove the skin on the top side. Cut down to the bone along the natural flank line. Slice the fish down one side of the back bone from head to tail. Gently pry the entire back fillet away from the bones. It should come off in one piece. Repeat with the belly cut. This is harder to keep intact. Now the spine and rib bones are exposed. Starting at the tail, carefully, gently, pull out the spine and rib bones. Take your salmon pieces and re-form them over the de-boned fish. Needless to say, this is now your slightly untidy side!

Ready for the incredibly clever part? Put a long oval serving plate over the fish, hold the board to the platter, and, in one graceful movement, flip the whole thing over! There on your serving plate is the other side of the salmon. Carefully strip off the skin and you've got a whole, completely boned salmon to delight your guests! Yes, you may pat yourself on the back for this one. You may also see why television is so helpful when explaining these tricky techniques!

## Unusual Ingredients

BALSAMIC VINEGAR - Here's a Minimax ingredient that adds great flavor: a vinegar from Northern Italy that, by law, must be aged for 10 years, going through stages in oak, chestnut, mulberry and juniper barrels. It will also be a tasty addition to your salad dressings, marinades and fruit desserts.

ASPARAGUS - This vegetable is best when it's purchased in season - late spring and early summer - from local sources. Controversy rages in culinary circles over the relative tenderness of thick-stemmed or thinner-stemmed spears. I think this is an issue you'll have to decide for yourself since I'm an enthusiast for both!

Think of asparagus as spears of health, because it contains a substance believed to be a cancer-protection agent, carotene, as well as vitamin C and the mineral selenium - ideal for Minimax menus! Buy asparagus whose tips are tight and purplish in color, its spear smooth and firm. Refrigerate it as soon as you get it home.

# SHARK STIR-FRY GNEKOW

*This is a dish created for one of my heroes: a person pushing back boundaries, making news, providing creative alternatives for society. The hero is Barry Gnekow, who's developed wonderfully fragrant and elegant de-alcoholized wines. This dish is made with Barry's favorite ingredients. It may become one of your favorites — if you can get used to the idea of eating shark. Barry had a low key response on tasting his dish on camera for the first time ... "I guess you could say we won!"*

*The very nature of stir-fry is that all is included, and when it's done ... it's done, and must be consumed immediately. I always provide chopsticks for the pure fun of it - and it helps both digestion and conversation.*

## Nutritional Profile

| PER SERVING | CLASSIC | MINIMAX |
|---|---|---|
| Calories | 662 | 379 |
| Fat (gm) | 51 | 8 |
| Calories From Fat | 70% | 20% |
| Cholesterol (mg) | 115 | 39 |
| Sodium (mg) | 1328 | 150 |
| Fiber (gm) | 1 | 8 |

■ *Classic Compared – Chinese Stir-Fried Beef and Mushrooms*

## Time Estimate

Hands On
Unsupervised

*Minutes*  10  20  30  40  50  60  70  80  90

## Cost Estimate

Low     Medium     Medium High     Celebration

*Serves 6*

## INGREDIENTS

RICE

1 cup uncooked wild rice (236 ml)

1 cup water (236 ml)

1 tablespoon fish sauce (15 ml)

3 tablespoons pine nuts (45 ml)

STIR FRY

1 tablespoon extra light olive oil with a dash of sesame oil (15 ml)

7 green onions, chopped (both the white and green parts)

1 tablespoon fresh grated ginger root (15 ml)

1 pound shark meat (500 gm), cut in 1 inch (2.5 cm) cubes. (We used fresh, black-tipped shark on the television program, for a wonderful taste!)

4 ounces fresh water chestnuts (113 grams), peeled and thinly sliced

4 ounces snow peas (113 grams), strings removed

24 cilantro leaves (Estimate 4 leaves for each person you're serving.)

4 ounces fresh white, seedless grapes (113 grams) (Sneak a grape in the grocery store to make sure they're sweet.)

1 cup de-alcoholized white wine (236 ml)

1 tablespoon arrowroot (15 ml) mixed with

1 tablespoon de-alcoholized white wine (15 ml)

¼ teaspoon ground cayenne pepper (1.25 ml)

## FIRST PREPARE

■ Remember, all stir-fries are based upon one principle: everything is cut up and measured before you start cooking!

## NOW COOK

■ Use a pressure cooker to reduce the cooking time of wild rice from 40 to 15 minutes. Place the wild rice and water in the pressure cooker and stir in fish sauce. Check and make sure that the lid hole is clear, fasten and put on high heat. Cook the rice for 15 minutes from when the cooker starts "hissing". Stir in the pine nuts and set aside.

■ Heat the olive oil in a wok on high heat. When a drop of water hits the wok and disappears immediately, the wok is ready! Drop in the green onions, ginger and shark meat. Keep stirring.

■ As the shark meat whitens, drop in the water chestnuts and snow peas. Keep stirring. Add cilantro leaves and grapes. At the last moment pour in the wine.

■ Stir the arrowroot paste into the wok. In moments you have a glistening, gorgeous wine sauce.

■ Sprinkle the sparkling red cayenne pepper over the top to add taste-bud heat. Serve with the wild rice and pine nuts.

## Helpful Hints and Observations

CHINESE FOOD IN GENERAL - All of us owe a great deal to the extra effort that some folk take in order to be experts in a given field. I'd like to take up this space to tell you about a wonderful book, *The Modern Art of Chinese Cooking*, written by Barbara Troop, a very gifted specialist who has gone deep into what is an often poorly described style of kitchen practice. Barbara writes with the infectious enthusiasm of a dedicated cook on a learning curve. Because of this she passes on much more than simply techniques. She is the best teacher because she assumes nothing. You get the feeling that she cares personally that you understand.

## Unusual Ingredients

BLACK-TIP SHARK - Common to the waters of the South Atlantic coast of America from Florida to the Bahamas, its rich white meat is wonderfully delicious and should be only lightly cooked, as in my stir-fry method.

ARIEL DE-ALCOHOLIZED WINE - You've tried the rest, now try the best (at least in my opinion!). Ariel is a California winery producing superior de-alcoholized products. They're so good that they're winning awards over alcoholic wines in blind taste tests. Of course, the reason for Ariel's high quality is in large part due to the special de-alcoholization techniques pioneered by Barry Gnekow. You can get more information on how to obtain Ariel wine in your area by calling this toll-free phone number, 1-800-456-9472.

WATER CHESTNUTS - At one time these were only available canned in the United States, but they are now available fresh at most Asian markets. Choose those that are very hard and have a gloss to them. If fresh water chestnuts are not available, Jicama, a large, white tuber similar in shape to a turnip, can be substituted.

# SOLE WITH SAFFRON SAUCE

*I was inspired to create this dish from a "Sole with Café de Paris Sauce" original. This classic featured moist, thick Dover sole stuffed with highly seasoned butter, nestled in a bath of butter sauce. Today, I have used no butter at all! I can almost hear your sharp gasp, saying, "No, it isn't possible!" But it may be that you won't even miss the butter. Let your taste buds be the judge!*

*Great accompaniments to this dish are tiny, steamed new potatoes and green beans sprinkled with a touch of nutmeg, parsley and mint.*

## Nutritional Profile

| PER SERVING | CLASSIC | MINIMAX |
|---|---|---|
| Calories | 780 | 88 |
| Fat (gm) | 66 | 1 |
| Calories From Fat | 77% | 13% |
| Cholesterol (mg) | 258 | 40 |
| Sodium (mg) | 2073 | 147 |
| Fiber (gm) | 1 | .2 |

■ *Classic Compared – Sole with Café de Paris Sauce*

## Time Estimate

| Hands On | | | | | | | | | |
|---|---|---|---|---|---|---|---|---|---|
| Unsupervised | | | | | | | | | |
| *Minutes* | 10 | 20 | 30 | 40 | 50 | 60 | 70 | 80 | 90 |

## Cost Estimate

| | | | |
|---|---|---|---|
| Low | Medium | Medium High | Celebration |

*Serves 6*

## INGREDIENTS

FUMET

1 teaspoon extra light olive oil with a dash of sesame oil (5 ml)

1 large onion, peeled and sliced (6oz) (170 gm)

2 sprigs of fresh parsley

2 bay leaves

2 sprigs of fresh thyme

2 whole cloves

1 pound fish bones (450 gm)

6 cups water (1.4 L)

FISH

6 (6 oz) sole fillets (170 gm each)

SAFFRON SAUCE

1 cup prepared fish fumet (236 ml)

¼ teaspoon fresh chopped tarragon (1.25 ml)

½ teaspoon fresh chopped dill (2.5 ml)

1 tablespoon fresh chopped parsley (15 ml)

2 tablespoons chopped green onions (30 ml)

2 anchovy fillets, mashed to a paste

1 tablespoon capers (15 ml)

1 clove garlic, peeled and chopped

2 teaspoons English mustard (10 ml)

1 tablespoon lemon juice (15 ml)

Pinch of saffron threads (1.25 ml)

1 tablespoon arrowroot (15 ml)

¼ cup de-alcoholized white wine (59 ml)

## FOR THE FUMET

*The fumet or fish stock reduction is the most important element of this dish's flavorful sauce.*

■ Heat the olive oil in a medium saucepan over medium heat. Add the onions, parsley, bay leaves, thyme, cloves and fish bones.

■ Pour in the water and bring to a boil. Reduce the heat and simmer no longer than 30 minutes. Any longer and the fumet will become bitter.

■ Strain out the liquid.

■ Discard the solids and transfer the liquid to another saucepan, bring to a boil and reduce 50 percent. You should have about 1 cup (236 ml) of absolute reduction - the fumet.

## FOR THE FISH

■ When you get the sole fillets home from the market, put them in ice cold, salted water. This Scottish crofter's technique, called "crimping", will remove the "woofy" smell.

■ Just annoint your broiler pan with a touch of olive oil. Place the sole fillets on the broiler.

■ Position the pan 4 inches (10 cm) from the broiler's heat source for about 6 minutes.

■ Remove the fish while it's tender and snowy white. Don't wait until it browns or becomes crisp.

## FOR THE SAFFRON SAUCE

■ In a small saucepan, over medium heat, mix the reduced fumet with the tarragon, dill, parsley, green onions, anchovies, capers, garlic, mustard and lemon juice.

■ Now for a burst of color: stir in a pinch of saffron threads. Note that the yellow hue is very similar to that of butter!

■ In a small bowl, dissolve the arrowroot in the white wine. Take the saucepan from the heat and stir in the arrowroot mixture. Return to the heat and stir until thickened.

■ To Serve: Remove the fish to a warmed serving plate and spoon some saffron sauce over each portion.

### Helpful Hints and Observations

CRIMPING - A few more words about this very important idea. I've seen many people wrinkle their noses when they talk about fish. "I don't like the way it smells." "It's sticky to the touch." Well, it is true that even perfectly fresh fish can become surface tacky in a warm car, but it can be refreshed using this ancient Scottish crofter's method called "CRRRRRIMPING!" The trick is to get cold tap water tasting like seawater by adding sea salt - about 1 tablespoon (15 ml) for 2 quarts (1.9 L). Now add a bunch of ice cubes to drop the temperature to North Sea levels and then slip your fish directly from the wrapper into the iced "sea water" and leave it there for about 15 minutes. When you dry it off give it a sniff - it should have a sea-fresh aroma. If it doesn't, it might not have been the "right stuff" when you bought it.

### Unusual Ingredients

ANCHOVY FILLETS - See Unusual Ingredients, page 59.

SAFFRON - See Unusual Ingredients, page 61.

# BANGKOK STEAMED TROUT

*Whole fish cooked in this Thai marinade is absolutely delicious. You might also like to try it with a chicken breast or your favorite fillet of fresh fish.*

*Since this fish is so well garnished with its vegetables it needs only some well steamed rice served on the side.*

## Nutritional Profile

| PER SERVING | CLASSIC | MINIMAX |
|---|---|---|
| Calories | 516 | 200 |
| Fat (gm) | 30 | 5 |
| Calories From Fat | 52% | 23% |
| Cholesterol (mg) | 246 | 76 |
| Sodium (mg) | 434 | 274 |
| Fiber (gm) | 1 | 2 |

■ *Classic Compared – Trout Woolpack*

## Time Estimate

| Hands On Unsupervised | | | | | | | | | |
|---|---|---|---|---|---|---|---|---|---|
| Minutes | 10 | 20 | 30 | 40 | 50 | 60 | 70 | 80 | 90 |

## Cost Estimate

| Low | Medium | Medium High | Celebration |
|---|---|---|---|

*Serves 6*

## INGREDIENTS

1 whole (2 pound) trout (900 gm)

1 cup celery (236 ml), sliced thin, on the diagonal

1 sweet red pepper, seeded and julienned

1 cup green chinese cabbage (236 ml), cut in 1 inch (2.5 cm) squares

½ cup Enokitake mushrooms (118 ml)

Chopped cilantro leaves, for garnish

MARINADE

2 cups chicken stock (472 ml) (recipe page 210)

2 tablespoons dried cranberries (30 ml)

2 jalapeno chilies, finely chopped

1 tablespoon freshly grated ginger (15 ml)

4 cloves pickled garlic, mashed

2 tablespoons freshly squeezed lime juice (30 ml)

2 tablespoons soy sauce (30 ml)

## FIRST PREPARE

■ For this recipe, you will need either a long fish steamer with a perforated rack or a large baking pan with a grill that fits inside another covered pan.

■ Clean and wash the fish. Cut a long piece of foil, 3 inches (8 cm) larger than the fish. Place the fish in the center of the foil and fold up the edges to make a "pool" around the fish. This "pool" will hold the marinade. Add water to the steamer pan, being sure that the perforated base or wire grill is raised above the water line.

■ Place all the marinade ingredients in a sauce-pan. Boil 5 minutes.

## NOW COOK

■ Bring the water in the steamer to a boil and then slip the fish in its aluminum foil pool onto the rack. Pour the marinade over the fish so that it now sits in a broth of seasonings. Cover and steam 15 minutes, until the fish is just tender.

■ Place the sliced celery in another pan and steam for 4 minutes. Add the red pepper, cabbage and mushrooms and steam for 30 seconds.

■ Carefully lift the fish from the steamer to a serving platter and garnish with the steamed vegetables and the chopped cilantro.

## Helpful Hints and Observations

REMOVING THE FISH FROM THE FOIL - My description of this maneuver is really simplistic, so I'll use this space to try and illustrate the entire technique.

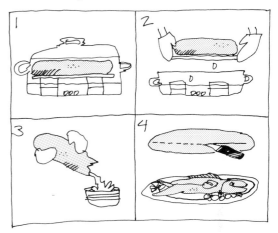

1. This shows the entire construction of the steamer.

2. Lift out the grid with the fish in its boat.

3. Pour out all the marinade and cooking liquids.

4. Lay foil boat on its side and cut slot full length. The fish can then be passed through the slot onto the dish.

## Unusual Ingredients

ENOKITAKE MUSHROOMS - This long stemmed, white mushroom with a small cap is named for the tree it grows upon. Indigenous to Japan, they are available at supermarkets worldwide. They are usually sold wrapped in plastic to preserve freshness because they oxidize very quickly, turning light brown. Select mushrooms that are firm and white. Avoid slimy stems and loose packaging.

DRIED CRANBERRIES - You might think these look a lot like raisins, only they are bright red and have a wonderfully tangy flavor. If you can't find them at your supermarket, try the local health food store. Sometimes marketed as craisins, they should be dry but moist internally like a raisin.

PICKLED GARLIC - Very common in Asia and a favorite of the Koreans. If you have an Asian market nearby, you will find it with other pickled condiments. The most common is spring garlic, pickled in vinegar, soy sauce and sugar.

# GOLDEN TUNA

*O*ur very special "celebrity on the street" for whom
we created this dish was Jeff Gold, a retired I.B.M.
representative who has had serious health problems
related to his diet. Jeff flew in from New York to
taste this dish which comprised all his favorite foods -
and he loved it!

## Nutritional Profile

| PER SERVING | CLASSIC | MINIMAX |
|---|---|---|
| Calories | 956 | 871 |
| Fat (gm) | 84 | 8 |
| Calories From Fat | 79% | 9% |
| Cholesterol (mg) | 303 | 66 |
| Sodium (mg) | 890 | 265 |
| Fiber (gm) | 2 | 12 |

■ *Classic Compared – Tuna with Pasta*

## Time Estimate

| Hands On | | | | | | | | | |
|---|---|---|---|---|---|---|---|---|---|
| Unsupervised | | | | | | | | | |
| *Minutes* | 10 | 20 | 30 | 40 | 50 | 60 | 70 | 80 | 90 |

## Cost Estimate

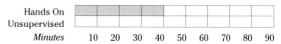

Low          Medium          Medium High          Celebration

*Serves 2*

## INGREDIENTS

1 teaspoon extra light olive oil with a dash of sesame oil (5 ml)

⅜ teaspoon salt (1.8 ml)

¼ teaspoon freshly ground black pepper (1.25 ml)

2 (4 ounce) pieces of fresh tuna steak (113 gm each), yellow fin if possible

3 large nectarines

2 tablespoons freshly squeezed lime juice (30 ml)

¼ teaspoon cayenne pepper (1.25 ml)

2 cups dried pasta (ziti) (472 ml)

2 quarts water (1.9 L)

½ cup de-alcoholized white wine (118 ml)

1 tablespoon fresh chopped basil (15 ml)

1 tablespoon fresh chopped parsley (15 ml)

1 tablespoon freshly grated dry Monterey Jack cheese (15 ml), or Parmesan

## FIRST PREPARE

■ Pour the olive oil onto a plate. Add a third of the salt and two thirds of the pepper and gently mop it up with the tuna, making sure each piece is lightly oiled on both sides.

■ Remove the pits from the nectarines and cut them in quarters. Puree them in a food processor or blender, then push through a sieve into a large bowl. Stir in the lime juice and cayenne pepper.

## NOW COOK

■ Drop the pasta into boiling water with the remaining salt and cook for 11 minutes, until al dente (slightly resistant to the teeth). Drain in a colander, then return the pasta to the warm pot and set aside.

■ While the pasta is cooking, place the tuna in a hot skillet, cover and cook for 6 minutes on medium heat. Turn the tuna, add the de-alcoholized white wine and increase the heat to high. Cover and cook for another 3 minutes.

■ Pour the pureed nectarine sauce over the tuna and allow it to heat through. Sprinkle with basil and the remaining freshly ground pepper.

■ Turn the tuna out onto hot serving plates. Pour half the heated sauce over the tuna pieces and the rest over the pasta. Sprinkle with the parsley and cheese.

## Helpful Hints and Observations

TUNA SUBSTITUTES - I am often asked if you could do this dish with chicken breast. The answer is, yes. In fact, whenever you encounter a potentially difficult main food item, you can think to yourself, how would it taste with something else? In this case, imagine the tart-sweet taste of a nectarine and the smooth taste of chicken - what do you think of that? If it works for you, then have a go at it! In this way you learn how to springboard off other peoples' recipes and literally do your own thing.

## Unusual Ingredients

TUNA - Yummmy! And don't think you've experienced the taste with the canned variety. Fresh tuna is a unique taste in its own right. I recommend the yellow fin for this dish, but don't be afraid to substitute whatever's fresh and best at your local fish market.

NECTARINES - Golden, juicy, sweet and tangy! Select nectaries that are fairly firm, but give slightly under pressure. Store the fresh, ripe fruit in the refrigerator for 3 to 5 days until ready to eat.

# CATFISH POORBOY

This is one of the great "foods-of-the-people" dishes and deserves to be world famous. At its most simple, it is really a long bread roll filled with fried catfish, perhaps some mayonnaise and often with a pickle. In this case, I have done an "upgrade" to increase the aroma, color and texture.

I suppose that you could attack this "filled bread roll sandwich" with a knife and fork, but frankly, you'd miss out on all the fun! Catfish Poorboy is a super creative alternative for a BBQ or patio/garden picnic. A big, crisp, tossed salad with "Treena's Vinaigrette" would go really well (see Helpful Hints).

## Nutritional Profile

| PER SERVING | CLASSIC | MINIMAX |
|---|---|---|
| Calories | 657 | 446 |
| Fat (gm) | 25 | 9 |
| Calories From Fat | 34% | 19% |
| Cholesterol (mg) | 136 | 50 |
| Sodium (mg) | 2914 | 611 |
| Fiber (gm) | 4 | 3 |

■ *Classic Compared – Catfish Poorboy*

## Time Estimate

Hands On
Unsupervised

Minutes    10   20   30   40   50   60   70   80   90

## Cost Estimate

Low          Medium      Medium High    Celebration

*Serves 4*

## INGREDIENTS

4 poorboy rolls (a 7-8 inch white roll (18-20 cm), 3-4 inches (8-10 cm) in diameter) I find the best roll carries the name "Italian Spaghetti Roll." (See Unusual Ingredients.)

1 tablespoon extra light olive oil with a dash of sesame oil (15 ml)

½ cup chopped onion (118 ml)

2 red bell peppers, seeded and chopped in ¼ inch (.75 cm) cubes

1 red jalapeño pepper, seeded and finely diced (leave in the seeds and membrane for extra heat, if you wish)

1 garlic clove, crushed

2 tablespoons tomato paste (30 ml)

2 tablespoons fresh chopped basil (30 ml)

1 tablespoon fresh lime juice (15 ml)

½ cup water (118 ml)

4 catfish fillets, 7 ounces (200 grams) each

## FIRST PREPARE

■ Split rolls in half lengthwise, leaving one side joined. Scoop out the doughy center. Set aside.

## NOW COOK

■ Heat the oil in a large frying pan. Over high heat cook the onions, peppers and garlic until the onions are translucent. Add the tomato paste, half the chopped basil leaves and the lime juice. Then pour in the water, reduce the heat to low and cook for 2 minutes.

■ Arrange the 4 fish fillets on the sauce in the fry pan. Brush with the surrounding sauce. Put under the broiler for about 8 minutes. (It helps to have a fry pan with a handle that withstands 500°F (260°C), otherwise crowd the fillets to one side and keep the handle out in the cool.)

■ Slip the well sauced fish fillets into the "Poorboys". Spoon sauce on top and sprinkle each sandwich with the remaining basil.

■ Serve immediately. Totally delicious!!

## Helpful Hints and Observations

PAN BROILING - This is another relatively new technique that you may wish to consider for some future creation of your own. The idea is simple: you create a colorful, aromatic sauce of vegetables and herbs then lay fish fillets (or veal, chicken breasts, etc.) on this "bed". Brush the fish with the pan juices, slip it under a hot broiler, about 4 inches (10 cm) from the heat source and let it cook for about 8 minutes. The fish will be perfect, and if you used sweet peppers and onions they will have roasted on the exposed surfaces to give a smokey taste.

SCOOPING OUT THE BREAD - Be careful here! It's easy to dig too far and make a hole. Then all the great juice will end up on your shirt!

TREENA'S VINAIGRETTE - A lovely dressing for a side salad to this dish. Just blend together 1 part olive oil, 2 parts white wine vinegar, and 1 garlic clove. Add dry mustard powder, cayenne pepper and soft brown sugar to taste. Use sparingly over crisp greens and freshly sliced celery, tomatoes and purple onions. A few sunflower seeds add texture.

## Unusual Ingredients

CATFISH - These fillets should come from a farm rather than from a possibly polluted creek or pond — "check the label" — as they say! If you can't find catfish in your neck of the woods, try Catfish Poorboy with any good "oily" fish, such as black sea bass, butterfish, pompano, sable, salmon, lake trout, sea trout (weakfish) or whitefish.

ITALIAN SPAGHETTI ROLLS - These rolls have a great sourdough flavor and a crisp crust. If your supermarket or local bake shop does not carry them by this name, find a roll with similar qualities. The sourdough flavor is from what is called "the starter". The starter is a combination of ingredients, one usually being buttermilk, giving the sour flavor.

# KEDGEREE

*The* Chef de Cuisine, Kevin Graham, of the famed Windsor Court Hotel in New Orleans, makes a very rich Kedgeree (not in the least stingy!). He obliged me by setting a much higher fat standard than usual. Mine is a "flip side" alternative. Don't risk buying poor quality fish: get the best, the moister the better.

Kedgeree is really either a breakfast or supper dish and is complete in itself.

## Nutritional Profile

| PER SERVING | CLASSIC | MINIMAX |
|---|---|---|
| Calories | 693 | 456 |
| Fat (gm) | 56 | 11 |
| Calories From Fat | 73% | 22% |
| Cholesterol (mg) | 296 | 189 |
| Sodium (mg) | 1187 | 1224 |
| Fiber (gm) | 1 | 2 |

■ *Classic Compared – Kedgeree*

## Time Estimate

| | |
|---|---|
| Hands On Unsupervised | 2 Hours |

Minutes  10  20  30  40  50  60  70  80  90

## Cost Estimate

Low          Medium          Medium High          Celebration

*Serves 4*

## INGREDIENTS

1 pound smoked haddock (or similar smoked white fish) (450 gm)

Cold milk - enough to cover the fish in a small bowl

3 hard-boiled eggs (boiled 5 minutes)

1 teaspoon extra light olive oil with a dash of sesame oil (5 ml)

1 large onion (8 ounces) (225 gm), finely diced

2 teaspoons garam masala (10 ml)

½ teaspoon turmeric (2.5 ml)

¼ teaspoon cardamom (1.25 ml)

1 cup uncooked Basmati or Louisiana long grain rice (236 ml), rinsed

3½ cups homemade fish stock (826 ml) (recipe page 210)

1 bay leaf

2 tablespoons fresh chopped parsley (30 ml)

¼ teaspoon freshly ground sea salt (1.25 ml) if needed, no more

TURMERIC SAUCE

1 cup homemade fish stock (236 ml) (recipe page 210)

1 tablespoon arrowroot (15 ml)

½ teaspoon turmeric (2.5 ml)

## FIRST PREPARE

■ Remove and discard the skin from the smoked fish. Soak it for 1 to 2 hours in sufficient cold milk to cover. This helps leach out the salt.

■ Separate the hard-cooked egg whites from the yolks. Slice the egg whites into thin strips and set aside. Discard the egg yolks. (Pet dogs appreciate these egg discards).

## NOW COOK

■ Heat the olive oil in a large saucepan and cook the onion, garam masala, turmeric and cardamom together until the onion is soft, about 5 minutes.

■ Add the Basmati rice to the onions, stir and leave to cook for 2 minutes. Add 2½ cups (590 ml) of fish stock and the bay leaf. Cook on medium heat, uncovered, 18 to 20 minutes, until all the stock is absorbed into the rice.

■ Remove the fish from the milk. Into a small saucepan on very low heat flake the fish into 1 inch (2.5 cm) pieces. Feel carefully for small bones. Add the remaining fish stock, bring to a simmer, cover and cook gently for 5 minutes. Add the sliced egg whites and cover.

■ Instead of a high fat butter sauce, make the turmeric sauce by pouring the fish stock into a hot saucepan. Stir in the turmeric and arrowroot. Almost instantaneously the sauce will become glossy and smooth. This sauce is used to add the "mouth feel" and color of butter without which a Scotsman would declare the dish "stingy".

■ Stir the thickened sauce into the rice. Gently stir in the fish and eggs.

■ Taste for salt. I feel a dish with this much rice needs some salt. But be careful not to add more than ¼ teaspoon (1.25 ml). This is all the sodium an average adult needs each day!

■ Transfer the Kedgeree to a serving dish and garnish with chopped parsley.

## Helpful Hints and Observations

REPLACING FAT - In this recipe I faced a good deal of classical and cultural difficulty. As I've already commented, a Scot's idea of ultimate "stinginess" (and they have the reputation to start with) is someone who doesn't add sufficient butter to Kedgeree. You will need to know that my father was pure Scot and my family goes back for many generations. We come from the lowlands just south of Edinburgh. Hence, if I'm stingy with the butter, I'm in trouble! I actually took this recipe to Scotland and tested it in its adopted birthplace. It was accepted without condemnation. In fact, those who tried it preferred the lighter taste. Some of the reasons for this breakthrough were the reduced fish stock (fumet) that provides richness and flavor from the bones; the turmeric that gives it a yellow, butter color; and the arrowroot that adds a glossy sheen.

## Unusual Ingredients

SMOKED HADDOCK - This fish is easily found on the eastern seaboard of the U.S. and off the coasts of England and France. At one time, haddock was the most plentiful of all the white fish, accounting for almost half the catch in the North Atlantic. When smoked, haddock has a dull, pale surface. Substitute smoked whiting if haddock is unavailable.

GARAM MASALA - See Unusual Ingredients, page 111.

BASMATI RICE - See Unusual Ingredients, page 47.

# TACOS DE PESCADO

$\mathscr{A}$t lunchtime in the heart of Phoenix, Arizona's business district, lines of people are waiting to eat at "Fina Cocina." Owner and head chef, Norman Fierros, dazzles his patrons by presenting the great flavors of Mexican cuisine with a masterful light touch. This recipe is an adaptation of one of his most popular dishes and makes wonderful sense for lunch.

Mexican salads rely mainly on color and freshness, which come to think of it, isn't a bad combination! This taco is served with a finely sliced onion, cabbage and tomato salad: the finer the cut, the better!

## Nutritional Profile

| PER SERVING | CLASSIC | MINIMAX |
|---|---|---|
| Calories | 613 | 298 |
| Fat (gm) | 36 | 6 |
| Calories From Fat | 53% | 18% |
| Cholesterol (mg) | 108 | 39 |
| Sodium (mg) | 2589 | 402 |
| Fiber (gm) | 5 | 10 |

■ Classic Compared – Taco

## Time Estimate

| Hands On | | | | | | | | | |
|---|---|---|---|---|---|---|---|---|---|
| Unsupervised | | | | | | | | | |
| Minutes | 10 | 20 | 30 | 40 | 50 | 60 | 70 | 80 | 90 |

## Cost Estimate

| Low | Medium | Medium High | Celebration |
|---|---|---|---|

*Serves 4*

## INGREDIENTS

CILANTRO PESTO

3 cups packed cilantro leaves (708 ml)

½ cup extra light olive oil with a dash of sesame oil (118 ml)

5 garlic cloves, peeled

2 jalapeno peppers, cored and seeded

1 cup walnuts (236 ml)

1 cup very mild feta cheese (236 ml)

Juice of 1 lemon

¼ cup ice water (59 ml)

TACOS

4 (6 ounce) sole fillets (170 gm each)

2 tablespoons sea salt (30 ml)

1 quart ice water (1 L)

6 Roma tomatoes, seeded and finely sliced

6 green onions, chopped

½ head of a purple cabbage, thinly sliced

1 teaspoon extra light olive oil with a dash of sesame oil (5 ml)

8 whole wheat tortillas

Juice of 1 lime

½ teaspoon freshly ground white pepper (2.5 ml)

4 lime wedges

## FIRST PREPARE THE CILANTRO PESTO

*NOTE: This recipe makes 3 cups (708 ml). We only use 5 tablespoons (75 ml) for the 4 servings in this recipe. Each tablespoon has 23 calories and 2 grams of fat.*

■ Place all the ingredients in a food processor and puree into a thick paste. Refrigerate until needed.

## NOW COOK THE TACOS

■ Dissolve the sea salt into the ice water. Slip the fish into the salty water and let them refresh for 10 minutes. Remove the fish and pat dry with paper towels. Sprinkle the sole with pepper and set aside.

■ Mix together the tomatoes, onion, cabbage and 1 tablespoon (15 ml) of the Cilantro Pesto.

■ Lightly grease a skillet with the oil and put on medium heat. Dip the tortillas in water and then quickly steam-saute on both sides. Remove from the pan and keep warm until needed (I use a plate set over a small saucepan of boiling water, covering the cooked tortillas with a clean cloth).

■ Place the fillets on a lightly oiled rack in a roasting pan and broil for 4 minutes. Sprinkle with the lime juice.

■ To assemble, spread a warm tortilla with 1 tablespoon of cilantro pesto, place a fish fillet on it and cover with the salad mixture. Roll up like a taco or simply leave it open-faced for your guests to do the rolling - it looks more attractive this way. Serve with lime wedges on the side.

## Helpful Hints and Observations

PROCESSOR HEAT - The food processor is a wonderful piece of equipment and really essential when making a good pesto. However, because of its speed it does work up a certain amount of friction heat which can discolor the green tint of the pesto. This is the reason for the iced water: it saves the mixture from heat discoloration.

HEATING TORTILLAS - Be careful not to let your steam heated tortillas stay too long under the towel - 10 minutes should be maximum.

My personal preference is to use whole wheat tortillas. I like the taste and nutrition better and, as an added bonus, they're much easier to handle.

## Unusual Ingredients

FETA CHEESE - Made of sheep's milk, Feta is curdled, heated and then cured or pickled in a mixture of brine and its own whey. Look for feta that is white, moist and crumbly in texture.

CILANTRO - This bright green, leaf herb adds a fresh, distinctive flavor to your cooking. Another name for cilantro is chinese parsley and, to make matters even more confusing, its dried seeds are marketed as coriander! Look for cilantro in your supermarket, or in Latin American or Asian specialty shops. Like many herbs, cilantro is also quite easy to grow in a home garden.

# CREPES FRUITS DE MER

*This dish comes from my past! My parents opened Gravetye Manor near East Grinstead back in 1958. Under Peter Herbert's direction, it is now one of the very best small hotels in Europe. We originally invented this dish for the head of the seafood company, Young's. He was delighted! Now it is re-invented for you.*

*I love to serve this on a large platter with 6 to 8 portions all lined up! However, unless you have a presentable fish slice or a long palette knife, it's probably best to slosh it up in the kitchen. Freshly steamed green beans and small boiled potatoes make up a great supper.*

## Nutritional Profile

| PER SERVING | CLASSIC | MINIMAX |
|---|---|---|
| Calories | 1433 | 525 |
| Fat (gm) | 63 | 8 |
| Calories From Fat | 39% | 13% |
| Cholesterol (mg) | 588 | 223 |
| Sodium (mg) | 2509 | 507 |
| Fiber (gm) | 7 | 10 |

■ *Classic Compared – Crepes Fruits De Mer*

## Time Estimate

Hands On
Unsupervised
Minutes    10   20   30   40   50   60   70   80   90

## Cost Estimate

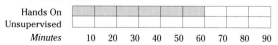

Low        Medium      Medium High    Celebration

*Serves 4*

## INGREDIENTS

CREPE BATTER – FOR 8 CREPES

½ cup all-purpose flour (118 ml)

1 whole egg

1 egg yolk

1 cup non-fat milk (236 ml)

1 teaspoon extra light olive oil with a dash of sesame oil (5 ml)

8 fresh dill sprigs

FILLING

1 (15 ounce) can cooked butter beans (425 gm), drained and rinsed

3 cups non-fat milk (708 ml)

12 ounces sole (340 gm), preferably Petrale, cut in finger-size strips

6 ounces sea scallops (170 gm)

¾ cup button mushrooms (177 ml), quartered, unless very small

2 tablespoons arrowroot (30 ml) mixed with 4 tablespoons de-alcoholized white wine (60 ml)

½ cup de-alcoholized white wine (118 ml)

1 teaspoon fresh finely chopped dill (5 ml)

⅛ teaspoon cayenne pepper (.6 ml)

6 Italian plum tomatoes, peeled, seeded and chopped

1 tablespoon fresh chopped parsley (15 ml)

6 ounces small, pre-cooked salad shrimp (170 gm)

2 tablespoons freshly grated Parmesan cheese (30 ml)

GARNISH

1 lemon, cut into wedges

Fresh chopped parlsey

## FIRST PREPARE THE CREPES

■  In a medium bowl, combine the flour, eggs and milk and let stand for 30 minutes. Swish the oil around the hot crepe pan to prepare the surface, then pour the oil into the batter. Mix in well. This will make each crepe self-releasing.

■  Pour a small ladle of batter into the hot crepe pan. When it begins to bubble and look waxy, gently loosen the edges. Place a fresh dill sprig on the uncooked surface and flip the crepe over. Continue to cook the remaining crepes in the same manner. Cover them with a damp towel to await filling.

## NOW COOK THE FILLING

■  Place the butter beans in a food processor and process until pureed, adding a ¼ cup (59 ml) of the wine to make a paste. Set aside and reserve.

■  Heat the milk in a large skillet. Place the sole strips, sea scallops and mushrooms in the milk. Poach for 4 to 5 minutes but do not boil. When tender, remove from the milk and keep warm.

■  Take out 1 cup (236 ml) of poaching milk and place it in a small saucepan. Remove from the heat and add half of the dissolved arrowroot solution. Return to the heat and stir until thickened.

■  Add ¼ cup (59 ml) wine to the milk in the large skillet. Stir in the remaining arrowroot mixture to thicken and add ½ cup (118 ml) of the butter bean paste. Return the poached fish mixture to the sauce.

■  Add the dill and cayenne to the sauced fish. Add the tomatoes and chopped parsley for color and the small shrimp. Stir very gently to avoid breaking the sole.

■  Lay the reserved crepes in an oven-proof pan, dill side down. Fill each one with the fish mixture and fold. Turn seam side down. Pour the sauce over the herbed tops — they should just show through.

■  Sprinkle with Parmesan cheese. Place under the boiler until the cheese melts and browns — about 2 minutes.

■  Serve with sliced lemons on the side and a good scattering of chopped parsley. A little paprika will add color to compensate for the light touch with the cheese.

## Helpful Hints and Observations

BUTTER BEAN SAUCE - In this recipe I have tried to use the very lightly flavored butter bean to add some "body" to the sauce. It works for me — please see if it's a technique you an adapt to other recipes. You will get a certain amount of grainy texture that is different from the velvet softness achieved by a flour and butter roux-based sauce but you will notice from the nutritional comparison that we had a substantial amount of work to do!

PRE-PREPARATION - You can prepare this dish up to 6 hours in advance, up to and including filling and laying the crepes in the pan. Cover the filled crepes with plastic wrap and keep cool until needed. Reserve the sauce separately. Reheat the crepes in a 250°F (120°C) oven. Reheat the sauce, pour it over the heated crepes, sprinkle with cheese, cook and serve. This works well at a dinner party when you want more time with your guests.

# SCALLOPS & SHRIMP VINCENT

*C*hef de Cuisine, Vincent Guerithault, of the restaurant "Vincent's at Camelback" in Phoenix, Arizona, gave me permission to adapt his popular scallops and shrimp appetizer to provide a quick and elegant main dish. As you'll see, the recipe utilizes an unusual method: one in which the shrimp and scallop juices go to make up a lovely fresh orange sauce in only a matter of minutes.

Chef Vincent serves this dish as an appetizer in miniature bamboo steamers. I have increased the size of each portion and added basmati rice to make it a main course.

## Nutritional Profile

| PER SERVING | CLASSIC | MINIMAX |
|---|---|---|
| Calories | 643 | 324 |
| Fat (gm) | 18 | 2 |
| Calories From Fat | 25% | 6% |
| Cholesterol (mg) | 78 | 45 |
| Sodium (mg) | 1636 | 163 |
| Fiber (gm) | 8 | 3 |

■ *Classic Compared – Scallops & Shrimp Vincent*

## Time Estimate

Hands On
Unsupervised

*Minutes*   10   20   30   40   50   60   70   80   90

## Cost Estimate

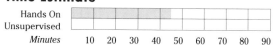

Low        Medium      Medium High   Celebration

*Serves 2*

## INGREDIENTS

2 cups water (472 ml)

½ cup basmati rice (118 ml)

½ teaspoon extra light olive oil with a dash of sesame oil (2.5 ml)

1 shallot, peeled and finely sliced

1 teaspoon freshly grated ginger root (5 ml)

Zest of ½ orange

1 tablespoon finely sliced fresh basil (15 ml)

1 cup de-alcoholized white wine (236 ml)

6 medium raw shrimp, peeled, deveined and the shells reserved

6 scallops

1 orange, segmented, pitted and the pith removed

1 tablespoon arrowroot (15 ml) mixed with

2 tablespoons de-alcoholized white wine (30 ml)

GARNISH

Finely sliced fresh basil to taste

Freshly ground white pepper to taste

## NOW COOK

■ Put the water in a medium saucepan, bring to a boil, add the basmati rice and cook for 10 minutes. Drain in a metal sieve or colander. Fill the saucepan about a quarter full with hot water. Put the sieve or colander filled with rice over the saucepan and cover. Not only will this keep the rice warm, it also helps the grains be separate and fluffy (see Helpful Hints).

■ Heat the oil in a pot large enough to hold a steamer platform to cook the seafood. Add the shallot, ginger root, orange zest and basil. Heat and stir.

■ Add the de-alcoholized wine and the reserved shrimp shells. Put the steamer platform in place, cover and bring to a boil. Place the shrimp and scallops on the steamer tray and steam for 5 minutes (try not to overcook seafood - 5 minutes should be enough). Remove the shrimp and scallops and keep warm.

■ Take the poaching liquid off the heat and strain it into a smaller saucepan. Add the arrowroot paste, return to the heat and stir until thickened.

■ Return the shrimp, scallops and orange pieces to the thickened poaching liquid. Sprinkle with additional fresh basil and white pepper to taste.

■ Serve the glistening, fragrant seafood in a nest of the steamed rice.

## Helpful Hints and Observations

PERFECT RICE - A major goal in most nations' rice cookery is to achieve separate, fluffy grains. Clogged, starchy rice masses are not, as a rule, enjoyable, except when using chopsticks!

Clogging happens through overcooking in too great a volume of water and from surface starch created by movement of the rice grains against themselves in packing and shipping.

The obvious first step must be to rid the rice of its surface starch by rinsing it under cold water until the water runs clear. CAUTION: Don't rinse the rice marked as "enriched" or having "added nutrients". These are put in the package in powder form and will rinse away. My recommendation would be to avoid these "nutrient added" products unless you consume a great deal of rice as your sole grain source.

Put the rinsed rice into a saucepan with 4 cups (944 ml) of boiling water for each cup (236 ml) of rice. Boil for 10 minutes and strain through a metal sieve or colander. Put the sieve or colander full of rice back over the saucepan a quarter filled with boiling water. Cover and steam for 15 minutes. Each grain will be separate and fluffy.

This will always work if you follow these directions exactly.

## Unusual Ingredients

BASMATI RICE - A fragrant, long-grain rice from India and Pakistan, basmati rice can be found in the specialty department of your local supermarket. A common substitute for basmati is a rice now grown in Texas called, Texmati.

SCALLOPS - Succulent, sweet and oh, so good to eat, scallops come in various sizes and types. The two most popular are the jumbo size sea scallops and the petite bay scallops. Also available, but on a limited basis, are singing scallops, purchased live inside their beautiful shells. When buying scallops, look for a whitish-orange color, and make sure the liquid surrounding them is thick with a sweet fragrance.

SHRIMP - This shellfish comes in various sizes and grades according to pound and brand. Shrimp are sized according to how many there are in a pound. We used a 16-20 size in this recipe. They are graded by number or by color 1, 2, 3, or white, brown and not so good. Select shrimp which are firm and fragrant, not fishy.

# SHRIMP GUMBO

*This Minimax version of a Creole classic is based upon the marvelous rendition served by Chef Leah Chase at her fabulous restaurant in New Orleans, "Dooky Chase." One food critic called Leah's gumbo, "the kind of dish that makes you want to throw down your spoon, rush into the kitchen and kiss the cook!" I hope this Minimax version inspires similar emotions — it could be the beginning of world peace!*

## Nutritional Profile

| PER SERVING | CLASSIC | MINIMAX |
|---|---|---|
| Calories | 415 | 510 |
| Fat (gm) | 17 | 3 |
| Calories From Fat | 36% | 5% |
| Cholesterol (mg) | 197 | 107 |
| Sodium (mg) | 1974 | 204 |
| Fiber (gm) | 14 | 11 |

■ *Classic Compared – Gumbo*

## Time Estimate

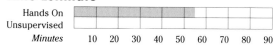

| | | | | | | | | | |
|---|---|---|---|---|---|---|---|---|---|
| Hands On | | | | | | | | | |
| Unsupervised | | | | | | | | | |
| *Minutes* | 10 | 20 | 30 | 40 | 50 | 60 | 70 | 80 | 90 |

## Cost Estimate

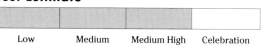

| Low | Medium | Medium High | Celebration |
|---|---|---|---|

*Serves 4*

## INGREDIENTS

1 pound fresh uncooked shrimp (500 gm)

1 cup uncooked long grain rice (236 ml)

4 tablespoons white flour (60 ml)

2 (14 ounce) cans cut okra (397 gm each), drained

2 tablespoons extra light olive oil with a dash of sesame oil (30 ml)

1 (6 ounce) can of no-salt tomato paste (170 gm)

1 large white onion, peeled and chopped

3 stalks celery, chopped

2 green bell peppers, seeded and chopped

2 garlic cloves, peeled and chopped

6 cups water (1.4 L)

6 thyme sprigs

2 bay leaves

½ teaspoon cayenne pepper (2.5 ml)

Chopped green onions and fresh parsley, for garnish

## FIRST PREPARE

■ Peel and devein the shrimp, saving the shells. Cut each shrimp into 3 pieces and set aside.

■ Put the shrimp shells into a medium saucepan and cover with 2 cups (472 ml) water. Bring to a boil and simmer just a couple of minutes. Strain out the shells, reserving the liquid. This flavor infused water will be used to cook your rice.

## NOW COOK

■ Cook the rice in the reserved shrimp shell water until all the liquid is absorbed and the rice is cooked through.

■ Put the flour in a saucepan over medium heat. Stir constantly until it turns light brown. Remove from the heat and cool. This step is crucial in developing a nice, toasty flavor and brown color for your gumbo.

■ Put the drained okra in a large plastic bag. Pour in the cooled flour. Seal off the top and shake until the okra is completely coated with flour.

■ Heat 1 tablespoon (15 ml) of the oil in a large pot. Add the flour-coated okra and the flour, one half at a time. You want the okra to fry and become really brown. Push the okra to one side of the pot.

■ On the other side of the pot, add the tomato paste and cook, stirring often. Continue cooking until the tomato paste turns a dark brown. This is a caramelizing called the Maillard reaction. Now

stir the tomato paste into the okra pieces. Turn the cooked okra out onto a plate, scraping up all the tasty brown pan residue.

■ Add the remaining oil to the same pot. Add the onions, celery, green pepper and garlic. Let the vegetables swelter and fry over high heat. Stir in the cooked okra and continue frying over high heat.

■ Pour in 4 cups (944 ml) water, thyme, bay leaves and the "creole torpedo" — the cayenne pepper. Simmer 30 minutes.

■ Just before you're ready to serve, stir in the shrimp. Cook only about 4 minutes. The shrimp should not be overdone.

■ To Serve: Spoon the rice, fragrant from the shrimp shells, into a bowl. Sprinkle the chopped green onions over the rice. Top with the shrimp gumbo. Sprinkle with emerald flecks of fresh, chopped parsley.

## Helpful Hints and Observations

WHAT TO DO WITH THE ROUX? - Another really tough issue: can it be Creole without roux, the incredible invention that provides both depth of taste and silky thickening to so many wonderful dishes? Roux is almost equal amounts of flour and butter, stirred together over mild heat to cook. This combination can actually thicken up to six times its own weight in liquid! It is also rich in saturated fat and calories. I think this recipe's method is a great alternative.

OKRA - Fresh okra wasn't available when we made this dish on the television program, so we tried the canned variety, which turned out to be just fine and much less complicated (or slippery). The fresh okra doesn't have a good, high nutrient value, so the normal canning loss wasn't too much of a threat.

## Unusual Ingredients

OKRA - A pod vegetable related to the cotton plant, whose origin is traced back to Africa. Brought to the Americas during the slave trade, okra is popular in the southern United States. Used as a thickener, okra replaced filet-powder, a thickener made of ground sassafras leaves. If using fresh okra, select pods that are a light to medium green. Fresh okra will keep only 3 to 5 days. It can be blanched and frozen.

SHRIMP - See Unusual Ingredients, page 47.

# JAMBALAYA

$C$*ajun — a term derived from Arcadian — is a mixed style of cooking often confused with Creole and Soul. This is not too surprising when you note that the same geographical area of Louisiana was first peopled by Choctaw Indians, followed by the Spanish, Africans, Arcadians from Nova Scotia and then the French. Jambalaya — so like paella — is almost certainly of Spanish origin.*

*This famous dish is always served as it cooks (eventually!) from pot to plate. For my taste, I really enjoy a crisp salad with Treena's vinaigrette (see recipe page 39) and lots of fresh salad herbs.*

## Nutritional Profile

| PER SERVING | CLASSIC | MINIMAX |
|---|---|---|
| Calories | 704 | 456 |
| Fat (gm) | 41 | 16 |
| Calories From Fat | 52% | 31% |
| Cholesterol (mg) | 241 | 178 |
| Sodium (mg) | 2312 | 981 |
| Fiber (gm) | 2 | 3 |

■ *Classic Compared – Austin's Jambalaya*

## Time Estimate

| Hands On | | | | | | | | | |
|---|---|---|---|---|---|---|---|---|---|
| Unsupervised | | | | | | | | | |
| *Minutes* | 10 | 20 | 30 | 40 | 50 | 60 | 70 | 80 | 90 |

## Cost Estimate

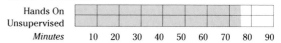

| Low | Medium | Medium High | Celebration |
|---|---|---|---|

*Serves 6*

## INGREDIENTS

16 ounces smoked ham hocks (450 gm)

4 cups water (944 ml)

4 bay leaves

1¾ pounds uncooked shrimp/prawns in their shells (800 gm)

2 cups boiling water (472 ml)

1 teaspoon extra light olive oil with a dash of sesame oil (15 ml)

1 onion, peeled and chopped

2 garlic cloves, peeled and chopped

½ cup chopped celery (118 ml)

1 tablespoon no-salt tomato paste (15 ml)

8 ounces lean ham steak (225 gm)

1 teaspoon fresh thyme (5 ml)

⅛ teaspoon whole cloves (.6 ml)

½ teaspoon fresh cayenne pepper (2.5 ml) (more if your tongue is asbestos)

1½ cups uncooked Louisiana long grain rice (354 ml), rinsed

1 (28 ounce) can Italian plum tomatoes (794 gm), drained and roughly chopped

¼ cup fresh chopped parsley (59 ml)

## ASSEMBLE

■ Cover the ham hocks with cold water. Bring to a boil and cook 5 minutes. Remove the hocks and discard the water.

■ Place the blanched ham hocks into 4 cups (944 ml) of fresh water, add the bay leaves and simmer 1 hour, or pressure cook for 20 minutes.

■ Remove the ham hocks, strain and reserve liquid. Cut lean meat in shreds and discard all the fat and bone. Return the reserved liquid to a saucepan and reduce to 2 cups (472 ml) to make a ham hock stock. Skim off any surplus fat.

■ Cook the shrimp in 2 cups (472 ml) boiling water for 3 minutes. Remove the shrimp and pour the liquid into the ham hock stock.

■ Put the cooked shrimp directly into ice water; peel, devein and slice in half lengthwise. Put the shells into the ham hock stock and continue cooking until reduced to 3 cups (708 ml) — about 25 percent reduction.

■ In a large saute pan, heat the oil and fry the onion, garlic and celery. After 2 minutes, add the tomato paste and cook 1 minute. Heat caramelizes the tomato paste into a deep brown color. Called the "Maillard reaction," this adds both color and depth of taste so essential when a lot of fat is removed from a recipe.

■ Cut the ham steak into bite size cubes and add to vegetables with the shredded ham hocks meat.

■ Place the thyme, cloves and cayenne pepper into a coffee bean grinder or a small food mill. Grind the spices to create a wonderfully fragrant powder. Put half the mixture in the ham hock stock and half in the vegetables.

■ Remove the shrimp shells from the stock.

■ Cook the rice in 3 cups (708 ml) of the ham hock stock for about 20 minutes, or until all the liquid has been absorbed. Never stir the rice while cooking — it can break its texture into a mush.

■ Combine the cooked rice with the vegetables and ham. Add the tomatoes and the shrimp.

■ Stir in the parsley and a scattering of chopped fresh thyme. Now taste it ... add more cayenne pepper if everyone likes it hot and spicy. Serve it hot!

## Helpful Hints and Observations

RICE COOKED SEPARATELY - I have separated the rice from the other ingredients in order to avoid the common problem of having the rice "catch" if you don't use a heavy enough pan. Removing so much of the fat makes the sticking problem even worse. However, please note that I have used a good stock to cook the rice ... so nothing is lost ... only fat and frustration.

## Unusual Ingredients

LOUISIANA LONG GRAIN RICE - This grain's biggest distinction is where it's grown - New Jersey! No, only kidding! Louisiana long grain is a relative of Indian rice, which is also long grain. Of the over 2,500 varieties of rice, the major distinction is the length of the grain - short and sticky or long and fluffy. You can find this rice in the gourmet section of most supermarkets. A converted long grain rice will substitute nicely.

CAYENNE PEPPER - I like to call this spice the "Creole Torpedo". It comes from the fruit of a South American hot pepper plant. Cayenne chilies have an oval shape, growing from 2 to 6 inches (5 to 15 cm) long. They start out green and turn red or orange as they ripen. Their dried, ground seeds form the product we are most familiar with. Fresh cayennes can be found in Asian and Latin markets. Select peppers that are firm and glossy green for sweet taste, red for hot.

# RIVER CAFE SUCCOTASH

David Burke has a problem with his restaurant ... it's the view! "The River Café" is located just east of the Brooklyn Bridge in New York City and sits right on the river bank with nothing to obscure the Manhattan skyline. But David wants people to look at his food, so he has to fight for attention.

As a result, David's cuisine is remarkable for its display. In a way he is a modern Antonin Careme (a chef with remarkable presentation skills in the 1800's) with a sense of humor. This dish is some-what altered, but owes its concept to David's genius for presentation.

I set the succotash off against freshly cooked spinach fettuccini - great colors and no other vegetable needed.

## Nutritional Profile

| PER SERVING | CLASSIC | MINIMAX |
|---|---|---|
| Calories | 484 | 202 |
| Fat (gm) | 17 | 4 |
| Calories From Fat | 32% | 16% |
| Cholesterol (mg) | 253 | 45 |
| Sodium (mg) | 2673 | 110 |
| Fiber (gm) | 10 | 6 |

■ *Classic Compared – Sauteed Shrimp & Ravioli with Pumpkin Succotash*

### Time Estimate

| | | |
|---|---|---|
| Hands On | | |
| Unsupervised | | |

*Minutes* 10 20 30 40 50 60 70 80 90

### Cost Estimate

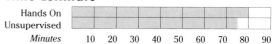

Low     Medium     Medium High     Celebration

*Serves 4*

## INGREDIENTS

4 mini pumpkins (or 1 medium sized pumpkin)

1 tablespoon extra light olive oil with a dash of sesame oil (15 ml)

2 cups shrimp stock (472 ml) (recipe page 210)

12 large shrimp, shells removed

1 cup diced red pepper (236 ml)

1 cup diced yellow pepper (236 ml)

½ cup de-alcoholized white wine (118 ml)

1 cup cooked corn kernels (236 ml)

1 cup cooked lima beans (236 ml)

1 tablespoon fresh chopped sage (15 ml)

¼ teaspoon freshly ground salt (1.25 ml)

½ cup fresh chopped chives (118 ml)

4 cups cooked spinach fettuccine (944 ml)

## FIRST PREPARE

■ Cut the stem and top off each pumpkin. Remove the seeds and stringy material (the seeds toasted and reserved to use on my breakfast cereal, Kerrmush, page 162). Scoop the pumpkin flesh out with a melon baller, leaving the shell ¼ inch (.75 cm) thick. Place the balls in a saucepan with the shrimp stock. Bring to a boil, then reduce heat and simmer until the pumpkins balls are tender - about 20 minutes. Puree in a food processor until smooth.

## NOW COOK

■ Preheat the oven to 350°F (180°C). Place the hollowed out pumpkins on a rack in a roasting pan with a small amount of water in the bottom. Cover with foil and bake for 35 minutes.

■ Heat the oil in a large skillet and saute the shrimp and peppers until the shrimp are lightly brown. Place in a small bowl and set aside. Pour the wine into the skillet, add the corn, lima beans and sage and cook 30 more seconds. Add the pumpkin puree and simmer another 1-2 minutes. Season with the freshly ground salt.

■ To Serve: On a large platter place the medium pumpkin shell or place one mini pumpkin on individual plates. Place 2 shrimp in the bottom of each pumpkin and pour in the succotash. Top with 1 more shrimp and a sprinkle of the chives. Serve with spinach fettucini fresh from the pot.

## Unusual Ingredients

PUMPKINS - Such a festive and beautiful vegetable for presenting your succotash! Look for pumpkins without brown blemishes and no soft spots. But don't think of pumpkins just for decoration. The winter squashes - like pumpkin, butternut, hubbard and acorn - not only yield tasty flesh, they are also wonderful sources of what are believed to be anti-cancer nutrients: Vitamin C, fiber and carotene.

SAGE - When you think back to the aroma of Thanksgiving stuffing, you're probably thinking about sage. And it's probably the common garden sage, although there are over 500 varieties of this herb. This is a strong herb for strong uses. It even holds up well when you throw it on barbecue coals to impart fragrance to grilling. But really, dried sage doesn't taste anything like the fresh, so try to find the real thing.

# APRICOT CILANTRO CHICKEN

Once in a while, Treena and I visit a restaurant that we really like. "Triples," on the west side of Lake Union in Seattle, Washington, is one of the best. One of their simple, yet wonderful dishes is a plump chicken breast with a chutney-like sauce, using apricots, cilantro and a special spice mix.

With their permission, I've tweaked the fat down a little, resulting in some excellent nutritional numbers (that's because it was so good to start with!).

I serve this dish with saffron-tinted rice and steamed kale. This is a recipe you must try - it is full of aroma, color and texture, almost the perfect Minimax dish!

## Nutritional Profile

| PER SERVING | CLASSIC | MINIMAX |
|---|---|---|
| Calories | 659 | 443 |
| Fat (gm) | 22 | 6 |
| Calories From Fat | 30% | 12% |
| Cholesterol (mg) | 97 | 86 |
| Sodium (mg) | 2177 | 151 |
| Fiber (gm) | 6 | 7 |

■ *Classic Compared – Chicken with Apricot Cilantro Sauce*

### Time Estimate

| | | |
|---|---|---|
| Hands On | | |
| Unsupervised | 3 Hours | |
| *Minutes* | 10  20  30  40  50  60  70  80  90 | |

### Cost Estimate

| Low | Medium | Medium High | Celebration |
|---|---|---|---|

*Serves 6*

## INGREDIENTS

6 (6 ounce) chicken breasts with skin, fat trimmed and de-boned (170 gm each) (see Helpful Hints)

MARINADE

2 tablespoons freshly squeezed lemon juice (30 ml)

1 tablespoon Dijon mustard (15 ml)

⅛ teaspoon cayenne pepper (.6 ml)

⅛ teaspoon freshly ground black pepper (.6 ml)

2 tablespoons de-alcoholized white wine (30 ml)

1 tablespoon fresh chopped thyme (15 ml)

SAUCE

1½ cups hot water (354 ml)

1 cup dried apricots (236 ml), without sulfites

12 Roma tomatoes, seeded and diced

1 medium onion, peeled and diced

1 teaspoon extra light olive oil with a dash of sesame oil (5 ml)

1 tablespoon fresh ginger root (15 ml), cut in fine strips

2 tablespoons fresh chopped cilantro (30 ml)

2 whole cloves

1 (1 inch) piece of cinnamon stick (2.5 cm)

¼ teaspoon coriander seeds (1.25 ml)

¼ teaspoon freshly ground black pepper (1.25 ml)

2 tablespoons apricot preserves (30 ml)

RICE

1 quart water (1 L)

1¼ cups uncooked long grain rice (295 ml)

Pinch of saffron (enough to color the rice *pale* yellow)

BOUQUET GARNI

4 whole cloves

6 black peppercorns

6 coriander seeds

1 (2 inch) piece of cinnamon stick (5 cm)

1 (1 inch square) piece of fresh ginger root (2.5 cm square)

2 sprigs fresh cilantro

GARNISH

8 cups kale leaves (1.9 L)

Fresh cilantro sprigs

## FIRST PREPARE

■ The Marinade: In a medium sized bowl, mix all the ingredients. Put the chicken breasts in the marinade and refrigerate for 3 hours.

■ Pour 1½ cups (354 ml) hot water over the dried apricots and let plump for 1 hour. Strain, reserving the water. Finely dice 4 of the apricots and set aside to use later in the rice. Chop the remaining apricots.

■ In a small food processor, or using a pestle and mortar, grind the cloves, cinnamon, coriander seeds and black peppercorns for the sauce. Push the spice powder through a sieve, trapping any large particles.

## NOW COOK

■ The Rice: Pour the water into a medium sized saucepan, add the bouquet garni and bring to a boil. Add the rice and saffron, cover and boil for 10 minutes. Strain through a metal sieve, or colander with very small holes! Place the sieve with the rice over the saucepan which has been a quarter filled with boiling water. Stir in the 4 chopped apricots. Cover and steam for 15 minutes.

■ Remove the chicken breasts from the marinade and place them in a hot skillet skin-side down. Brown for 1 minute, then reduce the heat and continue cooking for 5 minutes on each side. Remove and set aside. Pour 1 cup (236 ml) of the reserved apricot soaking water into the skillet to de-glaze the pan residues.

■ The Sauce: Heat the oil in a medium saucepan and cook the onion and ginger for 2 minutes.

■ Stir in the tomatoes and apricots. Strain the apricot and pan juices into the saucepan and bring to a rapid boil. Stir in the spice powder and apricot preserves to add a lovely gloss.

■ Strip the skin off the chicken breasts and return them to their original skillet. Coat with the sauce and sprinkle with the chopped cilantro leaves. Keep warm over medium heat.

■ Just before serving, steam the kale leaves for 3-4 minutes.

■ To Serve: Place 1 cup (236 ml) of the kale leaves on each dinner plate. Spoon ½ cup (118 ml) of rice in the center in the shape of a nest. Pour a spoonful of sauce on the rice and lay a sauce-coated chicken breast on top. Garnish with a large sprig of fresh cilantro and serve hot!

## Helpful Hints and Observations

CHICKEN SKIN - See Helpful Hints, page 59.

# CHICKEN ENGLISH MEHSON

*This dish was created for a viewer who we met in the streets of New York. Gary Mehson just happened to be English, but that didn't stop him from raving on about chicken in a rich sauce with mushrooms ... on pasta ... with LOTS of sauce. So I created Chicken English Mehson just for him. In the end, he flew in from London to Seattle to put it to the ultimate personal test. He liked it, so it carries his name.*

*A crisp salad to follow wouldn't hurt!*

## Nutritional Profile

| PER SERVING | CLASSIC | MINIMAX |
|---|---|---|
| Calories | 1231 | 699 |
| Fat (gm) | 53 | 18 |
| Calories From Fat | 39% | 23% |
| Cholesterol (mg) | 248 | 100 |
| Sodium (mg) | 2296 | 628 |
| Fiber (gm) | 7 | 9 |

■ *Classic Compared – Poulet Saute Maison*

## Time Estimate

| | | | | | | | | | |
|---|---|---|---|---|---|---|---|---|---|
| Hands On | | | | | | | | | |
| Unsupervised | | | | | | | | | |
| *Minutes* | 10 | 20 | 30 | 40 | 50 | 60 | 70 | 80 | 90 |

## Cost Estimate

| | | | |
|---|---|---|---|
| Low | Medium | Medium High | Celebration |

*Serves 2*

## INGREDIENTS

3 teaspoons extra light olive oil with a dash of sesame oil (15 ml)

1 medium onion, peeled and thinly sliced

2 teaspoons shallots (10 ml), thinly sliced

1 ounce Canadian bacon (28 gm), cut into matchsticks

1 teaspoon fresh thyme (5 ml)

1 tablespoon fresh chopped parsley (15 ml)

2 (6 ounce) chicken breasts (170 gm each), with skin

1 tablespoon tomato paste (15 ml)

2 ounces pimento (57 gm), cut into matchsticks

¾ cup de-alcoholized white wine (177 ml)

24 button mushrooms, quartered

14 pitted black olives, cut in half

5 teaspoons capers (25 ml)

2 cups beef stock (472 ml) (recipe page 210)

2 tablespoons arrowroot (30 ml)

4 ounces spaghetti (113 gm)

3 quarts water (2.8 L)

1 cup collard greens (236 ml), thinly sliced

GARNISH

Chopped parsley

## NOW COOK THE CHICKEN

■ In a large skillet, heat 1 teaspoon (5 ml) of the olive oil and saute the onion and shallots until translucent.

■ Add the Canadian bacon, thyme and parsley and cook for 2-3 minutes. Turn the contents of the pan out onto a plate and set aside.

■ Heat 1 more teaspoon (5 ml) of the olive oil and brown the chicken breasts on medium heat for 4 minutes on each side. Add the tomato paste and pimento. Cook until lightly browned. Remove the chicken and place it on a dish. Deglaze the pan with ½ cup (118 ml) of the de-alcoholized white wine. Remove the skin from the chicken.

■ Return the cooked onion mixture and chicken breasts to the skillet. Add the mushrooms, olives, and 4 teaspoons (20 ml) of the capers. Pour in the beef stock.

■ Make a paste of the arrowroot and the remaining wine. Remove the pan from the heat and stir the arrowroot paste in to thicken.

■ Cook the pasta in 3 quarts (2.8 L) of water for 10 minutes. Pour the pasta into a strainer set over a serving bowl. Pour the hot water out and place the noodles in the heated bowl. Toss with the collard greens and the remaining capers.

■ To Serve: Make a bed of pasta and place the chicken breasts in the center. Spoon the sauce over the chicken and garnish with chopped parsley.

## Helpful Hints and Observations

SAUCE COLOR - Beef stock is usually dark in color but we wanted it a deep reddish brown. The pimento and tomato paste combined with the olive oil did the trick. I cooked it at medium high heat and it quickly began to darken. When you try this, keep stirring, and don't fuss if the pan gets almost black — but don't let it burn! You'll get the hang of it quite easily. The trick is to aim for real darkness by stirring as the sugar content caramelizes.

Then add the stock all at once and stir to loosen the glaze on the bottom. When you thicken it with the tablespoon (15 ml) of arrowroot it simply needs to be strained to remove any overcooked solids and you are ready!

This method works well to create a quick, savory and great colored low fat sauce for all kinds of dishes.

## Unusual Ingredients

OLIVES - Green, black, small, large, smooth, wrinkled, there are so many different kinds of olives you really must try a few and see which ones suit your taste. Green olives are the unripe fruit of the olive tree picked in September; black olives are the same fruit left to ripen on the tree and picked in November; oil olives are the same fruit left on the tree until January. Olive trees normally live anywhere from 300 to 600 years!

SHALLOTS - Here's a good way to start a long debate: how do you describe the taste of this member of the onion family? Milder than yellow onions, but with a hint of garlic? You'll just have to come to your own conclusions. When buying shallots, like any dried onions, look for skin that is smooth and hard. Don't buy any type of onion that has tops sprouting or feels soft.

# CHICKEN POLESE

*This dish began many years ago in Sydney, Australia, at a truly wonderful Italian restaurant called "Beppies," owned by Guiseppe Polese. The recipe has remained a favorite over the years and has gone through most of my changes. I hope you enjoy the 90s version!*

That's Chicken Polese... Not Chicken Police.

## Nutritional Profile

| PER SERVING | CLASSIC | MINIMAX |
|---|---|---|
| Calories | 907 | 293 |
| Fat (gm) | 56 | 11 |
| Calories From Fat | 55% | 33% |
| Cholesterol (mg) | 308 | 85 |
| Sodium (mg) | 1748 | 515 |
| Fiber (gm) | 2 | 3 |

■ *Classic Compared – Chicken Polese*

## Time Estimate

| | | | | | | | | |
|---|---|---|---|---|---|---|---|---|
| Hands On | | | | | | | | |
| Unsupervised | | | | | | | | |

Minutes    10   20   30   40   50   60   70   80   90

## Cost Estimate

| | | | |
|---|---|---|---|
| Low | Medium | Medium High | Celebration |

*Serves 2*

## INGREDIENTS

1 teaspoon extra light olive oil with a dash of sesame oil (5 ml)

1 garlic clove, peeled and diced

2 (6 ounce) boneless chicken breasts (170 gm), with skin

½ sweet red pepper, finely diced

2 Roma tomatoes, finely diced

1 tablespoon fresh oregano (15 ml), finely chopped

Freshly ground black pepper

l tablespoon chopped fresh parsley (15 ml)

2 slices low-fat mozzarella cheese

4 anchovy fillets

2 tablespoons capers (30 ml)

½ teaspoon arrowroot (2.5 ml)

2 tablespoons de-alcoholized white wine (30 ml)

## NOW COOK

■ In a large skillet, heat the olive oil and fry the garlic until brown. Remove the garlic and discard.

■ In the same skillet, fry the chicken breasts for about 3 minutes on each side. Remove the skin and discard. Set the chicken aside.

■ In the same skillet, fry the red pepper for 2 minutes. Add the tomatoes, oregano, black pepper to taste and 1 teaspoon (5 ml) of the parsley.

■ Return the chicken to the pan, cover and reheat for about 2 minutes.

■ Cover each breast with a slice of cheese, 2 crisscrossed anchovy fillets and a sprinkle of capers. Cover and cook until the cheese melts - about 1 minute. Remove the chicken to a warm plate.

■ In a small bowl, mix the arrowroot and wine into a thin paste. Remove the pan from the heat and stir the arrowroot thickening into the pan juices. Return to low heat and stir until the sauce thickens.

■ Serve the chicken breasts in a juicy pool of sauce dusted with the remaining parsley.

## Helpful Hints and Observations

REMOVAL OF SKIN - A matter of timing! By now you will know that I always remove the fatty skin from poultry, except for Rock Cornish Hens that are too fiddly and too small to matter.

I do not, however, take the skin off before I cook the chicken when it is to be boiled, grilled, broiled, shallow-fried or roasted. The exception is when a bird has to be cut into sections for a casserole or stew.

The reason for retaining the skin for cooking is that it helps to keep the moisture in. The fat skin acts as a barrier to the escaping steam as the temperature rises.

It is sometimes messy and almost always a sacifice to remove it when it's golden and crispy, but if you can remember these numbers, it may help: Chicken, 3 lbs, roasted with skin on, skin removed before eating, 871 calories for the whole bird, 32 percent calories from fat. Chicken, 3 lbs, skin eaten, 1,333 calories for the whole bird, 47 percent calories from fat. This adds up to 51 grams of fat, or a total of 462 calories, usually divided among 4 people, to equal over 115 calories a head for skin!

BONING WHOLE CHICKENS - Whole chickens make good budget sense. Bone the chickens, then use the bones for the stock and freeze leftover portions for later use.

## Unusual Ingredients

ANCHOVY FILLETS - You might respond with a gasp of, "Oh, no!" Please let me encourage you to experience a wonderful taste sensation. Anchovies from a tin can be wonderful, but at the same time, some brands can be just awful. When purchasing anchovies, buy a good quality brand packed in olive oil. If your store has several brands, the best idea is to taste the most expensive. If they are not evenly sized and colored or if they are frayed at the edges take them back for a refund!

CAPERS - These are actually the unopened flower buds of a desert shrub, often found in the Sahara, but farmed commercially in Southern France, close to the Mediterranean. The buds are pickled and lend a terrific flavor to foods they accompany. Buy capers of good quality. The most valued are capers that are the least developed. They may be more expensive, but they're worth it. Look for capers near the pickles in your local supermarket. When opened, they keep well in the refrigerator providing the brine solution covers the buds.

# CHICKEN YANKOVA

*T*reena and I first ate this dish in Moscow back in 1970 B.G. (Before Glasnost). The original is a modified Chicken Kiev in which a chicken is smothered in butter and packed into a puffed pastry envelop and slow-baked. Delicious, but just look at the nutrition analysis of the classic: 70 grams of fat per serving!!!

The crisp bread loaf is best served whole and cut slice-by-slice on a wooden board. A great dish to serve with a colorful salad.

## Nutritional Profile

| PER SERVING | CLASSIC | MINIMAX |
|---|---|---|
| Calories | 1232 | 491 |
| Fat (gm) | 70 | 10 |
| Calories From Fat | 51% | 18% |
| Cholesterol (mg) | 336 | 48 |
| Sodium (mg) | 791 | 798 |
| Fiber (gm) | 4 | 5 |

■ *Classic Compared – Chicken Yankova*

## Time Estimate

Hands On
Unsupervised

*Minutes*  10  20  30  40  50  60  70  80  90

## Cost Estimate

Low        Medium      Medium High   Celebration

## INGREDIENTS

12 ounces mushrooms (340 gm), sliced

2 teaspoons extra light olive oil with a dash of sesame oil (10 ml)

1 tablespoon fresh lemon juice (15 ml)

¼ teaspoon cayenne pepper (1.25 ml)

½ teaspoon dried dill weed (2.5 ml)

1 French bread loaf (approximately 12 x 4 x 3 inches, 30 x 10 x 8 cm)

2 ounces dry Monterey Jack cheese (57 gm), grated

4 skinned chicken breasts

1 cup chicken stock (236 ml) (recipe page 210)

2 sprigs fresh tarragon, or 1 teaspoon dried (5 ml)

Freshly ground black pepper to taste

⅛ teaspoon saffron (.6 ml)

1 tablespoon arrowroot (15 ml) mixed with 2 table-spoons de-alcoholized dry white wine (30 ml)

GARNISH

Fresh sprigs of tarragon or parsley

## FIRST PREPARE

■ Put the mushrooms into a large bowl. Sprinkle them with half the olive oil, the lemon juice, cayenne pepper and dill. Cover the bowl with a plate and shake it thoroughly. Now the mush-rooms are evenly coated with the flavoring ingredients.

■ Cut lengthwise into the bottom of the French bread loaf at a 30 degree angle on both sides, taking a triangular section out of the loaf. Now cut the dough off the triangular section, leaving you with the crust, which you will use as a cap. Hollow out the rest of the loaf, leaving a practically dough-free loaf surrounded by crust. Sprinkle a quarter of the grated cheese over the cap and the rest into the hollowed loaf.

■ Preheat the oven to 300°F (150°C).

## NOW COOK

■ Pour the remaining olive oil on a plate and mop it up with the chicken breasts, coating both sides. Put the oiled breasts into a large heated skillet and brown for 4 minutes on each side (8 minutes total). Take the chicken out of the pan and set it aside.

■ Drop the mushrooms into the same pan and saute for 2-3 minutes. Set the mushrooms on a plate. Take another plate of similar size and place it on top of the mushrooms. Now squeeze the plates together while holding them over a small saucepan. The juice should drizzle into the saucepan!

■ Pour the chicken stock into the skillet, scraping the residue off the bottom of the pan. Pour this deglazed sauce into the small saucepan with the mushroom juice and keep on low heat.

■ Set the chicken breasts into the bread loaf. Lay one long sprig of tarragon over each chicken breast. If you can't get fresh tarragon, then sprinkle with the dried.

■ Season the mushrooms with pepper and pack them in over the chicken. Place the cap on the loaf, so that the filling is packed solid and enclosed. Cover with foil and bake in the preheated oven for 10 minutes, just to warm through. The crust should not become over-crisp.

■ The Sauce: Stir the saffron into the sauce in the small saucepan. Off the heat, mix in the arrowroot paste and bring it to a boil to thicken.

■ To Serve: Carve the loaf with a good serrated bread knife and place a couple of 1 inch (2.5 cm) slices of chicken yankova on a plate. Drizzle with the sauce and garnish with the rest of the grated cheese and a sprig of fresh tarragon or parsley - enjoy!

## Helpful Hints and Observations

DIG OUT THE DOUGH! - No, this isn't a hold up! I mean scoop out all the soft, inner bread leaving only a thin coating on the inner crust. You can dry this doughy center bread in the oven at 150°F (70°C) for about 20 minutes to make white bread crumbs. Just pop them in a blender or processor and store in an airtight container in a cool place.

TOSSING THE MUSHROOMS IN SEASONINGS - This is a very special way to reduce the amount of oil you add to vegetables, especially mushrooms. *please* try it ... and you'll be amazed at the result!

## Unusual Ingredients

TARRAGON - See Unusual Ingredients, page 149.

SAFFRON - Produced from the stigmas of a flowering crocus, it takes a minimum of 70,000 blooms to produce 1 pound (450 gm) of saffron! This is one of the reasons why it's one of the most expensive spices in the world. Fortunately, a very small amount goes a long way. Saffron can be bought in three different forms: threads, cakes or powder. One man said that saffron "refreshes the spirit and is good against fainting fits and palpitation of the heart." Well, at least enjoy its rich yellow color in your Minimax cooking.

# POULET BASQUAISE

$\mathcal{I}$'ve often used this recipe as an example of how fresh foods in season were simply assembled in a geographically isolated area between France and Italy to become a significant flavor combination that identified the region.

Couldn't this happen all over again where you live? Simply restrict yourself to foods grown within, say, 20 miles (32 km) in a specific season and see what you get!

This is a "food-of-the-people" dish - nothing haute cuisine about it. There's no need for other vegetables ... it's complete as it is.

## Nutritional Profile

| PER SERVING | CLASSIC | MINIMAX |
|---|---|---|
| Calories | 1001 | 604 |
| Fat (gm) | 57 | 14 |
| Calories From Fat | 51% | 20% |
| Cholesterol (mg) | 176 | 133 |
| Sodium (mg) | 1461 | 249 |
| Fiber (gm) | 4 | 6 |

■ *Classic Compared – Poulet Basquaise*

## Time Estimate

| Hands On | | | | | | | | | |
|---|---|---|---|---|---|---|---|---|---|
| Unsupervised | | | | | | | | | |

Minutes  10  20  30  40  50  60  70  80  90

## Cost Estimate

| Low | Medium | Medium High | Celebration |
|---|---|---|---|

*Serves 4*

## INGREDIENTS

1 whole (3½ pound) chicken (1.6 kg)

2 teaspoons extra light olive oil with a dash of sesame oil (10 ml)

⅔ cup finely diced mushrooms (157 ml)

2 garlic cloves, peeled and chopped

1 (6-ounce) can no-salt tomato paste

2 green peppers, cored, seeded and diced

1 red bell pepper, cored, seeded and diced

4 large tomatoes, seeded and diced

Freshly ground black pepper to taste

¾ cup dry white de-alcoholized wine (177 ml)

1 tablespoon fresh chopped parsley (15 ml)

1¼ cups long grain rice (295 ml)

8 cups water (1.9 L)

3 sliced mushrooms

1 tablespoon fresh sliced basil leaves (15 ml)

2 tablespoons fresh chopped parsley (30 ml)

1 teaspoon baking powder (5 ml)

## NOW COOK

■ Cut chicken into 3 pieces: The whole breast and two legs and thighs. Remove all the skin.

■ In a large, low-sided casserole, heat half of the oil and saute the garlic and mushrooms for 2 minutes. Turn out on a side dish and reserve.

■ Pour the remaining oil into the casserole, turn the heat up high and brown the chicken pieces, turning often. Stir in the tomato paste, making sure the chicken gets coated. The tomato paste caramelizes and turns brown: the Maillard reaction. Add the diced peppers. Make sure you dredge up any brown residue off the bottom of the pot. This provides a smokiness that gives depth of taste without fat.

■ Pour in the wine, the reserved mushrooms and the tomatoes. Grind in fresh black pepper to taste. Make sure the chicken breast is turned meat side down into the pot to ensure thorough cooking. Put the lid on and simmer at medium heat for 35 minutes.

■ While the Poulet Basquaise is simmering, cook the rice: In a medium saucepan, boil the water. Add the rice, bring to a boil again, cover and simmer for 10 minutes. Drain the rice through a metal strainer or colander. To keep the rice hot,

add 2 inches (5 cm) of hot water to the pan. Put the strainer full of cooked rice on top, cover with a small lid and keep on medium heat for up to 15 minutes. The rice will continue to cook in a gentle steam and will be perfectly fluffy without becoming overcooked.

■ After the chicken is done, remove it from the pot onto a cutting board and carve it into nice chunks. By cooking the chicken in large pieces you get a much more attractive and succulent piece of meat.

■ Drop the chicken pieces back into the sauce. Stir in the sliced mushrooms, chopped basil and parsley - a fresh, field-like touch to your finished dish! And now an ingredient that will make an astonishing taste difference: stir in the baking powder. This smooths out the flavor, canceling any acidity and allowing the sweetness to come through.

■ Put the cooked rice on a large serving platter, make a well in the middle and fill with the chicken.

### Helpful Hints and Observations

SMOKY DEPTH - This is a standard for me: to cook tomato paste along with the peppers until it begins to brown. It develops an unusual, smoky, sweet yet acid, taste that compensates to some degree for the loss of fat.

### Unusual Ingredients

TOMATOES - When selecting tomatoes for this recipe, look for unpackaged ones so you can examine them. Watch out for bruises, cracks, moldy spots and other blemishes. Choose tomatoes that are ripe, firm and plump. Two varieties that would be good for this recipe are the round or beefsteak tomatoes or the Italian Roma tomatoes (the pear shaped ones) that are fleshy, have few seeds and are a little sweeter than American varieties.

BASIL - This herb is often proclaimed as the perfect accompaniment to anything that includes tomato. A pungent herb, basil has been used in the kitchen since at least 400 B.C. Its name, from the Greek, basilikon, means kingly. Indeed, in many places custom demanded that the king himself cut the first basil of the season with a golden sickle! But please don't wait for a king to cut basil for your use in the kitchen. Its fragrant leaves compliment many vegetables and meats.

# SMOKED CHICKEN BREASTS

*My* very good friend, Chef de Cuisine, Ludger Szmania, has mastered the art of aroma, color and texture for alternative cuisine. This smoked chicken idea got mixed up with a Chinese pot steamer technique and came out very well. It really is a new style of cooking for you to try. You might like to try cooking fish or even a whole chicken or duck in the same manner.

## Nutritional Profile

| PER SERVING | CLASSIC | MINIMAX |
|---|---|---|
| Calories | 846 | 119 |
| Fat (gm) | 50 | 2 |
| Calories From Fat | 53% | 14% |
| Cholesterol (mg) | 150 | 0 |
| Sodium (mg) | 1721 | 622 |
| Fiber (gm) | 2 | 2 |

■ *Classic Compared – Chicken with Cream Gravy*

## Time Estimate

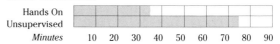

| Hands On | | | | | | | | | |
|---|---|---|---|---|---|---|---|---|---|
| Unsupervised | | | | | | | | | |
| *Minutes* | 10 | 20 | 30 | 40 | 50 | 60 | 70 | 80 | 90 |

## Cost Estimate

| Low | Medium | Medium High | Celebration |
|---|---|---|---|

*Serves 4*

## INGREDIENTS

4 large, skinless and boneless chicken breasts approximately 7 or 8 ounces each (227 grams) You can cut these from whole birds! If you do so, let the first section of the wing remain, so the breast is not entirely boneless.

MARINADE

½ teaspoon cinnamon (2.5 ml)

¼ cup red wine vinegar (59 ml)

3 whole cloves, crushed

½ teaspoon fresh grated ginger root (2.5 ml)

¼ cup low sodium soy sauce (59 ml)

3 sprigs fresh thyme

Freshly grated nutmeg

Freshly ground black pepper

THE SMOKE

2 Earl Grey Tea Bags

2 tablespoons brown sugar (30 ml)

2 tablespoons brown rice (30 ml)

1 cinnamon stick

CINNAMON SAUCE

1 medium sweet onion, peeled and finely sliced

1 tablespoon brown sugar (15 ml)

1 teaspoon extra light olive oil with a dash of sesame oil (5 ml)

1 cup chicken broth (236 ml)

1 cinnamon stick

2 sprigs of thyme

## FIRST PREPARE

■ Put the chicken breasts in a bowl. Pour the marinade ingredients on top and marinate for at least 30 minutes.

■ For the Smoke: Fold several layers of aluminum foil into a platform that will hold the smoke ingredients about 1 inch off the bottom of a solid cast aluminum or cast iron Dutch Oven. Place the ingredients on top of the platform in the bottom of the pot.

## NOW COOK

■ For the Sauce: Place the onion slices in a saucepan along with the brown sugar and oil. Cook on medium heat until caramelized. Add the chicken broth, cinnamon stick and thyme sprigs. Bring to a boil and reduce the volume by about one third.

■ Puree the reduced sauce in a food processor. Strain through a fine sieve into a saucepan and keep warm.

■ Remove the chicken from the marinade and set aside.

■ Add the marinade to the sauce and bring back to a boil. Continue reducing.

■ Start smoking the chicken: Put the Dutch oven "smoker" lid on over high heat. In about 6 minutes it should begin to smoke. Set a steamer basket over the smoke. Set the chicken on it and smoke for 10 minutes. It will be a lovely dark brown! Remove the Dutch oven from heat and let sit for 5 minutes. NOTE: When you take the chicken out, it's a good plan to take the aluminum foil and smoke ingredients out to the garbage immediately! This rids your home of any potential for residual smoke smell!!

■ Serve the smoked chicken breasts with a lovely rice. Saffron rice adds great yellow color! Pour the cinnamon sauce on top, garnished with a sprig of fresh thyme and fresh vegetables on the side.

## Helpful Hints and Observations

THE DUTCH OVEN - I used a SCANPAN 2001+ Dutch oven with a capacity of 6½ quarts (6 liters). It worked very well because of its non-stick finish. I simply rinsed it out with warm, soapy water and it was as good as new. The glass lid went through the dishwasher!

THE SMOKE - There is a great deal being said about various smoke woods, and each one does add its own flavor. But to my taste this unique blend of Earl Grey tea, brown rice, cinnamon and brown sugar is a delight - well worth a try!

## Unusual Ingredients

EARL GREY - A black tea named after the illustrious Prime Minister of England who was given the blend in return for service in China. Earl Grey tea is flavored with the oil of bergamot, a Mediterranean citrus. Find a tea that is individually wrapped, which helps to maintain freshness. Remember not all brands taste alike. Find the style you prefer and enjoy.

CINNAMON - A native spice of Southeast Asia, it is the dried inner bark of related evergreen trees. Of these trees one produces true cinnamon, the other, a spice properly named cassia. Mostly what is sold as cinnamon is truly cassia. The way to tell them apart is by color. Cinnamon is a tan brown color, cassia is reddish brown. This spice we know as cinnamon is one of the world's oldest commodities.

# EVIL JUNGLE PRINCESS

$\mathcal{I}$would be delighted to learn where this classic Thai dish got its somewhat odd title. If you know, please write. We tried to find out from the charming Thai chef and co-collaborator on this dish, Malee Chu, but it was the only thing she didn't know!

Incidentally, you should visit Malee's restaurant when you are in Scottsdale, Arizona. It's called, "Malee's at the Borgata."

Serve with a small bowl of short grain white rice, such as pearl rice, on the side. You can sprinkle the rice with some rice wine vinegar and cayenne pepper for extra flavor.

Our numbers show the use of a strained coconut milk, not store bought cream. To do so would increase the calories from fat to 43 percent.

## Nutritional Profile

| PER SERVING | CLASSIC | MINIMAX |
|---|---|---|
| Calories | 525 | 202 |
| Fat (gm) | 41 | 6 |
| Calories From Fat | 71% | 27% |
| Cholesterol (mg) | 225 | 58 |
| Sodium (mg) | 803 | 114 |
| Fiber (gm) | 1 | 4 |

■ *Classic Compared – Chicken a la King*

## Time Estimate

| | | | | | | | | | |
|---|---|---|---|---|---|---|---|---|---|
| Hands On | | | | | | | | | |
| Unsupervised | | | | | | | | | |
| *Minutes* | 10 | 20 | 30 | 40 | 50 | 60 | 70 | 80 | 90 |

## Cost Estimate

| | | | |
|---|---|---|---|
| Low | Medium | Medium High | Celebration |

*Serves 2*

## INGREDIENTS

1 teaspoon peanut oil (5 ml)

2 garlic cloves, peeled and crushed

2 tablespoons finely chopped lemon grass (30 ml)

2 Kaffir lime leaves, softened in a little warm water and finely chopped

1 (8 ounce) chicken breast (227 gm), skin removed, and sliced into 2 x ¼ inch (5 x.75 cm) strips

¼ cup unsweetened coconut milk (59 ml) (can be purchased ready-made in canned form)

¼ cup chicken stock (59 ml) (recipe page 210)

½ teaspoon chili powder (2.5 ml)

1 teaspoon sugar (5 ml)

7 fresh peppermint leaves, finely chopped

2 tablespoons fish sauce (30 ml)

½ teaspoon cayenne pepper, or to taste (2.5 ml)

2 tablespoons freshly squeezed lemon juice, or to taste (30 ml)

1 cup finely sliced chinese cabbage (236 ml)

1 cup finely sliced red cabbage (236 ml)

1⅔ cups Enokitake mushrooms (392 ml)

## NOW COOK

■ Heat the peanut oil in a large skillet and add the garlic. Cook until the oil has been infused with the garlic flavor, about 1 minute, then remove and discard the garlic.

■ Add the lemon grass, lime leaves and chicken and stir-fry until the chicken just loses its raw look.

■ Add the coconut milk, chicken stock and chili powder and stir-fry until the chicken turns completely white and the sauce has cooked down into a coating, not floating, cream.

■ Stir in the sugar, mint leaves and fish sauce. You also need to add the cayenne pepper at this time, but remember: the amount of cayenne you add will determine a 1 to 5 star heat factor. I can't go past a ** but my wife, Treena, can manage at least a ***** or 1 full teaspoonful (5 ml)!

■ Stir in the lemon juice to suit your taste.

■ Turn the sliced cabbages and the mushrooms into a hot skillet with a little chicken stock or water (just enough to create a little steam), just to heat through, about 2 minutes, then turn out onto a serving plate.

■ Serve the vegetables with the sauced chicken on top.

## Helpful Hints and Observations

COCONUT MILK - See Helpful Hints, page 203.

### Unusual Ingredients

ENOKITAKE MUSHROOMS - Tiny, whitish mushrooms with skinny stems which are sold in clumps in plastic bags. The Japanese never eat them raw. They are usually cooked for a minute or two in soups or used as a garnish for fish or chicken.

FISH SAUCE - See Unusual Ingredients, page 23.

LEMON GRASS - Here's the reason why a Thai or Vietnamese dish will have a compelling flavor you can't quite put your finger on. Lemon grass doesn't give a strong lemon flavor, just a subtle lemon perfume. Purchase it in oriental specialty markets or a good produce department in a large supermarket.

KAFFIR LIME LEAVES - See Unusual Ingredients, page 23.

# SLOPPY JOE

$\mathcal{E}$veryone raised in North America seems to have a Sloppy Joe in their gastronomic experience and every recipe has its own secret ingredient. I've got several in this recipe, and they all add up to Minimax flavor with much less fat and refined carbohydrate. It's also a lot of fun and easy to fix!

　　Serve on a hot plate with a crisp, colorful salad on the side.

## Nutritional Profile

| PER SERVING | CLASSIC | MINIMAX |
|---|---|---|
| Calories | 470 | 338 |
| Fat (gm) | 29 | 7 |
| Calories From Fat | 54% | 20% |
| Cholesterol (mg) | 77 | 51 |
| Sodium (mg) | 1165 | 592 |
| Fiber (gm) | 3 | 6 |

■ *Classic Compared – Not So Sloppy Joe*

## Time Estimate

| Hands On | | | | | | | | | |
|---|---|---|---|---|---|---|---|---|---|
| Unsupervised | | | | | | | | | |
| *Minutes* | 10 | 20 | 30 | 40 | 50 | 60 | 70 | 80 | 90 |

## Cost Estimate

| Low | Medium | Medium High | Celebration |
|---|---|---|---|

*Serves 4*

## INGREDIENTS

1 tablespoon extra light olive oil with a dash of sesame oil (15 ml)

1 cup diced onion (236 ml)

¼ cup diced carrot (59 ml)

¼ cup diced celery (59 ml)

2 garlic cloves, peeled and chopped

½ green bell pepper, cored, seeded and finely chopped

12 ounces ground turkey (340 gm) or turkey breast

¼ cup bulgur wheat (59 ml)

3 tablespoons tomato paste (45 ml)

1 tablespoon dark brown sugar (15 ml)

1 tablespoon fresh oregano (15 ml)

⅛ teaspoon freshly ground salt (.6 ml)

¼ teaspoon freshly ground black pepper (1.25 ml)

1½ cups de-alcoholized red wine (354 ml)

1 cup low-salt tomato sauce (236 ml)

4 whole wheat hamburger buns

## NOW COOK

■ Heat the oil in a large wok and stir-fry the onion, carrot, celery, garlic and green pepper until just tender. Tip the vegetables into a bowl and set aside.

■ In the same wok or a large frypan, brown the ground turkey. Stir in the bulgur, tomato paste and brown sugar and cook until the tomato paste's color darkens.

■ Sprinkle in the oregano and return the cooked vegetables to the pan. Season with the salt and pepper to taste.

■ Pour in 1 cup of the wine and half of the tomato sauce. Cover and cook for 15 minutes.

■ Meanwhile, put the hamburger buns into a low oven to toast.

■ Just before serving, stir in the remaining wine and tomato sauce and the horseradish. Place the bottom side of a toasted bun on a plate and spoon the Sloppy Joe mixture over the top. Set the top just slightly over to one side to expose the filling.

## Helpful Hints and Observations

ADDING LIQUIDS IN TWO PLACES - In this recipe you'll note that I add the de-alcoholized wine and tomato sauce in equal amounts at either end of the cooking process. The reason for this is fresh taste and aroma. I get the flavors of both the wine and the tomato into the meat and vegetables in the simmering process but then I pick up tremendous freshness of aroma, taste and color by the last minute addition.

Please give it a try. Taste it before you make the final addition and then again when it's added. Now you can try this idea with other dishes that call for tomato juice and/or wine.

DE-ALCOHOLIZED WINE HELPS - De-alcoholized wine allows for last moment addition without concern for the alcohol steam-off which can take some time.

## Unusual Ingredients

GROUND TURKEY - All you have to do is look: It's there in its little plastic packet waiting for you to buy it. Leaner (especially in the saturated fat department) and less expensive than ground beef, turkey is a good substitute in many dishes. Don't wait until next Thanksgiving! My personal choice (that means you are not under any pressure to agree) is to buy turkey as breast or thigh, according to the recipe and then grind it when I need it.

WHOLE WHEAT BUNS - Every bit of fiber helps! When you look for whole grain buns, don't just grab the first brown colored bread you see. Brown color might just indicate that there's a lot of molasses in the recipe. Let me suggest that you read the label. You'll get the most nutrients if one of the first ingredients listed is 100% whole wheat flour that is stone ground. The next best thing is whole wheat or other whole grain flour (not stone ground).

# SUPER BURRITOS

*I*'m not as practiced with Mexican food as I would like to be, but I've traveled in Mexico and eaten in some truly wonderful restaurants. I had missed out on burritos and therefore was delighted to "have a go." What a happy combination this recipe turned out to be. I love it ... hope you do, too!

## Nutritional Profile

| PER SERVING | CLASSIC | MINIMAX |
|---|---|---|
| Calories | 1357 | 783 |
| Fat (gm) | 68 | 13 |
| Calories From Fat | 45% | 15% |
| Cholesterol (mg) | 185 | 62 |
| Sodium (mg) | 1657 | 1211 |
| Fiber (gm) | 10 | 17 |

■ *Classic Compared – Super Burritos*

## Time Estimate

| Hands On | | | | | | | | | |
|---|---|---|---|---|---|---|---|---|---|
| Unsupervised | | | | | | | | | |
| *Minutes* | 10 | 20 | 30 | 40 | 50 | 60 | 70 | 80 | 90 |

## Cost Estimate

| | | | |
|---|---|---|---|
| Low | Medium | Medium High | Celebration |

*Serves 4*

## INGREDIENTS

8 (8 inch) flour tortillas (20 cm)

1 cup dried pinto beans (236 ml)

5 cups chicken stock (1.2 L) (recipe page 210)

1 cup uncooked brown rice (236 ml)

2 Anaheim peppers, diced

1 tablespoon extra light olive oil with a dash of sesame oil (15 ml)

1 cup chopped onion (236 ml)

½ cup chopped green pepper (118 ml)

1 garlic clove, peeled and diced

12 ounces ground chicken (340 gm) (from a 1¼ pound chicken breast with bone (600 gm))

1 tablespoon chili powder (15 ml)

¼ teaspoon ground cumin (1.25 ml)

1 cup strained yogurt (236 ml) (recipe page 210)

5 large Roma tomatoes, seeded and diced

¼ cup fresh chopped cilantro (59 ml)

¼ cup chopped green onion (59 ml)

1 cup shredded lettuce (236 ml)

2 ounces dry Monterey Jack cheese (57 gm)

## FIRST PREPARE

■ Stack tortillas and wrap tightly in foil. Heat in a 350°F (180°C) oven for 10 minutes to soften.

## NOW COOK

■ Put the pinto beans and 2 cups (472 ml) of the chicken stock into a pressure cooker and cook for 10 minutes. Add the brown rice, the remaining chicken stock and half of the diced Anaheim peppers and cook 15 minutes more.

■ In a medium sized casserole, heat the olive oil, add the onion, green pepper and garlic and cook until the onion is soft and slightly translucent.

■ Add the ground chicken to the mixture, tossing and breaking up the chicken until the mixture is an even texture throughout.

■ Add the chili powder and cumin. Stir in half of the remaining diced Anaheim peppers.

■ Mix 1½ cups (354 ml) of the rice and beans into the chicken filling.

■ Spoon a scant ¼ cup (59 ml) of filling onto the lower half of each warmed tortilla. Fold the opposite sides in until they meet. Fold the bottom and top edges just over the filling and turn over on a baking sheet so that all the folds are underneath. Bake in a 350°F (180°C) oven for 10 to 12 minutes.

■ Make the sauce by combining the strained yogurt, tomatoes and the remaining Anaheim peppers in a medium-sized bowl. Stir in the cilantro and green onion.

■ Slit the cooked burritos down the middle and spoon the sauce into the top. Serve them on a bed of shredded lettuce, with a sprinkling of Monterey Jack cheese and the remaining beans and rice on the side.

## Helpful Hints and Observations

THE BREAD TRICK - After placing meat in the grinder, finish it off with a piece of bread. When you see the bread coming through, you'll know you've ground all the meat!

MUCHO GRANDE CALORIES - It's a big meal at 783 calories. So if you are watching the numbers you could settle for one burrito at 392. The fat numbers are actually very good.

## Unusual Ingredients

TORTILLAS - If you want to start a fight in Mexico, probably a good way to do it would be to declare one tortilla better than another. In one province alone you can buy 30 different types! So in the interests of maintaining peace, keep this information under your hat: I recommend a trip to the grocery store to look for whole wheat tortillas. Now, I know corn tortillas are the classic. But in this case I'm being an advocate for whole grains in your Minimax experiments.

PINTO BEANS - Have you run into these yet? When you buy them raw they're quite festive: beige with white speckles. When cooked, they lose their speckles. Pintos are the traditional bean used to make "frijoles refritos" or Mexican refried beans. Like all beans, they're quite nutritious, but need to be complemented with grains, nuts or seeds in order for your body to complete their incomplete protein. Guess what? Eating pinto beans with tortillas is a simple way to do this!

# CREPES ANTONIN CAREME

*A*ntonin Careme was a famous chef whose complex display provided the great Escoffier (1784-1833) with an opportunity to propose a simple method of "modern" cookery, and so the urge to simplify goes on and on ...

Today's approach is one in which to simplify also means to reduce risk, while at the same time enhancing aroma, color and texture.

I have found this to be an enormously popular recipe. It does take time but it is definitely inexpensive and it looks and tastes wonderful. If you serve it from a large platter, or straight from the broiler, you will need a long bladed palette knife.

## Nutritional Profile

| PER SERVING | CLASSIC | MINIMAX |
|---|---|---|
| Calories | 537 | 285 |
| Fat (gm) | 31 | 8 |
| Calories From Fat | 53% | 25% |
| Cholesterol (mg) | 178 | 155 |
| Sodium (mg) | 651 | 154 |
| Fiber (gm) | 2 | 1 |

■ *Classic Compared – Crepes Antonin Careme*

## Time Estimate

| | | |
|---|---|---|
| Hands On | | |
| Unsupervised | | |

Minutes: 10 20 30 40 50 60 70 80 90

## Cost Estimate

| Low | Medium | Medium High | Celebration |
|---|---|---|---|

*Serves 4*

## INGREDIENTS

FILLING

2 celery stalks, finely chopped
12 ounces cooked chicken meat (340 gm), diced

CREPE BATTER

1 whole egg
1 egg yolk
9 fluid ounces non-fat milk (266 ml)
½ cup all-purpose flour (118 ml)
Freshly ground white pepper
1 teaspoon extra light olive oil with a dash of sesame oil (5 ml)
1 teaspoon fresh chopped tarragon (5 ml)

SAUCE

⅔ cup non-fat milk (156 ml)
2 cups chicken stock (472 ml) (recipe page 210)
3 tablespoons arrowroot (45 ml) mixed with ½ cup de-alcoholized white wine (118 ml)
⅛ teaspoon freshly grated nutmeg (.6 ml)
⅛ teaspoon freshly ground white pepper (.6 ml)
½ cup heavy cream (118 ml), stiffly whipped, optional

GARNISH

½ teaspoon freshly grated Parmesan cheese (2.5 ml)
Fresh chopped parsley

## FIRST PREPARE

■ The Crepes: In a large bowl, beat together the egg, egg yolk and milk. Beat in the flour and pepper until fully incorporated. Set aside to rest for 30 minutes before cooking the crepes.

■ Pour the olive oil into a crepe pan, swish it around to cover all surfaces, then pour the excess into the crepe batter. This helps to make the crepes self-releasing and precludes having to re-oil the pan.

Over medium to high heat, pour a small ladle of batter into the prepared pan. Tilt the pan so the batter spreads evenly over the entire bottom surface. When the crepe begins to bubble and looks waxy - about 2 to 3 minutes - use a spatula to gently loosen the edges. Sprinkle with ⅛ teaspoon (.6 ml) of the tarragon, then flip over. Cook until golden brown on the second side - about 1 minute. Continue cooking all the crepes in this manner.

■ The Filling: Poach the chopped celery in boiling water until just tender - about 10 minutes. Drain and set aside. When cool, combine with the diced chicken.

■ The Sauce: In a small saucepan, over medium heat, mix the milk and stock. Remove the saucepan from the heat and stir in the arrowroot mixture. Return to the heat and stir until thickened. Season with nutmeg and pepper. At this point you can add the whipped cream for its extra whitening effect and depth of taste, but don't forget to count the cost first: It adds 103 calories per serving and 11 grams of fat which will make the percentage of calories from fat, 44 percent!

■ Combine half of the thickened sauce with the chicken filling. Reserve the other half to pour over the crepes.

■ Assembling the crepes: Place a crepe on a large, oven-proof serving dish, herbed-side down. Spoon a good amount of filling in a line down the center. Fold the edges gently over the filling and then turn the crepe over so it is seam side down. Proceed to fill all the crepes in this manner.

Pour the remaining sauce over the crepes, sprinkle with Parmesan cheese and pop them under the broiler until the cheese melts - about 1 minute. Scatter a little parsley on top and "Voila!" (as they say in most kitchens ... whether French is spoken or not!).

### Helpful Hints and Observations

This recipe is literally chock full of techniques, but sometimes it is really hard to describe something as simple as turning a very fine crepe - almost too fragile to flip!

Here then is a simple illustration that may help you to avoid the frustration of seeing your limp masterpiece draped over the edge and slowly slipping onto the stove!

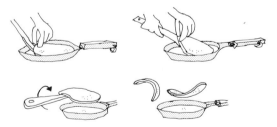

### Unusual Ingredients

BAY LEAVES - See Unusual Ingredients, page 17.

# ENCHILADAS FINA COCINA

*Norman Fierros is a man with a mission: to upgrade the tastes and appeal of classic Mexican food. His "Fina Cocina" restaurant in downtown Phoenix is proof that this new "pudding" is worth eating - in fact, it's wonderful and highly inventive. I've spring-boarded off one of Norman's ideas with one of my own. Now why don't you do the same with mine?*

A man with a mission

## Nutritional Profile

| PER SERVING | CLASSIC | MINIMAX |
|---|---|---|
| Calories | 826 | 385 |
| Fat (gm) | 50 | 12 |
| Calories From Fat | 55% | 27% |
| Cholesterol (mg) | 182 | 30 |
| Sodium (mg) | 1858 | 447 |
| Fiber (gm) | 10 | 8 |

■ *Classic Compared – Enchilada*

## Time Estimate

| Hands On Unsupervised | | | | | | | | | |
|---|---|---|---|---|---|---|---|---|---|
| Minutes | 10 | 20 | 30 | 40 | 50 | 60 | 70 | 80 | 90 |

## Cost Estimate

| | | | |
|---|---|---|---|
| Low | Medium | Medium High | Celebration |

*Serves 4, 2 Enchiladas Each*

## INGREDIENTS

TOMATILLO SAUCE

1 teaspoon extra light olive oil with a dash of sesame oil (5 ml)

1 medium onion, peeled and sliced

2 cloves garlic, peeled and chopped

1 pound tomatillos (500 gm), peeled and diced into ½ inch (1.5 cm) cubes

1 jalapeño pepper, seeded and finely chopped

1 cup water (236 ml)

1 cup chicken broth (236 ml)

3 tablespoons arrowroot (45 ml) mixed with 3 tablespoons water (45 ml)

FILLING

1 tablespoon extra light olive oil with a dash of sesame oil (5 ml)

1 red onion, sliced very thin

1 red pepper, seeded and sliced

¼ cup chicken broth (59 ml)

1 teaspoon cumin seed (5 ml)

1 teaspoon cayenne pepper (5 ml)

8 ounces cooked chicken meat, preferably thigh and leg, without skin, fat or bone (227 gm)

1 tablespoon fresh chopped cilantro (15 ml)

1 tablespoon fresh chopped parsley (15 ml)

Reserved arrowroot mixture

8 (10 inch) flour tortillas (25 cm)

Chopped cilantro leaves, for garnish

## FOR THE TOMATILLO SAUCE

■  Heat the olive oil in a medium saucepan. Add the onion, garlic, tomatillos and jalapeño pepper. Stir together, letting the volatile oils fill the room. Ah! Ambrosia! Cook 1 minute, add the water and bring to a boil. Boil 7 minutes.

■  Strain the tomatillo sauce through a sieve to remove the skin and seeds. I use a machine that separates the juice from the skin and seeds for you. See Helpful Hints and Observations, page 145.

■  Put the strained tomatillo sauce into a medium saucepan. Stir in the chicken broth, and boil for 2 minutes.

■  Remove the tomatillo sauce from the heat and stir in 1 tablespoon (15 ml) of the arrowroot paste to thicken. Reserve the rest.

## FOR THE FILLING

■  In a large saute pan, heat the olive oil over high heat. Drop in the red onion and red peppers and cook 1 minute.

■  Add the chicken broth, cumin  seed, cayenne pepper, chicken meat, cilantro and parsley.

■  Add the remaining arrowroot paste and stir to thicken and gloss the vegetables.

## ASSEMBLY

■  To warm tortillas, place them on a plate over a pot of hot water. Cover with a clean towel.

■  Place a warm flour tortilla on a warm serving plate. Spoon filling down the middle. Roll into a cylinder. Spoon tomatillo sauce over the top. Garnish with a dollop of the colorful filling on the side and a sprinkle of cilantro leaves.

## Helpful Hints and Observations

TART TASTES - You may have noticed that some Mexican recipes (and others) that use lots of tomatoes, green peppers and especially tomatillos will have a tart, even metallic taste: a little like touching your tongue to a small battery connection! If this taste is simply too sour for you, there is a solution. Add 1 level teaspoon (5 ml) of baking powder to the sauce. It will froth when it's added, and in doing so, it's actually neutralizing some of the acids. Now take a second taste and add and taste until you've got it right. Please don't overdo it. You can get a terribly powdery taste by adding too much too soon.

## Unusual Ingredients

TOMATILLOS - A Mexican tomato covered with a paper husk, most fascinating really. You may find them marketed as tomate verde or when they grow larger, as tomate manzano. You must remove the paper-like husk and rinse the tomatillo. You will find them to be sticky. This is natural and there is no need to wash this off. They are almost always cooked. Choose tomatillos that are firm and green.

CUMIN - An essential ingredient in many Mexican dishes, this spice is a native of West Asia where it is a component of Indian curry. Cumin gives a spicy edge and is used in chili and numerous sauces. Often confused with caraway, cumin seeds are long and light brown, while caraway seeds are curved.

TORTILLAS - Available in corn, flour or whole wheat, and the choice is yours to make. Corn tortillas are the most traditional but flour tortillas work better when making filled dishes that need to be folded. Tortillas freeze well and should be refrigerated to maintain their freshness.

# PHEASANT & CHESTNUTS

$\mathcal{P}$*heasant is now raised commercially on special farms. It is larger and less "gamey" in taste than its wild cousin. This dish is quite expensive but good results can also be achieved with using a fresh, 3 pound (1.4 kg) chicken.*

*Couple this with steamed broccoli and some long, thin, whole, steamed and glazed carrots and you have a fabulous special dinner dish.*

## Nutritional Profile

| PER SERVING | CLASSIC | MINIMAX |
|---|---|---|
| Calories | 1149 | 439 |
| Fat (gm) | 51 | 10 |
| Calories From Fat | 40% | 20% |
| Cholesterol (mg) | 12 | 64 |
| Sodium (mg) | 1 | 99 |
| Fiber (gm) | 1 | 6 |

■ *Classic Compared – Roast Pheasant & Cumberland Sauce*

## Time Estimate

| | | | | | | | | | |
|---|---|---|---|---|---|---|---|---|---|
Hands On
Unsupervised

*Minutes* 10 20 30 40 50 60 70 80 90

## Cost Estimate

Low    Medium    Medium High    Celebration

*Serves 2*

## INGREDIENTS

1 (2 pound) pheasant (900 gm)
Reserved pheasant bones
4 cups water (944 ml)
2 cups de-alcoholized red wine (472 ml)
2 tablespoons arrowroot (30 ml) mixed with
2 tablespoons de-alcoholized red wine (30 ml)
4 ounces peeled chestnuts (113 gm)
¼ teaspoon fresh tarragon (1.25 ml)
¼ teaspoon fresh thyme (1.25 ml)
½ teaspoon parsley (2.5 ml)

HERB STUFFING

½ tablespoon fresh chopped parsley (7 ml)
1 teaspoon fresh chopped thyme (5 ml)
1 teaspoon fresh chopped sage (5 ml)
¼ teaspoon fresh chopped tarragon (1.25 ml)
¼ teaspoon cracked black pepper (1.25 ml)
⅛ teaspoon salt (.6 ml)
2 tablespoons chopped onion (30 ml)

BOUQUET GARNI

2 bay leaves
6 parsley stalks
4 thyme sprigs

CHESTNUT SAUCE

1 teaspoon extra light olive oil with a dash of
sesame oil (5 ml)
1 onion, peeled and sliced
1 garlic clove, peeled and chopped fine
1 stalk celery, sliced
1 medium carrot, peeled and sliced

RICE PILAF

See recipe page 83. (Use chicken stock instead of
turkey stock and the reserved pheasant leg meat
instead of the shrimps.)

## FIRST PREPARE

■ The Herb Stuffing: Combine all the ingredients
in a small bowl and mix well.

■ Wash the pheasant and dry with absorbent
paper. To remove the leg and thigh portion from
the bird, cut down between the breast and thigh
joint. Carefully bone the breast meat off the
pheasant. Make sure to cut away any visible fat.
Reserve the legs, thighs and the bones.

■ Cut the breast in half. Coat the inner surface of
the breast halves with the herb stuffing. Place one
breast half on top of the other and squash together
so that all the stuffing is on the inside.

## NOW COOK THE PHEASANT

■ Preheat the oven to 375°F (190°C). Place the
stuffed pheasant breast on a rack in a baking pan
and roast at 375°F (190°C) for 35 minutes, or until
the internal temperature reaches 165°F (75°C) on
a meat thermometer.

## CHESTNUT SAUCE

■ Heat the olive oil in a large Dutch oven. Add
the onion, garlic, carrot, celery, bouquet garni
and the pheasant bones. Cook for 5 minutes.

■ Pour in the water and de-alcoholized wine and
simmer gently until reduced to 4 cups (1 L). Add
the reserved pheasant legs and thighs and cook
for 35 minutes more. Remove and strip the meat
from the bones and add it to the rice pilaf before
serving. Skim off all surface fat and strain the
stock.

■ Transfer the strained stock into a small saucepan and boil until reduced to 1½ cups (354 ml).

■ Remove the pan from the heat and mix in the
arrowroot paste. Return to the heat and stir until
thickened. Add the chestnuts, tarragon, thyme
and parsley.

■ To Serve: Transfer the cooked pheasant
breast from the oven to a cutting board. Slice
off the skin and carve the breast vertically into
thick slices. Serve on a bed of rice pilaf with
the chestnut sauce.

### Helpful Hints and Observations

LEGS AND THIGHS - These are cooked separately
from the breast meat because they need to cook
for 60 minutes and the breast needs 40!

### Unusual Ingredients

PHEASANT - Go to your grocery store and ask
someone in the meat department about the best
source for this fowl. The farm-raised variety tastes
much less gamey than the wild fowl because it is
raised on corn.

CHESTNUTS - Chestnuts should feel soft when
rubbed lightly with your fingers. Before you use
them, throw them in boiling water for 10 minutes
and then peel them. Peeled chestnuts in the can
are usually available in food stores.

# ROCK CORNISH GAME HENS & PILAF KIRKLAND

*A rock Cornish game hen cannot be heavier than 2 pounds (900 gm). These hens are fed a diet of acorns and cranberries, which gives them a slightly "wild" taste and a fuller flavor than chicken. They are a distinctive American invention having been secretly bred from an English Cornish game cockerel and an American Plymouth Rock white hen. Ah, such romance, but then just look where it got them!*

*The rice pilaf provides enough carbohydrate so there's no need for potatoes or beans. I usually add a heap of steaming fresh-cooked spinach or Swiss chard with a pinch of freshly ground nutmeg. Be sure to squeeze out the excess water before you add it to the plate.*

## Nutritional Profile

| PER SERVING | CLASSIC | MINIMAX |
|---|---|---|
| Calories | 948 | 374 |
| Fat (gm) | 62 | 12 |
| Calories From Fat | 59% | 29% |
| Cholesterol (mg) | 251 | 103 |
| Sodium (mg) | 535 | 155 |
| Fiber (gm) | 3 | 3 |

■ *Classic Compared – Game Hens Coq Au Vin*

## Time Estimate

| Hands On | | | | | | | | | |
|---|---|---|---|---|---|---|---|---|---|
| Unsupervised | | | | | | | | | |
| *Minutes* | 10 | 20 | 30 | 40 | 50 | 60 | 70 | 80 | 90 |

## Cost Estimate

| Low | Medium | Medium High | Celebration |
|---|---|---|---|

*Serves 4*

## INGREDIENTS

2 rock Cornish game hens (about 1 pound (450 gm) each)

RICE PILAF

1 tablespoon extra light olive oil with a dash of sesame oil (15 ml)

1 large yellow onion, peeled and finely diced

1 garlic clove, peeled and crushed

1 cup mixed uncooked grains (236 ml) (I recommend ½ cup (118 ml) Lundberg mixed long grain rice, ¼ cup (59 ml) pearl barley and ¼ cup (59 ml) wild rice)

2 cups chicken stock (472 ml) (recipe page 210)

2 bay leaves

1 sprig thyme

1 sprig parsley

¾ cup small green peas (177 ml)

1⅔ cups large mushrooms (392 ml), sliced ½ inch (1.5 cm) thick

THE SAUCE

¼ cup de-alcoholized white wine (59 ml)

1 tablespoon arrowroot (15 ml) mixed with 2 tablespoons de-alcoholized white wine

½ tablespoon fresh chopped cilantro (8 ml)

1½ tablespoons fresh chopped parsley (23 ml)

1 red bell pepper, seeded and finely diced

## FIRST PREPARE THE HENS

■ Cut the Cornish hens in half by making a cut on one side of the back bone. Make a second cut on the other side of the back bone. Take out the back and open up the bird. Cut through the breast bone from the inside. Remove the fine rib bones and cut the wing tips off. Save the wing and back bones for a stock. Dry the hens well with paper towels. Place on a rack in a roasting pan so as to elevate the hens above the baking surface.

## NOW COOK

■ In a casserole pan, heat the oil and cook the onion and garlic until the onions are translucent. Add the rice and stir to coat. Cover with the stock and lay the herbs on top. Cook uncovered in a 375°F oven (190°C) for 45 minutes. When done, remove the herbs, stir in the peas and mushrooms, and return to the oven to heat through for 5 minutes.

■ Time the hens to go into the oven 15 minutes after the rice. Bake for 30 minutes at 375°F (190°C) then remove from the oven.

■ To make an easy sauce, rinse the juice from the chicken roasting pan by adding de-alcoholized white wine. Pour into a fat strainer (this separates the fat from the juice), let sit for a few moments for the fat to rise to the surface, then pour the juice back into the pan through a fine sieve. You should end up with ½ cup of juice (118 ml).

■ Stir in the arrowroot paste until thickened. Stir in cilantro, parsley and diced red pepper.

■ Set the hens on a bed of pilaf and coat with the colorful sauce!

## Helpful Hints and Observations

THICK-CUT MUSHROOMS - This is a new technique I'd like you to try out carefully. The mushrooms must be fresh, white, and cut the full ½ inch (1.5 cm) suggested. They are slipped raw into the very hot pilaf and cook (or rather warm) in about 5 minutes. The result is remarkable: each slice has an almost meat-like texture that adds significantly to the dish.

FAT STRAINER - Here is another one of those simple ideas that make you ask "why didn't someone think of that before?" In this recipe, I make a gravy by keeping all the pan drippings,  adding the wine, and pouring the liquid directly into this fat strainer. The fat rises to the surface and lets you pour the clear juices out from under the fat layer. Nifty? It works, and in my opinion is a must in a Minimax kitchen.

## Unusual Ingredients

WILD RICE - Actually the seed of water grass that grows on lakes and is harvested in August and September. The wild rice you buy at the supermarket today is domesticated, or what is called "Paddy wild rice." Wild rice keeps very well in a tightly covered container set in a cool, dry place.

BARLEY - Believed to be the first cultivated grain, mentioned in Far-eastern writings and dating back 4,000 years. Today barley is mainly used in the making of beer, but as a food source it is a tasty addition to soups, stews, casseroles and pilaf dishes. Store barley as you would rice, in a covered container in a cool dry place.

# THANKSGIVING TURKEY & STUFFING PIE

*I* hope that by cooking a turkey in a toaster oven you'll understand that even a little space is enough to create a grand feast for your whole family.

Have a great time with your loved ones. Tell each other some good news and in whatever way you feel comfortable, try saying "thank you" to God.

Here are two of the recipes for our little feast: Turkey Breast with gravy and a Thanksgiving Stuffing Pie. You'll find the recipe for a terrific pumpkin dessert in individual filo pastry cups on page 184.

Have a great holiday!

## Nutritional Profile

| PER SERVING | CLASSIC | MINIMAX |
|---|---|---|
| Calories | 1367 | 253 |
| Fat (gm) | 58 | 6 |
| Calories From Fat | 38% | 21% |
| Cholesterol (mg) | 470 | 88 |
| Sodium (mg) | 657 | 165 |
| Fiber (gm) | 12 | 3 |

■ *Classic Compared – Roast Turkey, Chestnut Dressing*

## Time Estimate

| Hands On | | | | | | | | | |
|---|---|---|---|---|---|---|---|---|---|
| Unsupervised | | | | 1 Hour, 40 Minutes | | | | | |
| *Minutes* | 10 | 20 | 30 | 40 | 50 | 60 | 70 | 80 | 90 |

## Cost Estimate

| | | | |
|---|---|---|---|
| Low | Medium | Medium High | Celebration |

## TURKEY BREAST IN A TOASTER OVEN

*Serves 12*

### INGREDIENTS

1 (4 pound) whole turkey breast (1.8 kg)
4 fresh sage leaves
4 immature fresh thyme sprigs
2 garlic cloves, peeled and chopped
¼ teaspoon freshly ground white pepper (1.25 ml)
⅛ teaspoon freshly ground salt (.6 ml)
1 cup good quality chicken stock (236 ml)
(recipe page 210)
1 tablespoon arrowroot (15 ml) mixed with
2 tablespoons de-alcoholized white wine (30 ml)
1 tablespoon fresh chopped parsley (15 ml)

### FIRST PREPARE

■ Remove the skin from the turkey and set it aside. Carefully remove the center breast bone, keeping the two sides of the breast connected. Remove the tenderloin piece of turkey that forms an inner muscle of the breast. You can use this for other dishes. By removing it you make room for the herb dressing.

■ Spread the two boned breasts out flat on a cutting board. Place the sage leaves on top of one breast. Place the thyme sprigs and sprinkle the garlic, pepper and salt on the other.

■ Fold the breasts together with the seasonings inside. Place the breasts in a standard size meat loaf pan. Cut a piece of the reserved turkey skin to completely cover the top.

### NOW COOK

■ Bake the turkey breasts in a large toaster oven at 325°F (165°C) for 35 minutes per pound. Check the turkey skin half way through the cooking process. If the skin has shrunk, replace it with another piece of the reserved skin. Remove the cooked turkey to a serving platter, reserving the juices in the meat loaf pan.

■ To make a great gravy, pour the chicken stock into the meat loaf pan and dredge up any turkey residue. Now pour the stock into a saucepan and bring to a boil. Remove from the heat and pour the stock into a fat strainer. Let the fat rise to the surface - about 5 minutes. When separate, pour the clear, fat-free stock back into the saucepan.

■ Remove the gravy saucepan from the heat, stir in the arrowroot paste, then return to the heat and stir until thickened. Add the parsley.

■ Slice the turkey breast and serve with the gravy and Thanksgiving Stuffing Pie on the side.

## THANKSGIVING STUFFING PIE

*Serves 8*

### INGREDIENTS

2 teaspoons extra light olive oil with a dash of sesame oil (10 ml)
7 thin slices whole wheat bread
6 sprigs fresh thyme, leaves removed and chopped
8 fresh sage leaves, finely chopped
1 medium onion, coarsely chopped
10 ounces parsnips (284 gm), coarsely chopped
10 ounces carrots (284 gm), coarsely chopped
¼ cup turkey stock (118 ml) (recipe page 210)
½ teaspoon freshly grated nutmeg (2.5 ml)
2 tablespoons whole berry cranberry sauce (30 ml)

### FIRST PREPARE

■ Brush 1 teaspoon (5 ml) of the olive oil on the bottom and sides of a standard size loaf pan. Set 2 pieces of bread aside. Cut the rest of the bread into 1 inch (2.5 cm) wide strips and lay side by side to cover the bottom and sides of the pan. These bread strips will guide you later in cutting serving slices after the pie is baked.

■ Sprinkle 1 teaspoon (5 ml) each of the thyme and sage over the bread lining.

### NOW COOK

■ Preheat the oven to 350°F (180°C).

■ Heat the remaining olive oil in a saucepan and fry the chopped onions for 2 minutes. Add the parsnips and carrots and cook for 5 minutes. Add the turkey stock and the remaining thyme and sage and simmer until the vegetables are tender - about 20 minutes. Then mash them roughly, but well.

■ Spread half the mashed vegetables over the bottom layer of bread. Spread a tablespoon (15 ml) of cranberry sauce on top. Repeat with another layer of vegetables and then more cranberry.

■ Finish with slices of bread cut to cover the top.

■ Bake in the preheated oven for 30 minutes. Let cool for 5 minutes, then turn it out of the pan onto a serving plate. Slice it and serve with a fish slice.

### Unusual Ingredients

THYME - A strong herb, essential in French cooking, it is a classic addition to the bouquet garni (with parsley and bay leaves). You can use thyme in so many dishes ... I'm picturing a summer evening, there's a table set for two on the patio ... and pasta, yes, pasta, tossed with fresh vegetables and thyme ...

# TURKEY TREENESTAR

*This recipe is named for my wife Treena. It came about on the day she came home having given birth to our first child, Tessa. I had a very small chicken, a can of tiny shrimp and some Swiss asparagus soup powder. From such humble and romantic beginnings comes this ... turkey?*

*Serving a whole, roasted turkey for a party is popular but messy. This idea works well and when built up on a mound of fragrant rice pilaf and coated with the sauce of shrimp and asparagus tips it's great fun! Nutmeg seasoned carrots and some more freshly steamed asparagus go very well.*

## Nutritional Profile

| PER SERVING | CLASSIC | MINIMAX |
|---|---|---|
| Calories | 688 | 648 |
| Fat (gm) | 25 | 11 |
| Calories From Fat | 33% | 15% |
| Cholesterol (mg) | 150 | 146 |
| Sodium (mg) | 396 | 395 |
| Fiber (gm) | 3 | 2 |

■ *Classic Compared – Chicken Treenestar*

## Time Estimate

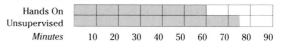

Hands On
Unsupervised

*Minutes*   10  20  30  40  50  60  70  80  90

## Cost Estimate

Low     Medium     Medium High     Celebration

*Serves 6*

## INGREDIENTS

1 (5 pound) (2.3 kg) turkey breast with ribs and back bone, to yield 1 pound 10 ounces (737 gm) cooked turkey meat

4 sprigs immature thyme

8 fresh sage leaves

¼ teaspoon freshly ground black pepper (1.25 ml)

⅛ teaspoon freshly ground salt (.6 ml)

7 ounces asparagus (198 gm), fresh or frozen if out of season

2 cups turkey stock (472 ml) (recipe page 210)

1 cup evaporated skim milk (236 ml)

¼ cup cornstarch (59 ml) mixed with 4 tablespoons de-alcoholized white wine (60 ml)

Pinch of freshly ground white pepper

4 ounces cooked bay shrimp (113 gm)

1 teaspoon dried dill weed (5 ml)

4½ cups cooked rice pilaf (1 L) (recipe follows)

RICE PILAF

1 teaspoon extra light olive oil with a dash of sesame oil (5 ml)

1 onion, peeled and thinly sliced

1½ cups uncooked long grain rice (354 ml), well rinsed and drained

6 stalks parsley

1 sprig thyme

1 bay leaf

3 cups turkey stock (708 ml) (recipe page 210)

4 ounces tiny shrimp (113 gm)

½ teaspoon dried dill weed (2.5 ml)

⅛ teaspoon freshly ground salt (.6 ml)

GARNISH

Fresh chopped parsley

Paprika

## FIRST PREPARE

■ Using a sharp knife, cut the back bone and ribs out of the whole breast. Remove the inner fillet, known as the supreme. Set the bones aside for the stock. Cut the breast into 2 even sections. You should have approximately 2¼ pounds (1 kg) of uncooked meat.

■ Set the meat skin-side-down on a board. Place the thyme sprigs and the sage leaves down the center of one side. Sprinkle with the fresh pepper and salt. Now place the other breast section on the seasoned section so that the skin is on the

outside and the thick muscles are at either end, to make a more even sized package.

■ Wrap the turkey in butcher's net as described on page 125.

■ Cut the asparagus tips from the spears and pass a knife through the tips a few times just to break them up without mashing them. The tips will be added to the sauce. Cut the rest of the asparagus into ½ inch (1.5 cm) slices and steam to serve as a side dish.

## NOW COOK

■ Place the prepared turkey on a trivet or rack in a roasting dish. Roast at 375°F (190°C) for 1 hour 15 minutes, or until the center of the turkey has reached 185°F (85°C) on a meat thermometer.

■ Approximately 25 minutes prior to the turkey being fully cooked, begin to prepare the sauce: In a large saucepan over medium heat, combine the heated stock and the evaporated skim milk. Bring to a boil then stir in the cornstarch paste. Turn the heat up a bit, bring back to a boil and stir until thickened.

■ Lower the heat and add a pinch of white pepper, the shrimp, reserved asparagus tips and the dill weed.

■ The Pilaf: Preheat the oven to 450°F (220°C). Heat the oil in a small saucepan and fry the onion until softened, but not brown. Add the rice and cook for 1-2 minutes, stirring to coat the rice with oil. Add the herbs and turkey stock. Bake uncovered in the preheated oven for 20 minutes. (If you want to bake it at the same time with the Turkey Treenestar, cook it at 375°F (190°C) for 30 minutes.) Remove the herbs and use a fork to fluff up the rice. Stir in the shrimp (the heat of the rice will warm the shrimp). Season with the dill weed and salt and serve hot.

■ Remove the turkey from the oven, cut off the net and slice into 12 (⅓ inch or 1 cm) slices. Press the pilaf into a slim loaf pan and turn out onto a platter. Lay the turkey slices on the rice and coat with the sauce. Dust with parsley and paprika.

### Unusual Ingredients

IMMATURE THYME - Mature sprigs of thyme have thicker, woody stems, while young sprigs are green and tender.

SAGE - See Unusual Ingredients, page 53.

ASPARAGUS - See Unusual Ingredients, page 29.

# ROAST BEEF & YORKSHIRE PANCAKES

*This* is truly a great tasting change from Yorkshire Pudding when cooking responsibly for loved ones. The Yorkshire Pancake is much easier to make at home or for a party and everyone will love it.

I'm sure none of us wants to see the end of the family meal where the large cut of meat is carved by Dad in Norman Rockwell style. However, in this case I've kept the amount of meat down to just enough for eight portions — and 2 pounds (1 kg) isn't a large enough piece to carve at the table. Two lovely side vegetables are steamed carrots with a touch of nutmeg and freshly steamed broccoli (unless President Bush is coming to dinner). With the vegetables added the fat is reduced to 38 percent.

## Nutritional Profile

| PER SERVING | CLASSIC | MINIMAX |
|---|---|---|
| Calories | 1485 | 316 |
| Fat (gm) | 113 | 14 |
| Calories From Fat | 68% | 40% |
| Cholesterol (mg) | 419 | 140 |
| Sodium (mg) | 428 | 268 |
| Fiber (gm) | 1 | 1 |

■ *Classic Compared – Roast Beef and Yorkshire Pudding*

## Time Estimate

| | | | | | | | | | |
|---|---|---|---|---|---|---|---|---|---|
| Hands On | | | | | | | | | |
| Unsupervised | | | | | | | | | |
| *Minutes* | 10 | 20 | 30 | 40 | 50 | 60 | 70 | 80 | 90 |

## Cost Estimate

| | | | |
|---|---|---|---|
| Low | Medium | Medium High | Celebration |

*Serves 8*

## INGREDIENTS

YORKSHIRE PANCAKES

½ cup flour (118 ml)

1 whole egg

1 egg yolk

1 cup non-fat milk (236 ml)

1 tablespoon extra light olive oil with a dash of sesame oil (15 ml)

1 tablespoon fresh chopped sage (15 ml)

1 tablespoon fresh chopped mint (15 ml)

Horseradish cream (about 1 teaspoon (5 ml) for each crepe)

ROAST BEEF

2 pounds beef bottom round (900 gm)

Freshly ground black pepper

1 large garlic clove, peeled and sliced in 4 pieces

2 cups good quality beef stock (472 ml)

1 tablespoon arrowroot (15 ml) mixed with 2 tablespoons water (30 ml)

## FIRST PREPARE

YORKSHIRE PANCAKES

■ Sift the flour into a bowl and make a well in the center. Lightly beat the egg and egg yolk together and pour into the well. Gradually pour in the milk, beating the ingredients together until a smooth batter is formed. Let sit for 30 minutes.

ROAST BEEF

■ Cut all but a thin layer of fat from the meat and season the roast with freshly ground black pepper.

■ Cut small shallow pockets underneath the roast and push the garlic slivers into the incisions.

## NOW COOK

■ Place the roast on a trivet in a roasting dish, fat side up, and roast in a 325°F oven (165°C) until an internal temperature of 120°F (48°C) for rare, 140°F (60°C) for medium, 160°F (71°C) for "spoiled!" This will take about 1 hour.

■ Meanwhile, cook the pancakes: Lightly oil an 8 inch (20 cm) diameter crepe pan with the olive oil, then tip the surplus into the batter and mix. This will make each pancake self-releasing. When the pan is hot, pour in sufficient batter to cover the bottom. Sprinkle some of the herbs on top of each pancake. Once bubbles appear on the surface of the pancake and it goes dull and waxy, flip it over and cook 1 minute longer.

■ Transfer the pancake to a plate and spread the plain side with one teaspoon (5 ml) of the horseradish cream. Fold it in half and in half again. Keep the prepared pancakes warm while you finish cooking the roast and its gravy.

■ When the roast is done, turn off the oven, open the door and let stand for 20 minutes to set the juices before carving. Remove the roast to a carving board, leaving the meat juices in the pan.

■ To the meat juices, add the beef stock and scrape out all the residue into a fat strainer. Let the fat rise to the top and then pour the juice through a fine sieve into a small saucepan.

■ Add the arrowroot paste to the meat juice in the saucepan. Stir over gentle heat until it thickens into a clear gravy.

■ Carve the beef in thin slices, about ¼ inch (.75 cm) thick. You should get 2 or even 3 slices for a 4 - 5 ounce (113-142 gm) serving — it's delicious!

## Helpful Hints and Observations

SITTING BATTER - (Sounds a little like an unusual tribal name!) Always let flour mixes rest before use. This allows starch cells to soften and take up more of the moisture and it gives a finer texture.

SHALLOW GARLIC POCKETS - Keep garlic slivers very close to the bottom surface. If dug in too deep they appear mid-slice and for some this is just too much!

THE TRIVET - This is simply a rack that gets the meat off the direct heat of the pan and stops both excessive evaporation of the meat surface and making a mess of your pan.

MEAT THERMOMETER - I really do urge you to buy a good one: a very small and thin probe by Taylor. Don't keep it in during cooking. It is better to drive it into the middle of the roast about 10 minutes before it is due to be done, and then remove it — testing again if necessary.

THICKNESS OF CUT - I cut beef, and in fact all meat cuts, in thin (¼ inch or .75 cm) slices. This does two things: I cover more of the plate than one thicker slice and I avoid choking my friends and family. The typical thick cut prime rib is often the culprit in a surprisingly large number of rather public incidents.

## Unusual Ingredients

BEEF BOTTOM ROUND - See Unusual Ingredients, page 97.

# FILET OF BEEF BENEDICT

$\mathscr{J}$ust think of it: beef so tender it melts in your mouth, a hint of Canadian bacon peeking through egg and mozzarella cheese, all together on a sourdough English muffin! Could a brunch dish so delicious be on a healthy Minimax menu? You bet!

Because the percentage of calories from fat is a little high, make Filet of Beef Benedict something you serve only occasionally. It's a great dish for a special holiday brunch.

## Nutritional Profile

| PER SERVING | CLASSIC | MINIMAX |
|---|---|---|
| Calories | 678 | 324 |
| Fat (gm) | 47 | 12 |
| Calories From Fat | 62% | 32% |
| Cholesterol (mg) | 537 | 67 |
| Sodium (mg) | 1513 | 659 |
| Fiber (gm) | 0 | 1 |

■ Classic Compared – Filet of Beef Benedict

## Time Estimate

| | | | | | | | | | |
|---|---|---|---|---|---|---|---|---|---|
| Hands On | | | | | | | | | |
| Unsupervised | | | | | | | | | |
| Minutes | 10 | 20 | 30 | 40 | 50 | 60 | 70 | 80 | 90 |

## Cost Estimate

| Low | Medium | Medium High | Celebration |
|---|---|---|---|

*Serves 4*

## INGREDIENTS

12 ounces beef tenderloin (340 gm), fully trimmed

Freshly ground black pepper

3 ounces Canadian bacon (85 gm), approximately 6 slices

2 ounces skim milk mozzarella cheese (57 gm)

1 tablespoon extra light olive oil with a dash of sesame oil (15 ml)

1 cup egg substitute (236 ml)

2 teaspoons horseradish (10 ml)

2 sourdough English muffins, cut in half and toasted

Freshly ground white pepper

½ cup de-alcoholized white wine (118 ml)

1 teaspoon arrowroot (5 ml) mixed with 1 tablespoon water (15 ml)

Fresh chopped parsley

Paprika

## FIRST PREPARE

■ Slice the beef into 1 inch (2.5 cm) thick medallions (or tournedos). Pound the meat with your fist or a mallet until it is 3½-4 inches (9-10.5 cm) in diameter (slightly bigger than the English muffins). Sprinkle with finely ground black pepper to taste.

■ Trim the skin, or wrap, off the bacon. Mince 2 slices (1 oz or 28 gm) very finely.

■ Cut 4 thin slices (approximately ⅛ inch or .5 cm thick) of cheese. Trim them to be circles 4 inches (10 cm) in diameter.

## NOW COOK

■ Pour the olive oil into a dish and sop both sides of the beef circles. Drop the beef into a hot frying pan and brown for about two minutes on each side. Push the beef to one side of the pan, and brown the 4 whole bacon slices. Allow about 30 seconds for each side.

■ While the meat is browning, combine the egg substitute with the minced Canadian bacon. Pour the egg mixture into non-stick egg poaching cups and set in a skillet filled with ½ inch (1.5 cm) of steaming water. Poach the eggs until set.

■ Spread ½ teaspoon (2.5 ml) horseradish on each of the muffin halves, then layer with Canadian bacon, beef and eggs and top with a slice of cheese. Season with freshly ground white pepper.

■ Set the oven rack 4 inches (10 cm) from the broiler element. Pop the muffins under the broiler. Check after one minute and remove them when the cheese is just beginning to brown.

■ For the Sauce: Heat the wine in the meat saute pan, scraping up any brown residue from the bottom of the pan. Remove from the heat and slowly stir in the arrowroot mixture. Place back on the heat and cook until thickened.

■ Pour the sauce over and around the broiled muffins and garnish with parsley and a sprinkle of paprika.

## Helpful Hints and Observations

SPECIAL FOOD BUYING TIP - When you ask your local butcher for a pound (450 gm) of fully trimmed beef, he'll charge you for all the fat he trims off. Ask for those trimmings back. You might find some useful meat pieces that you can cut out of the fat.

## Unusual Ingredients

MOZZARELLA CHEESE - This is a favorite ingredient of many people, but do you know how it got its name? Mozzarella is made from a curd that is broken up and heated in water until it forms an elastic thread. This thread is wound into a ball, from which pieces are sliced off to form the cheese. This last stage is where the name comes from, because mozzare, means "slice off"!

BEEF TENDERLOIN - Where does it come from? This tender cut of meat is from the short loin section of the cow behind its ribs.

# FILET OF BEEF MEURICE

*Treena and I first ate this dish in France back in 1970, when we visited the famous Hotel Meurice in Paris. Those were the days when cream, butter, eggs, beef and pate de foie gras were "just part of my job". Now things have changed - and so have we!*

*This is a romantic dinner for two, or a special dinner for four (just double the quantities). Even though it's relatively expensive, it is far, far less than you would pay in a restaurant. Serve it with freshly steamed leaf spinach ... it's wonderful!*

## Nutritional Profile

| PER SERVING | CLASSIC | MINIMAX |
|---|---|---|
| Calories | 1032 | 473 |
| Fat (gm) | 72 | 15 |
| Calories From Fat | 63% | 28% |
| Cholesterol (mg) | 430 | 66 |
| Sodium (mg) | 2360 | 359 |
| Fiber (gm) | 21 | 3 |

■ *Classic Compared – Filet of Beef Meurice*

## Time Estimate

| | | | | | | | | | |
|---|---|---|---|---|---|---|---|---|---|
| Hands On Unsupervised | | | | | | | | | |

Minutes  10  20  30  40  50  60  70  80  90

## Cost Estimate

| | | | |
|---|---|---|---|
| | | | |

Low        Medium        Medium High    Celebration

*Serves 2*

## INGREDIENTS

RICE PILAF

1½ cups beef stock (354 ml) (recipe page 210)

¼ cup uncooked long grain rice (59 ml)

⅛ cup uncooked pearl barley (30 ml)

⅛ cup uncooked wild rice (30 ml)

1 bay leaf

1 sprig tarragon

1 spray parsley

1 tablespoon Dijon mustard (15 ml)

1 teaspoon fresh chopped tarragon (5 ml)

FILET OF BEEF

8 ounces beef filet (tenderloin) (227 gm)

1 teaspoon extra light olive oil with a dash of sesame oil (5 ml)

¼ teaspoon freshly ground black pepper (1.25 ml)

1 tablespoon chopped shallots (15 ml)

¼ cup de-alcoholized white wine (59 ml)

¾ cup beef stock (177 ml) (recipe page 210)

⅓ cup strained yogurt (78 ml) (recipe page 210)

1 tablespoon cornstarch (30 ml) mixed with
2 tablespoons de-alcoholized white wine (30 ml)

1 teaspoon fresh chopped tarragon (5 ml)

## NOW COOK

■  The Rice Pilaf: In a medium saucepan, heat the beef stock and add the long grain rice, pearl barley and wild rice. Lay the bay leaf, tarragon and parsley on top. Cook uncovered in a 375°F (190°C) oven for about 45 minutes. When done, remove the herbs. Add the Dijon mustard and tarragon and stir thoroughly.

■  Lightly grease 2 individual ramekins with extra light olive oil. Pack the rice into the dishes. To keep it warm, place the ramekins in a pan filled with 1 inch (2.5 cm) of water. Put the pan on top of the stove over low heat.

■  Pour the oil on a plate and sprinkle with the freshly ground black pepper. Dredge the meat through the oil so that both sides are glazed.

■  Put the meat into a medium sized saute pan on medium heat and brown both sides. Remove the meat and place back on the glazing plate.

■  Add the shallots to the same pan. Add the de-alcoholized white wine to deglaze the pan. Add the beef stock and boil to reduce by half.

■  Mix the cornstarch paste with the strained yogurt. Add the reduced beef stock, return the mixture to the saute pan, bring to a boil and stir until thickened. Add the beef to warm through, then sprinkle with the chopped tarragon.

■  To Serve: Unmold the rice onto warm plates, top with a portion of the steak and coat with the sauce.

## Helpful Hints and Observations

SILVER SKIN - This is the fine, silvery membrane or sheath that encases the tenderloin on at least one side. This must come off in order to prevent the meat from bunching. What happens is that the membrane shrinks and toughens when it comes in contact with the hot pan and squeezes the meat out of shape. In this otherwise ultra-tender meat, it means having to chew hard and swallow when you least expect it!

So, regardless of its eventual ragged shape or the apparent weight loss on expensive meat, cut it off!

By the way, the trim is always useful for adding a soupcon of extra flavor to any good beef stock.

## Unusual Ingredients

MUSTARDS - The Romans started mustard on the road to fame. The most commonly used mustards are made from the white mustard plant, the black mustard and the wild mustard. English mustard is usually a mixture of black and white with curcuma (Indian curry spice) added. French mustards are made with a combination of white and black mustard seeds, with different herbs added. Dijon mustard is mixed with verjuice, an acid juice extracted from large, unripened grapes.

# SCOTTISH BEEF COLLOPS

*The cuisine of Scotland can be broadly divided into two groups: cottage and castle. The castle food owes its influence to the French and Italian royal courts and it is from these courts that the term "collops" comes. The French word, "escallop," means thin slices. The same in Italian is, "scallo-pini."*

*I've tried to use one pot to prepare the whole dish, therefore it isn't the most attractive serving piece. You can wrap a colorful cloth around the outside or simply serve individual plates in the kitchen. Beautifully cooked tiny peas with a little mint would be a great addition or finely shredded carrot, lightly steamed with a little nutmeg.*

## Nutritional Profile

| PER SERVING | CLASSIC | MINIMAX |
|---|---|---|
| Calories | 730 | 285 |
| Fat (gm) | 41 | 9 |
| Calories From Fat | 51% | 28% |
| Cholesterol (mg) | 183 | 42 |
| Sodium (mg) | 794 | 62 |
| Fiber (gm) | 3 | 3 |

■ *Classic Compared – Scottish Beef Collops*

## Time Estimate

| | | | | | | | | | |
|---|---|---|---|---|---|---|---|---|---|
| Hands On | | | | | | | | | |
| Unsupervised | | | | | | | | | |

Minutes   10   20   30   40   50   60   70   80   90

## Cost Estimate

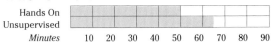

Low          Medium          Medium High      Celebration

*Serves 6*

## INGREDIENTS

1¼ pounds beef bottom round steak (560 gm)

1½ pounds potatoes (680 gm), peeled and sliced into ¼ inch (.75 cm) slices

2 teaspoons extra light olive oil with a dash of sesame oil (5 ml)

3 cups chopped onions (708 ml)

4 ounces mushrooms (113 gm), finely chopped

2 tablespoons all-purpose flour (30 ml)

2 pickled walnuts, finely chopped

2 tablespoons fresh chopped thyme (30 ml)

1¼ cups beef stock (295 ml) (recipe page 210)

4 ounces mushrooms (113 gm), thinly sliced

GARNISH

1 tablespoon fresh chopped parsley (15 ml)

Carrot shavings

## FIRST PREPARE

■ Cut the beef into ¼ inch (.75 cm) slices across the grain, at a slight diagonal. This should provide you with approximately 48 slices.

## NOW COOK

■ In a low-sided casserole, heat half of the oil and saute the onions until they're soft and slightly brown. Place the onions on a plate and set aside.

■ Lightly rinse the casserole and place back on the burner. Add the remaining oil and cover the bottom with half of the beef slices, allowing them to brown fully. Reposition the browned beef to one side and brown the rest of the beef.

■ Add the cooked onions and the chopped mushrooms. Sprinkle with the flour and spoon the mixture into a bowl. Stir in the walnuts and thyme.

■ Rinse the sides and bottom of the casserole with the beef stock, removing any browning residue. Pour into a bowl and reserve.

■ Spread half of the beef mixture over the bottom of the casserole. Layer with half the sliced mushroom, followed by half of the sliced potatoes. Repeat with layers of the remaining beef mixture and sliced mushrooms, topped with the remaining potatoes. Pour the reserved stock over the casserole, cover and cook at 350°F (180°C) for 40 minutes.

■ Garnish with parsley and carrot shavings.

## Unusual Ingredients

PICKLED WALNUTS - If they aren't available at the local grocery, you can make a substitute: Use 6 medium, pitted, black olives, marinated in ¼ cup (59 ml) cider vinegar and 1 tablespoon (15 ml) molasses for 3 hours. A slightly different texture but very similar flavor.

# STEAK DIANE

$\mathcal{B}$ack in the 1960s and 70s, there was hardly a "gourmet" restaurant that didn't have table-side cooking ... with flames. Steak Diane was an all-time favorite, being both simple and partially incinerated! I've doused the conflagration, lessened the portion size and reduced the fat. Oh, it's still simple!

In this recipe we've done the presentation for you: the steak is served with pan-broiled tomatoes, steamed green beans and glazed, red skin potatoes. It makes a pretty picture - and such an easy and well appreciated dish!

## Nutritional Profile

| PER SERVING | CLASSIC | MINIMAX |
|---|---|---|
| Calories | 1036 | 389 |
| Fat (gm) | 74 | 17 |
| Calories From Fat | 64% | 39% |
| Cholesterol (mg) | 406 | 81 |
| Sodium (mg) | 905 | 599 |
| Fiber (gm) | 8 | 7 |

■ Classic Compared – Steak Diane

## Time Estimate

| | | | | | | | | | |
|---|---|---|---|---|---|---|---|---|---|
| Hands On | | | | | | | | | |
| Unsupervised | | | | | | | | | |
| Minutes | 10 | 20 | 30 | 40 | 50 | 60 | 70 | 80 | 90 |

## Cost Estimate

| | | | |
|---|---|---|---|
| Low | Medium | Medium High | Celebration |

*Serves 2*

## INGREDIENTS

8 ounces beef tenderloin (227 gm) or eye of round

⅛ teaspoon freshly ground salt (.6 ml)

¼ teaspoon freshly ground pepper (1.25 ml)

4 ounces red potatoes (113 gm)

8 ounces green beans (227 gm), topped and tailed

Fine dusting of nutmeg, salt and pepper

¼ teaspoon freshly squeezed lemon juice (1.25 ml)

1 teaspoon extra light olive oil with a dash of sesame oil (5 ml)

½ ounce butter (14 gm)

1 garlic clove, peeled and finely chopped

2 shallots, peeled and finely chopped

½ cup fresh chopped parsley (118 ml)

2 small Roma tomatoes, sliced

2 tablespoons Worcestershire sauce (30 ml)

⅔ cup beef stock (157 ml) (recipe page 210)

## FIRST PREPARE

■ Tenderize the tenderloin by pounding it with your fist, if you feel aggressive, or with a mallet if you're in a gentler mood. The thickness should be less than ¼ inch (.75 cm). Sprinkle with the freshly ground salt and pepper.

■ Quarter and steam the potatoes for about 14 minutes. Add the green beans to the steamer and dust with nutmeg, salt and pepper. Steam for another 6 minutes. Separate the potatoes and beans. Sprinkle the lemon juice on the beans and set aside.

## NOW COOK

■ Heat the oil in a large skillet. Drag both sides of the tenderloin through the oil, then brown it quickly, for no more than 30 seconds on each side. Set aside in the pan to keep warm.

■ Heat the butter in another skillet. Saute the garlic and shallots for 2 minutes. Drop in half the parsley and the tomato slices. Keep the tomato slices to one side of the pan and turn them to warm both sides. Remove them from the pan and keep warm.

■ Add the Worcestershire sauce and beef stock. Cook until reduced by a third. Add the tenderloin, the remaining parsley and potatoes, making sure they are all coated with the sauce.

■ To Serve: Transfer the beef and potatoes to a very hot plate. Put the tomatoes on one side and the green beans on the other.

## Helpful Hints and Observations

EYE OF ROUND AND TENDERLOIN - The "eye" meat is sometimes called "the alias steak" because of its many names. It looks like the tenderloin but is much tougher and needs special treatment. If you wish to use eye of round meat, marinate it in red wine with red wine vinegar, overnight, if possible, and always in a glass or ceramic container. Dry the marinated beef with paper towels and pound it with a deeply indented meat mallet. It will never be as tender as tenderloin, but it has great flavor and is much less expensive.

## Unusual Ingredients

WORCESTERSHIRE SAUCE - First bottled in Worcestershire, England, it's roots are said to be Roman! Commercially, it's dark, tangy flavor is attributed to soy, garlic, molasses, lime, onions, tamarind, vinegar and a variety of spices, but home recipes call for "essence of anchovies" - now there's a mysterious secret ingredient!

RED WINE VINEGAR - Somewhere, in a vat, wine's complex molecules are breaking down, down, down, into ... vinegar! Of course, vinegar doesn't have to be made from wine. Fermented apples are the source for cider vinegar; grains or potatoes for malt vinegar. But in this case, red wine's robust, hearty flavor is the perfect addition. Because vinegar is low in calories, it's a good choice as seasoning in the Minimax kitchen, where I'm constantly on the lookout for "bright notes" of sour and bitter to replace the "velvet notes" that come from the taste of fat.

# KAREWAI STEAK PISCATELLA

*C*an this steak compete with the American favorite: prime rib with baked potato and hollandaise sauce? This is a legitimate question that Joe Piscatella, best selling author of "Don't Eat Your Heart Out," answers with "yes!" Such success can go to one's head.

    For serving, look for the ultimate in green. Broccoli works well but then so do snow peas: when just cooked they have that wonderful, crisp texture that goes well with a dish like this.

## Nutritional Profile

| PER SERVING | CLASSIC | MINIMAX |
|---|---|---|
| Calories | 1,111 | 505 |
| Fat (gm) | 75 | 15 |
| Calories From Fat | 60% | 28% |
| Cholesterol (mg) | 327 | 84 |
| Sodium (mg) | 901 | 79 |
| Fiber (gm) | 4 | 5 |

■ *Classic Compared – Prime Rib, Baked Potato and Hollandaise Sauce*

## Time Estimate

| | | | | | | | | | |
|---|---|---|---|---|---|---|---|---|---|
| Hands On | | | | | | | | | |
| Unsupervised | | | | | | | | | |

*Minutes* 10 20 30 40 50 60 70 80 90

## Cost Estimate

Low      Medium      Medium High      Celebration

*Serves 4*

## INGREDIENTS

3 quarts water (2.8 L)

1½ cups orzo pasta (354 ml)

2 cloves garlic, peeled and chopped

1 teaspoon extra light olive oil with a dash of sesame oil (5 ml)

1 large onion, peeled and sliced thin

1 (12 ounce) can no-salt tomato sauce (340 gm)

1 cup de-alcoholized red wine (236 ml)

1 tablespoon red wine vinegar (15 ml)

Fresh coarsely ground black pepper

1 pound flank steak (450 gm)

5 tablespoons fresh chopped basil (75 ml)

## NOW COOK

■  Cook the orzo in 6 cups (1.4 L) of boiling water for 8 minutes. Time the cooking to coincide with the steak's completion. Drain the orzo through a strainer. Place the strainer over hot water in a pot and cover with a lid to keep it warm.

■  Heat the olive oil in a saucepan and add the garlic and onions. Fry until the onions are soft — about 4 minutes.

■  Add the tomato sauce to the frying onions and stir in half the de-alcoholized wine and the vinegar.

■  Spread the coarsely ground pepper on a large cutting board. Place the flank steak on top of the pepper and press so that the pepper adheres to the steak.

■  Put steak into a hot skillet. Cook 4 minutes on each side. Steak should be nice and brown. The inside should be medium rare.

■  Pour the remaining wine over the steak. Scrape up the brown steak residue in the pan with a spatula. Add half of the tomato sauce and 1 table-spoon (15 ml) of the chopped basil. Continue to cook and reduce the sauce. It will be very hot and will begin to darken in color. Sprinkle 3 table-spoons (45 ml) of basil on top.

■  Put the orzo into the remaining tomato sauce. Add the rest of the chopped basil.

■  Remove steak from the tomato-onion sauce onto a cutting board with a gutter to catch the juices. Carve the steak across the grain in thin, diagonal pieces.

■  Serve the reduced steak juices as a sauce on the side. De-glaze the steak pan with a swish of de-alcoholized wine, and pour this into the sauce as well.

■  Serve the sliced steak with the orzo in sauce on the side, sprinkled with the remaining basil.

## Helpful Hints and Observations

PASTA SHAPES - The eye does wonderful things to the other senses. In this case it's what the pasta looks like that creates such a difference. Please try different shapes, sizes and colors — it's good food and provides visual interest to distract the "taste memory" that may be clamoring for noodles fixed Alfredo style with eggs, cream and cheese — whooppee!?!

CARVING LONDON BROIL (FLANK STEAK) - Traditionally this cut is carved in thin, diagonal slices across the grain of the meat. I have suggested a one pound (450 gm) piece because it would come from a smaller, less fatty animal. One pound (450 gm) is enough to feed four people with at least two, thin slices per head.

TOMATO SAUCE - I know this may seem odd but it's a unique flavor and color when it's cooked in a hot pan. The color deepens and the spices add to the overall flavor. It really is worth the effort to try it and see for yourself!

## Unusual Ingredients

LONDON BROIL or FLANK STEAK - This cut of meat has taken a "bad rap" in the past. Flank steak is extremely lean and comes from the underside of the cow. Most recipes call for rolling and stuffing, then braising, a slow method of cooking reserved for tougher cuts of meat. On the contrary, we quickly fry this cut and 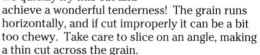  achieve a wonderful tenderness! The grain runs horizontally, and if cut improperly it can be a bit too chewy. Take care to slice on an angle, making a thin cut across the grain.

ORZO - A pasta that derives its name from its shape. In Italy, if you asked for orzo you would get barley. Orzo pasta is semolina flour pressed into the shape of barley.

# GOULASH

A Hungarian favorite, not covered with the traditional sour cream or filled with sausage, dumplings and cottage cheese - but a deliciously satisfying meal to serve to those you love! Let your taste buds be dazzled - if such a thing is physiologically possible!

When Treena and I were first married and I was an Air Force officer, she worked making sandwiches at 50 cents an hour. We saved her money and made casserole dinners for our friends. This was one of our favorites. Try serving it with plain, boiled noodles and plenty of green peas sprinkled with fresh mint.

## Nutritional Profile

| PER SERVING | CLASSIC | MINIMAX |
|---|---|---|
| Calories | 789 | 433 |
| Fat (gm) | 55 | 14 |
| Calories From Fat | 63% | 30% |
| Cholesterol (mg) | 153 | 85 |
| Sodium (mg) | 642 | 172 |
| Fiber (gm) | 4 | 8 |

■ *Classic Compared – Goulash*

## Time Estimate

| Hands On | | | | | | | | | |
|---|---|---|---|---|---|---|---|---|---|
| Unsupervised | | | | 95 Minutes | | | | | |
| Minutes | 10 | 20 | 30 | 40 | 50 | 60 | 70 | 80 | 90 |

## Cost Estimate

| | | | |
|---|---|---|---|
| Low | Medium | Medium High | Celebration |

*Serves 4*

## INGREDIENTS

1 teaspoon extra light olive with a dash of sesame oil (5 ml)

2 onions, peeled and finely chopped

2 garlic cloves, crushed, peeled and chopped

1½ pounds of bottom round beef, fat trimmed (700 gm) cut into 2 inch (5 cm) pieces

1 (6 ounce) can no-salt tomato paste (170 gm)

3 cups fat free beef stock (708 ml)

2 large potatoes, peeled and cut into ½ inch (1.5 cm) cubes

2 green peppers, seeded and cubed

2 tablespoons Hungarian paprika (slightly hot) (30 ml)

½ teaspoon freshly ground black pepper (2.5 ml)

1 teaspoon caraway seeds (5 ml)

7 plum tomatoes, peeled, seeded and chopped

## NOW COOK

■  Heat the olive oil in a large, heavy-bottomed saucepan (10 x 3½ inches deep or 25 x 9 cm) and fry the onion and garlic until translucent. Do not brown. Turn out into a bowl and set aside.

■  Drop the cubed meat into the hot pan, making sure all the pieces have a chance to touch the hot surface — this will ensure that the meat sears and browns properly.

■  Stir in the tomato paste. You'll see the sugar in the paste start to caramelize and turn brown. This is called the Maillard reaction. Now stir the onions and garlic back into the pan.

■  Pour in the beef stock, cover and simmer 90 minutes. Of course, you could do the recipe up to this point the day before. If this is the case, make sure you skim off any accumulated fat before you proceed.

■  Add the potatoes, green peppers, half of the paprika, the black pepper and the caraway seeds. Cover and simmer until the potatoes are tender, about 30 minutes.

■  Before you serve, stir in your ruby-red tomato pieces until just heated through. Sprinkle with the remaining paprika. Stir and serve !

## Helpful Hints and Observations

BOTTOM ROUND STEAK - I recommend bottom round for this Goulash rather than the traditional blade steak. It's not as fatty, but also not as juicy. However, the bigger you cut the pieces, the more succulent the final taste. I've settled on a 2 inch

piece (5 cm) for my taste, but decide on the size pieces you want to suit your preference.

LESS BEEF CAN MEAN MORE - I've also drastically cut the amount of beef in this dish to just over ¼ pound (113 gm) per serving. It makes a big difference in the cholesterol content, but as you'll see, not to your guest's ultimate taste satisfaction.

BROWNING THE MEAT - It really helps to give the meat enough heat, time and space to be properly browned. Get the pan very hot and dry the meat completely with paper towels. Drop each piece separately to give it enough space to roll onto its side and brown before you add the next piece. The point here is that normally meat never browns - it sits there and simmers in its own juices (meat is 70 percent water) rather than developing the essential "scorched" taste that adds depth of flavor without fat.

PAPRIKA - Usually added in two stages, one early and the second addition immediately before serving.

## Unusual Ingredients

HUNGARIAN PAPRIKA - The most esteemed of all paprikas! Varying in degree of "hotness", paprika is made by drying and then grinding the flesh of red peppers. To achieve the hotness, a suitable amount of the pepper seed is added. If you have a sweet paprika at home, add some cayenne pepper to it and you will have a good substitute.

TOMATO PASTE - Provides a wonderful color and depth to any dish. It is made by extracting the liquid and pulp of tomatoes and concentrating them to no less than 24 percent solids. Tomato sauce and puree are usually about 10-12 percent solids. It can be added to soups, sauces and casseroles, but make sure you buy the no-salt variety (really no salt added). Best purchased in the small, 6 ounce (170 gm) size.

BOTTOM ROUND - Sometimes sold as outside round, bottom round is a cut that comes from a larger rump section called the round or Chicago round. Other cuts that would come from the Chicago round are the inside top, round, the knuckle, eye, heel and shank. Bottom round is not as well marbled as, say, a sirloin or tenderloin. Because of this, the texture is not as "buttery", but it does have an excellent flavor and an attractive appearance. Remember the more marbling, the more fat, making the bottom round an excellent choice for roasting and carving. Choose a bottom round that is well colored and firm to the touch. Bottom round can also be cubed and used in soups and stews.

# BEEF CHILI

*H*ere it is, and I know that everyone has their favorite! Mine has only 11 grams of fat and 393 calories, which, when compared to a "Grand Prize" recipe, which had 44 grams of fat and 663 calories, was a major drop (see Nutritional Profile). But the Minimax version also has substantial flavor and good fiber at 10 grams per serving.

I found some small bean pots that hold 1¼ cups (295 ml) when filled to the brim. I filled these pots almost to the top, set them on a colorful plate and served crusty bread and a tossed salad on the side.

## Nutritional Profile

| PER SERVING | CLASSIC | MINIMAX |
|---|---|---|
| Calories | 663 | 393 |
| Fat (gm) | 44 | 11 |
| Calories From Fat | 60% | 26% |
| Cholesterol (mg) | 129 | 59 |
| Sodium (mg) | 1185 | 381 |
| Fiber (gm) | 8 | 10 |

■ *Classic Compared – Grand Prize Chili*

## Time Estimate

| Hands On Unsupervised | | | | | | | | | |
|---|---|---|---|---|---|---|---|---|---|
| Minutes | 10 | 20 | 30 | 40 | 50 | 60 | 70 | 80 | 90 |

## Cost Estimate

| Low | Medium | Medium High | Celebration |
|---|---|---|---|

*Serves 6*

## INGREDIENTS

1 tablespoon extra light olive oil with a dash of sesame oil (15 ml)

1½ pounds beef bottom round (680 gm)

1 large onion, peeled and finely chopped

2 garlic cloves, peeled and diced

2 jalapeno chili peppers, seeded and chopped

1 (6 ounce) can no-salt tomato paste (170 gm)

1 teaspoon cayenne pepper (5 ml)

1 tablespoon powdered cumin (15 ml)

1½ cups cold water (354 ml)

1½ cups de-alcoholized red wine (354 ml)

½ cup bulgur wheat (118 ml)

1 teaspoon baking powder (5 ml)

2 (15 ounce) cans pinto beans (425 gm), drained, yielding 3 cups (708 ml)

6 tablespoons finely minced green onions (90 ml)

6 teaspoons grated dry Monterey Jack cheese (30 ml)

## FIRST PREPARE

■ Cut half of the beef into ¼ inch (.75 cm) cubes. Cut the remaining beef into strips and coarsely grind. Use the bread trick to make sure you've ground all the meat (see page 71).

## NOW COOK

■ Here's a new way of browning meat: Pour the oil over the cubed meat and stir until completely coated. This will prevent the meat from simmering in its own juices. Now drop it into a very hot, high sided casserole pan and cook each cube on all sides for 5 minutes. Notice the cubes are nice and brown! Also note the dark brown residue on the bottom of the pan. Scrape it up to provide a wonderful depth of taste. When the cubes are brown, stir in the ground beef and cook until all the pink is gone.

■ Add the onions, garlic and jalapeno. Stir in the tomato paste. Now you will see the Maillard reaction: a darkening color change in the tomato paste that is the source of a deep, smoky taste. Stir in the cayenne pepper and the cumin.

■ Take the pan off of the heat and stir in 1 cup (236 ml) of the cold water. Scrape any residue off of the bottom of the pan. Stir in 1 cup (236 ml) of the de-alcoholized wine. Breathe deeply: what an aroma! Put the pot back on very low heat, cover and simmer for approximately 1 hour, or until the meat chunks are tender.

■ Put the bulgur in a 1 quart (1 L) container. In a small saucepan, boil together the remaining water and the remaining wine and then pour onto the bulgur. Let it sit until the bulgur absorbs all the liquid - about 5 minutes.

■ After the beef has simmered for 1 hour, mix in the cooked bulgur and baking powder. Stir in additional liquid, either water or wine, to your desired consistency. I prefer wine, feeling that wine added to the end of a dish is like the last spray of perfume before a woman walks out the door.

■ Put the pinto beans in a strainer and place over a pan with steaming water. Cover and steam until the beans are warm - about 15 minutes.

■ To Serve: Place ½ cup (118 ml) of the beans in a serving dish and smother with ½ cup (118 ml) of the chili. Dust each with one tablespoon (15 ml) of minced green onions and a teaspoon (5 ml) of cheese.

## Unusual Ingredients

HOMEMADE CHILI POWDER - Cayenne and cumin are the two essential ingredients for any chili powder. Instead of buying prepared chili powder, try mixing these two spices at home to make your own. They can be combined in varying amounts to suit your own taste.

DRY MONTEREY JACK CHEESE - This cheese originates from Monterey County, California. It is ripened up to one year depending on the amount of dryness desired. "Dry" refers to an extra hard cheese that is especially suited to grating. Monterey Jack is wonderfully versatile. Use it for casseroles, rarebits or grated on pastas.

# SANCOCHO

*O*ne pot cooking makes so much sense, and this great Puerto Rican recipe is such a good example. At the heart of it must be a good meat broth and lots of fresh vegetables. In this recipe the meat is more a condiment than the star attraction.

   One pot cooking also means one pot serving! There is enough going on here to simply serve Sancocho from a good looking, earthy casserole dish with a swiftly flashing ladle!

## Nutritional Profile

| PER SERVING | CLASSIC | MINIMAX |
| --- | --- | --- |
| Calories | 1265 | 353 |
| Fat (gm) | 46 | 11 |
| Calories From Fat | 33% | 27% |
| Cholesterol (mg) | 225 | 55 |
| Sodium (mg) | 2283 | 215 |
| Fiber (gm) | 15 | 5 |

■ *Classic Compared – Sancocho Especial*

## Time Estimate

| | | | | | | | | | |
| --- | --- | --- | --- | --- | --- | --- | --- | --- | --- |
| Hands On | | | | | | | | | |
| Unsupervised | | | | | | | | | |

Minutes   10   20   30   40   50   60   70   80   90

## Cost Estimate

| | | | |
| --- | --- | --- | --- |
| Low | Medium | Medium High | Celebration |

*Serves 6*

## INGREDIENTS

1 tablespoon extra light olive oil with a dash of sesame oil (15 ml)

1 large onion, peeled and diced

1 tablespoon minced fresh garlic

1 green pepper, seeded and cut in ½ inch (1.5 cm) cubes

2 red peppers, seeded and cut in ½ inch (1.5 cm) cubes

12 ounces bottom round steak (340 gm), trimmed and cut in ½ inch (1.5 cm) cubes

8 ounces pork shoulder (227 gm), trimmed and cut in ½ inch (1.5 cm) cubes

2 ounces ham (57 gm), finely cubed

2 cups beef stock (472 ml) (recipe page 210)

1 (4 ounce) jicama (113 gm), peeled and cut in ½ inch (1.5 cm) cubes

4 ounces fresh yams (113 gm), peeled and cut in ½ inch (1.5 cm) cubes

4 ounces fresh pumpkin meat (113 gm), peeled and cut in ½ inch (1.5 cm) cubes

4 ounces potatoes (113 gm), peeled and cut in ½ inch (1.5 cm) cubes

1 large plantain, cut in ½ inch (1.5 cm) slices

2 cups cooked corn kernels (472 ml)

2 tablespoons arrowroot (30 ml) mixed with 4 tablespoons water (60 ml)

1 tablespoon finely chopped fresh cilantro (15 ml)

¼ teaspoon freshly ground black pepper (1.25 ml)

BOUQUET GARNI

3 sprigs fresh cilantro

1 bay leaf

1 teaspoon marjoram (5 ml)

1 teaspoon cracked black peppercorns (5 ml)

3 whole cloves

## NOW COOK

■ Heat the oil in a large Dutch oven and saute the onion, garlic and peppers for five minutes. Remove the vegetables and set aside.

■ Increase the heat and add the beef, pork and ham to the Dutch oven. When the meat is browned, return the vegetables to the pot.

■ Pour in the beef stock, add the bouquet garni, cover and bring to a boil then simmer gently for 45 minutes.

■ Add the jicama, yam, pumpkin and potato. Cover and simmer for 30 minutes.

■ Add the plantain and corn and simmer for 10 minutes. Remove the Dutch oven from the heat, add the arrowroot paste, return to the heat and stir until thickened. Mix in the chopped cilantro and the pepper. Of course, remove the bouquet garni before serving.

## Helpful Hints and Observations

JICAMA VS. YAUTIA ROOT OR CASAVA - I have used Jicama instead of the classic casava. It gives a crisp texture and crunch to Sancocho instead of the rather bland softness of the casava.

OVERNIGHT IMPROVES THE FLAVOR - As with most casseroles, Sancocho improves if kept under refrigeration overnight. The flavors seem to melt together.

BOUQUET GARNI - Cut a piece of muslin or cheesecloth about 4 inches (10 cm) square. Place the herbs and spices in the middle, bring all four corners of the muslin together and tie securely into a small pouch. Hit it several times with the back of a knife to bruise the herbs and spices, helping them to release their volatile oils.

## Unusual Ingredients

PLANTAIN - In appearance the plantain is very similar to a banana, only it's larger and not as sweet. The starchy plantain is used as a vegetable in Central America and the Caribbean. Indeed, plantains are served with almost any main course — pork, beef, chicken or fish. They must be cooked before eating. You can buy them when they're an unripe green color — they will ripen at room temperature at home.

JICAMA - Look for this tuber in your grocery's produce department. Like the plantain, jicama is used extensively in Central America. You will find its crisp texture and sweet taste similar to water chestnuts. Use it as a refreshingly different ingredient in your salads. It should store in your refrigerator for up to 2 weeks.

# COTTAGE PIE

𝓛ike any great "food-of-the-people" dish, this
English classic has hundreds of local variations.
Mine reduces the meat and adds bulgur wheat, but
in my judgment does no disservice to the original's
flavor ... in fact, it seems better than most!

The Cottage Pie has such an attractive golden
brown appearance that you can dish it up at the
table. You'll need to add at least one fresh vegetable
on the side. One of our favorites is freshly steamed
swiss chard, with perhaps half an orange-fleshed
sweet potato.

## Nutritional Profile

| PER SERVING | CLASSIC | MINIMAX |
| --- | --- | --- |
| Calories | 653 | 464 |
| Fat (gm) | 35 | 12 |
| Calories From Fat | 49% | 23% |
| Cholesterol (mg) | 109 | 47 |
| Sodium (mg) | 584 | 325 |
| Fiber (gm) | 7 | 8 |

■ *Classic Compared – Cottage Pie*

## Time Estimate

Hands On
Unsupervised

*Minutes*   10   20   30   40   50   60   70   80   90

## Cost Estimate

Low       Medium       Medium High       Celebration

*Serves 6*

## INGREDIENTS

1½ pounds potatoes (or 2 large russets) (700 gm)
½ teaspoon freshly ground salt (2.5 ml)
⅛ teaspoon freshly ground white pepper (.6 ml)
1 cup buttermilk (236 ml)
Dusting of nutmeg
4 teaspoons extra light olive oil with a dash of sesame oil (20 ml)
1 onion, peeled and finely diced
1 medium carrot, peeled and finely diced
1 garlic clove, peeled and finely chopped
1 tablespoon fresh chopped parsley (15 ml)
1 tablespoon fresh chopped thyme (15 ml)
1 tablespoon marjoram (15 ml)
2 cups beef stock (472 ml) (recipe page 210)
¼ cup bulgur wheat (59 ml)
1 tablespoon soy sauce (15 ml)
¾ pound extra lean (9% fat or less) ground beef (340 gm)
3 tablespoons no-salt tomato paste (45 ml)
1 tablespoon freshly grated horseradish (15 ml)
1 tablespoon arrowroot (15 ml) mixed with ½ cup beef stock (118 ml)

## NOW COOK

■ Bake the potatoes at 350°F (180°C) for 1 hour. When cool enough to handle, scoop out the flesh (you can save the skins for a snack - see Helpful Hints, page 177), place in a large bowl and stir in ¼ teaspoon (1.25 ml) of the salt, the pepper, buttermilk and nutmeg. Continue stirring until you have creamy mashed potatoes. Set aside.

■ In a low sided casserole, heat 1 tablespoon (15 ml) of the olive oil and fry the onions, carrot and garlic until the onions become soft and slightly translucent.

■ Add the parsley, thyme and marjoram.

■ In a small saucepan, heat half the beef stock. Pour this over the bulgur wheat and stir in the soy sauce. Allow the bulgur to sit for 10 minutes to soften.

■ In a medium sized wok or skillet, heat the remaining olive oil. Pinch the ground beef into 1 inch (2.5 cm) chunks and drop them into the pan. Turn the chunks, allowing all sides to brown. Stir in the tomato paste and continue to cook until the tomato deepens in color.

■ Put the ground beef mixture into the casserole with the vegetables.

■ Pour the remaining beef stock into the now empty pan. Scrape up the residue. Pour stock and residue into the beef-vegetable mixture.

■ Add the bulgur wheat, horseradish and remaining salt and stir thoroughly.

■ Bring to a boil, cover and simmer for 15 minutes.

■ Remove from the heat and stir in the arrowroot mixture. Pour the contents of the casserole into an ovenproof serving bowl.

■ Pipe the mashed potatoes on top of the filling and spread the potatoes to cover the beef with an attractive ribbed top. Pop under the broiler to brown for 3 minutes.

### Helpful Hints and Observations

BAKED WHIPPED POTATOES - I make the best whipped potatoes from large, mature baking potatoes that are, in fact, baked first, and then scooped into a pan or passed through a ricer and combined with buttermilk and salt, white pepper and nutmeg. They are infinitely better than the waterlogged waxiness you get from boiling new potatoes. The baking process actually steams the extra water out rather than boiling water in. I use a ricer to remove any lumps. It looks like a large garlic press.

THE BASIC MINCED BEEF RECIPE - You can use the minced beef recipe given here for any number of recipes that call for a hamburger style meat sauce. It has lots of flavor and is quite low in fat.

### Unusual Ingredients

BULGUR - I know it looks a little strange but bulgur is actually just wheat kernels that have been boiled, dried and finally, cracked. It's very simple to prepare and as you will taste from this recipe, bulgur also has a charming, nutty flavor. It's been a staple food of people in the Middle East for thousands of years. So, now that you've been introduced, get cooking with bulgur: in salads, soups, or just eaten by itself.

BEEF - The sixty million dollar question (from a cattleman's point of view): can you still enjoy beef on a low fat diet? The answer is demonstrated in this recipe: ¾ lb (300 gm) beef to feed 6 people! Most nutritionists will advise that 4 oz (113 gm) is the maximum serving portion. The other factor to consider: look at the percentage of fat written on the label. Utilizing these two factors, most healthy people can keep small amounts of beef in their diet and experience its many nutritional benefits: iron, B vitamins and zinc, to name just a few!

# STEAK & OYSTER PIE

$\mathcal{N}$othing represents the best of British food as well as beef based pies with kidneys, mushrooms and oysters. Unfortunately in classic form, these pies are riddled with cholesterol; and the crust, when cooked on the meat, can be mostly sodden on the underside. I've set out to bring some relief!

I've replaced the traditional butter with a polyunsaturated stick margarine. In a careful taste test, I found no discernible difference in flavor or texture (probably because of the extra flavor from the wheat germ).

I serve the crust as a separate wedge - very crisp and delicious. Part of me says that it isn't right, because it isn't a pie: it's a stew with a piece of pastry. I just wanted you to know how I feel!

## Nutritional Profile

| PER SERVING | CLASSIC | MINIMAX |
|---|---|---|
| Calories | 906 | 228 |
| Fat (gm) | 48 | 9 |
| Calories From Fat | 48% | 37% |
| Cholesterol (mg) | 395 | 58 |
| Sodium (mg) | 682 | 210 |
| Fiber (gm) | 4 | 2 |

■ *Classic Compared – Steak, Kidney & Oyster Pie*

## Time Estimate

| | | |
|---|---|---|
| Hands On | | |
| Unsupervised | | |

Minutes  10  20  30  40  50  60  70  80  90

## Cost Estimate

| Low | Medium | Medium High | Celebration |
|---|---|---|---|

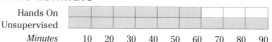

## INGREDIENTS

THE PIE TOP

1½ cups all-purpose flour (354 ml)

¼ cup wheat germ (59 ml)

6 tablespoons margarine (90 ml), cut into 12 small pieces and well chilled

5 tablespoons ice water (75 ml)

1 tablespoon 2% milk (15 ml)

THE FILLING

1 teaspoon extra light olive oil with a dash of sesame oil (5 ml)

2 onions, peeled and cut in chunks

2 carrots, peeled and cut in chunks

12 ounces bottom round steak (340 gm), cut in ½ inch (1.5 cm) cubes

2 heaped tablespoons tomato paste (30 ml)

12 ounces large mushrooms (340 gm), wiped clean and sliced, stems included

2 cups beef stock (472 ml) (recipe page 210)

8 shucked oysters (with liquid from a jar, preferably medium sized "Pacific"), drained and chopped, liquid reserved

2 tablespoons oyster sauce (30 ml)

2 tablespoons arrowroot (30 ml) mixed with 4 tablespoons water (60 ml)

Freshly ground black pepper

Chopped parsley

BOUQUET GARNI

1 bay leaf

1 teaspoon thyme (5 ml)

1 tablespoon parsley (15 ml)

3 whole cloves

1 teaspoon whole black peppercorns (5 ml)

## TO MAKE THE PIE TOP

■ Sift the flour into a bowl and stir in the wheat germ.

■ Pinch the chilled margarine pieces into the flour with the tips of your fingers.

■ Stir in the ice water until the mixture forms a stiff mass. Turn out onto a floured board and roll into an oblong shape. The less you handle it the better!

■ Fold the bottom third towards the center and the top third on top. Give the dough a quarter turn and roll it out to an oblong again and fold as before. Repeat this process once more.

■ Roll the pastry out to an 11 inch (28 cm) diameter circle and trim the rough edges. For a more attractive crust you can crimp the edge as in an old fashioned apple pie.

■ Transfer to a baking tray. Lightly score eight wedges in the dough without cutting all the way through. Brush lightly with the milk. Prick to help release steam during the baking process.

■ Bake in a preheated oven at 425°F (220°C) for 12-15 minutes or until golden and crisp. Cool on a wire rack before cutting into wedges.

## TO MAKE THE FILLING

■ Heat the oil in a large, ovenproof casserole with a lid. Add the onions and carrots and saute for about 1 minute on high heat. Transfer the vegetables to a bowl and set aside.

■ Add the meat to the casserole and brown on all sides. Stir in the tomato paste, scraping the bottom of the pan so that all the juices and residue are mixed together. Cook 3-4 minutes.

■ Add the mushrooms to the cooked carrots and onions. Stir two thirds of this mixture into the meat.

■ Pour in the stock and reserved oyster juice all at once and stir. Add the bouquet garni and the oyster sauce. Cover and simmer for 1 hour.

■ Add the remaining mushrooms, carrots, onions and the oysters to the mixture. Remove the pot from the heat and stir in the arrowroot mixture. Return to the heat and stir until thickened.

■ Spoon the filling into a high sided 9 inch (23 cm) pie plate. Place the pie crust on top and heat in a 400°F (205°C) oven for 5 minutes.

■ To Serve: Using the scoring as your guide, cut a wedge out of the pie crust and set it over two large spoonfuls of the filling.

### Helpful Hints and Observations

UPPER CRUST? - The crust I've used has less fat than is usual by at least four ounces (113 gm). It is made very quickly (another benefit compared to the time-consuming puff pastry) and because of the wheat germ addition, it is speckled in an attractive way and has a toasted, nutty flavor.

### Unusual Ingredients

OYSTERS - They should look plump and cream colored in a clear liquor. Pacifics are easily the least expensive and since, in this recipe, they are to be cooked, the supreme delicacy of some of the smaller, sweeter, rare varieties would be wasted.

WHEAT GERM - See Unusual Ingredients, page 181.

# BLINCHATY PIROG

*This* is the Russian equivalent of the American Sloppy Joe or the British Mince on Toast. Language does have quite a romantic influence, doesn't it? I have substantially increased the mushroom content and played some other games ... and ... it works!

Serve it whole and cut it in wedges as you would a pie. You will need a pie server to save a spill en route! Fresh green beans (if in season) are wonderful with this and I'm fond of large broiled tomatoes to add color as well as taste.

## Nutritional Profile

| PER SERVING | CLASSIC | MINIMAX |
|---|---|---|
| Calories | 945 | 359 |
| Fat (gm) | 62 | 12 |
| Calories From Fat | 59% | 30% |
| Cholesterol (mg) | 339 | 63 |
| Sodium (mg) | 404 | 359 |
| Fiber (gm) | 3 | 3 |

■ *Classic Compared – Meat Pirog*

## Time Estimate

| | 10 | 20 | 30 | 40 | 50 | 60 | 70 | 80 | 90 |
|---|---|---|---|---|---|---|---|---|---|
| Hands On | | | | | | | | | |
| Unsupervised | | | | | | | | | |

*Minutes*

## Cost Estimate

| Low | Medium | Medium High | Celebration |
|---|---|---|---|

*Serves 6*

## INGREDIENTS

CREPE BATTER

1 egg

1 egg yolk

1¼ cups nonfat milk (295 ml)

1 cup all-purpose flour (236 ml)

¼ teaspoon salt (1.25 ml)

1 tablespoon extra light olive oil with a dash of sesame oil (15 ml)

BEEF FILLING

1 tablespoon extra light olive oil with a dash of sesame oil (15 ml)

½ cup chopped onion (118 ml)

2 garlic cloves, crushed and peeled

12 ounces bottom round beef, coarsely ground (340 gm)

3 tablespoons tomato paste (45 ml)

1 cup water (236 ml)

1 cup de-alcoholized dry red wine (236 ml)

1 tablespoon arrowroot (15 ml) mixed with

1 tablespoon water (15 ml)

MUSHROOM FILLING

1 tablespoon extra light olive oil with a dash of sesame oil (15 ml)

12 ounces mushrooms (340 gm), finely chopped

3 green onions, trimmed and chopped

1 teaspoon cayenne pepper (5 ml)

1 tablespoon freshly squeezed lemon juice (15 ml)

½ cup cooked rice (118 ml)

⅛ teaspoon freshly ground black pepper (.6 ml)

2 ounces low-fat cottage cheese (57 gm)

1 teaspoon fresh chopped dill (5 ml)

SAUCE

1½ cups strained yogurt (354 ml) (recipe page 210)

⅓ cup de-alcoholized white wine (78 ml)

1 tablespoon chopped dill (15 ml)

6 sprigs of fresh dill

## FIRST PREPARE THE CREPES

■ In a small bowl, mix the egg, egg yolk, and milk. Sift the flour and salt into a medium bowl and make a well in the center. Pour the egg mixture into the well and gradually stir it together with the flour until fully incorporated with no lumps. Strain through a sieve. Set the batter aside in a cool place and let it rest for 30 minutes.

■ Heat an 8 inch (20 cm) saute pan to medium. Pour the olive oil into the pan, swish it around, then pour it into the crepe batter and mix thoroughly. This will help make the crepe self-releasing.

■ Pour ¼ cup (59 ml) of crepe batter into the saute pan. Rotate the pan until the entire surface is covered.

■ When the edges of the crepe start curling up and the top looks waxy, flip the crepe over. Cook the other side until it turns light brown, just a minute or two, then turn it out onto a dish. Make 4 more, giving you a stack of 5.

■ In a 10 inch (25 cm) saute pan, prepare one larger crepe as above and set aside. (You can lay a couple of branches of dill on the uncooked side before you flip and serve this side up for a nice finishing effect.)

## NOW COOK THE BEEF FILLING

■ Heat the olive oil in a large skillet, and brown the onions and garlic until the onions are translucent - about 2 minutes. Transfer to a plate. Clean out the skillet, leaving no trace of onion.

■ Add the beef to the skillet and brown. Stir in the tomato paste and cook until dark brown - about 4 minutes. Take off the heat and add the water to cool down the beef. Put the pan back on high heat and add the wine, the cooked onions and garlic. Bring to a boil, then lower the heat to medium. Pull off the heat and add the arrowroot paste. Stir thoroughly and reheat to thicken.

■ Mushroom Filling: Put the olive oil and mushrooms in a 10½ inch (27 cm) heated saucepan and saute for about 5 minutes. Remove from the heat and add the green onion, cayenne and lemon juice.

■ Mix the mushroom filling into the beef mixture. Add the cooked rice and black pepper. Stir in the cottage cheese and distribute evenly.

■ Place one small (8 inch or 20 cm) crepe on a plate. Cover with a thick layer of meat mixture. Place another of the smaller crepes on top. Repeat these layers, finishing with a layer of meat. Cover with the larger crepe. Garnish with the chopped dill.

■ The Sauce: Mix the yogurt with the de-alcoholized white wine and the chopped dill.

■ To Serve: Dollop a spoonful or two of the sauce onto a plate, place a wedge of the pirog on it. Garnish with a sprig of dill and enjoy!

# MOUSSAKA

*O*riginally this classic was made in Rumania, but it has become one of the greatest examples of Greek "food-of-the-people." I have made several changes in order to lower the health risks. As always, the taste values are less velvety without the oil and lamb fat, but the overall flavor is still there.

This dish is usually served at the table from the pan it's cooked in. I really enjoy a mixed wild rice and long grain rice pilaf with it (see Rock Cornish Game Hens, page 78) and some perfectly cooked tiny green peas.

## Nutritional Profile

| PER SERVING | CLASSIC | MINIMAX |
|---|---|---|
| Calories | 756 | 176 |
| Fat (gm) | 64 | 6 |
| Calories From Fat | 76% | 30% |
| Cholesterol (mg) | 231 | 60 |
| Sodium (mg) | 4934 | 461 |
| Fiber (gm) | 4 | 2 |

■ *Classic Compared – Moussaka*

## Time Estimate

| | | |
|---|---|---|
| Hands On | | |
| Unsupervised | | |
| *Minutes* | 10  20  30  40  50  60  70  80  90 | |

## Cost Estimate

| | | | |
|---|---|---|---|
| Low | Medium | Medium High | Celebration |

*Serves 6*

## INGREDIENTS

1 teaspoon extra light olive oil with a dash of sesame oil (5 ml)

1 cup finely diced onion (236 ml)

1 garlic clove, peeled and minced

12 ounces ground lamb (340 gm)

3 tablespoons low-salt tomato paste (45 ml)

¼ cup bulgur wheat (59 ml)

1 teaspoon dried oregano (5 ml)

1 cup water (236 ml)

1 cup de-alcoholized red wine (236 ml)

⅛ teaspoon cinnamon (.6 ml)

1 bay leaf

⅛ teaspoon freshly ground salt (.6 ml)

¼ teaspoon freshly ground black pepper (1.25 ml)

1 (13 ounce) eggplant (369 gm), peeled and sliced

¼ cup (59 ml) + 2 tablespoons (30 ml) freshly grated Parmesan cheese

### SAUCE

1 cup non-fat milk (236 ml)

⅛ teaspoon freshly ground nutmeg (.6 ml)

⅛ teaspoon freshly ground salt (.6 ml)

2 tablespoons cornstarch (30 ml) mixed with 4 tablespoons water (60 ml)

1 egg yolk, slightly beaten

## NOW COOK

■ In a large wok or frypan, heat the oil and saute the onions and garlic until the onions are soft and translucent. Turn out onto a plate and set aside.

■ In the same pan, brown the lamb. Add the tomato paste, bulgur, cooked onions, oregano and water. Stir, scraping any residue off the bottom of the pan and into the mixture for added depth of taste. Add the wine, cinnamon, bay leaf, salt and pepper.

■ Layer a third of the eggplant slices on the bottom of a ceramic or glass souffle dish. Cover with half the lamb and sprinkle with a third of the ¼ cup (59 ml) of cheese. Repeat with a third of the eggplant, the remaining lamb, and a third of the cheese, finishing with a layer of the remaining eggplant and the remaining cheese.

■ For the Sauce: In a 1½ quart (2 L) saucepan, heat the milk. Sprinkle with the nutmeg and salt. Gradually stir in the cornstarch paste and bring to a boil stirring until thickened. Remove from the heat. Pour a little of the sauce into the beaten egg yolk, then stir it back into the sauce. This will prevent the egg yolk from curdling.

■ Pour the sauce over the moussaka layers and sprinkle with the remaining Parmesan cheese. Bake in the oven at 350°F (180°C) for 40 minutes. When done, the eggplant will separate from the sides of the souffle pan, revealing the bubbling juices.

■ Slice the moussaka into 6 even wedges and serve.

## Helpful Hints and Observations

ON SALTING EGGPLANT - A great many recipes call for salting eggplant slices liberally and then pressing them to reduce both bitterness and excess water content. The slices are then cooked in oil or lamb fat.

I chose to buy a smaller sized eggplant, not more than 3 inches (8 cm) in diameter, and simply peeled it, sliced it and slipped it naked into the sauce - no salt, no oil, no bother and no bitterness! I did add ¼ cup (59 ml) of bulgur wheat to soak up any surplus liquid.

The result of these efforts is clear from the numbers: an incredible drop of 57 grams of fat, 580 calories and 4,473 mg of sodium - for each serving!

My local deli owner is Greek. The day after this recipe went on television he looked at me, bit his finger and shook his head in mock bewilderment - then he smiled!

## Unusual Ingredients

EGGPLANT - Not always egg shaped: it can be round or even long. In Europe you see both a purple-black and white color. Buy eggplant with skin that's shiny and a stem-cap that's bright green. The skin should feel firm, not mushy. The smaller eggplants have less seeds and more tender skins.

# ROGAN JOSH

*This recipe was developed in cooperation with Mr. Ranjan Dey, of the excellent "New Dehli" restaurant on Ellis Street in San Francisco.*

*The cuisine of Northern India is heavily influenced from the Aryan peoples of their northern borders. This is where their yogurt and lamb comes from. When you smell the combination of garlic, ginger and the sweet, warm spices, then you always know exactly where you are!*

*The classic way to serve is to dish up the lamb with a good basmati rice, 1 cup (236 ml) raw for 3 servings and a variety of chutneys, chappaties (flat bread) and sliced fruits as side dishes.*

## Nutritional Profile

| PER SERVING | CLASSIC | MINIMAX |
|---|---|---|
| Calories | 1038 | 378 |
| Fat (gm) | 63 | 13 |
| Calories From Fat | 55% | 31% |
| Cholesterol (mg) | 204 | 80 |
| Sodium (mg) | 333 | 140 |
| Fiber (gm) | 4 | 2 |

■ *Classic Compared – Rogan Josh*

## Time Estimate

Hands On
Unsupervised

Minutes   10   20   30   40   50   60   70   80   90

## Cost Estimate

Low        Medium        Medium High        Celebration

*Serves 6*

## INGREDIENTS

2 tablespoons extra light olive oil with a dash of sesame oil (30 ml)

4 garlic cloves, peeled and finely diced

2 cups chopped onions (472 ml)

1 tablespoon freshly grated ginger root (15 ml)

½ teaspoon cayenne pepper (2.5 ml)

¼ teaspoon powdered nutmeg (1.25 ml)

½ teaspoon turmeric (2.5 ml)

¼ teaspoon mace (1.25 ml)

1½ teaspoons paprika (7.5 ml)

1 teaspoon garam masala (5 ml)

1½ pounds lean leg of lamb (700 gm), cut in 1 inch (2.5 cm) cubes

1 tablespoon dried coriander (15 ml)

2 cups peeled and chopped tomatoes (472 ml)

⅛ teaspoon freshly ground salt (.6 ml)

1 tablespoon cornstarch (15 ml) mixed with 2 tablespoons water (30 ml)

¾ cup plain non-fat yogurt (177 ml)

¾ cup water (177 ml)

1 tablespoon fresh chopped cilantro (15 ml)

3 cups steamed rice (708 ml) (see Helpful Hints, page 47)

## NOW COOK

■ Heat half the olive oil in a large 11 inch (28 cm) wok. Stir in the garlic, onions, ginger and cayenne pepper. Saute until the onions are slightly softened and appear translucent. Stir in the nutmeg, turmeric, mace, paprika and garam masala.

■ Put another large 13 inch (33 cm) pan on high heat and add the remaining olive oil. Drop the lamb cubes in around the edges, allowing them to brown fully on one side (see Helpful Hints). Add the dried coriander.

■ Stir in the sauteed onion mixture. Now add the tomatoes and the salt.

■ Blend in the cornstarch paste, yogurt and water, bring to a boil and stir until thickened. Reduce the heat, cover and simmer for one hour. Uncover and cook another 30 minutes. Sprinkle with chopped cilantro and serve over ½ cup (118 ml) of steamed rice.

## Helpful Hints and Observations

SPICE SAUTE - A classic Indian method calls for the warm, citrus-like spice of coriander and the bite of cayenne pepper to be added to the oil before frying the meat. I've adapted this idea using much less fat. In a 6 person dish, up to ¾ cup (177 ml) of oil or clarified butter (ghee) can be added. I've dropped this down to 2 tablespoons (30 ml).

ONE-SIDED SAUTE - I learned a completely new technique during the development of this dish. In India, the meat is never browned; instead they leave it open to receive maximum spice penetration. Because I struggle to lower fat levels, I need to brown the meat to replace the perception of depth of taste you get when plenty of fat holds the flavor longer. Eventually I settled for a one-side-only browning: I get my depth of taste, Mr. Dey got his spice absorption and a new technique that works well for all manner of casseroles was born!

NON-FAT YOGURT AND THE BREAKING PROBLEM - Whole yogurt, with its 3.5% fat content, can be added to hot dishes and stirred in without separating (what I call "breaking"). When the fat is removed, yogurt moves apart into a million tiny flecks (I haven't counted them but it seems a fair estimate). To counter this I've added a small amount of cornstarch as a binder. It seems to work and it's a lot better than resorting to more fat.

## Unusual Ingredients

GARAM MASALA - The secret to India's great curries is here: there is no such thing as curry powder. Instead they mix their own blend of spices to create a specific curry taste for each individual dish. Garam masala is as close as you can get to the aromas of an Indian curry without blending your own spices. You might want to use it as a base, and then add your own finishing flourishes. Generally the basic ingredients of garam masala include coriander, cumin seeds, cloves, cinnamon and black pepper. Blend your own if you can't find it commercially available.

MACE - This fragrant spice might sound unfamiliar but is actually part of a familiar friend: It is ground from the dried outer covering of the nutmeg!

# PORK TENDERLOIN WITH GLAZED PEARS

*A*nother dish from my "galloping" days and, remarkably, it wasn't too bad! I've tweaked it a bit in order to further reduce the fat and I'm delighted at having found a new technique that gives fresh fruit a light pickled spice.

The colors of the dish are really wonderful. They don't need anything in the reds or oranges to fight the plump, pale, saffron-tinted pears. So, I'd recommend just adding some fresh steamed French green beans with a hint of nutmeg.

## Nutritional Profile

| PER SERVING | CLASSIC | MINIMAX |
|---|---|---|
| Calories | 617 | 472 |
| Fat (gm) | 28 | 13 |
| Calories From Fat | 41% | 25% |
| Cholesterol (mg) | 161 | 109 |
| Sodium (mg) | 480 | 234 |
| Fiber (gm) | 2 | 2 |

■ *Classic Compared – Pork Tenderloin with Glazed Pears*

## Time Estimate

| | | | | | | | | |
|---|---|---|---|---|---|---|---|---|
| Hands On | | | | | | | | |
| Unsupervised | | | | | | | | |

Minutes  10  20  30  40  50  60  70  80  90

## Cost Estimate

| Low | Medium | Medium High | Celebration |
|---|---|---|---|

*Serves 4*

## INGREDIENTS

2 (8 ounce) butterflied pork tenderloins
(227 gm each)

⅛ teaspoon salt (.6 ml)

¼ teaspoon freshly ground black pepper (1.25 ml)

2 cups water (472 ml)

7 tablespoons brown sugar (105 ml)

⅛ teaspoon saffron (.6 ml)

½ teaspoon allspice berries (2.5 ml)

½ teaspoon cloves (2.5 ml)

¼ cup cider vinegar (59 ml)

2 pears, preferably Comice, peeled, halved lengthwise and cored

2 tablespoons extra light olive oil with a dash of sesame oil (30 ml)

1 ounce Canadian bacon (38 gm) (about 2 slices), diced

1 tablespoon honey (15 ml)

## NOW COOK

■ Pound the butterflied pork tenderloins until they are ½ inch (1.5 cm) thick. Season with salt and pepper.

■ In a medium saucepan, over medium heat, dissolve 4 tablespoons (60 ml) of the brown sugar in the water. Add the saffron, allspice berries, cloves, and vinegar. Poach the pears in this syrup, turning them so that the "cup side" is uppermost. This is done so that if there is oxidation, it occurs on the side not seen in the final dish! The poaching process should take about 15 minutes. Remove the pears to a small bowl. Pour the poaching liquid over them and set aside.

■ Heat the olive oil in a small saucepan and fry the Canadian bacon for approximately 5 minutes. Brush the oil from the pan over the pork tenderloins and on the base of the broiler pan. Sprinkle half of the Canadian bacon bits on top of the tenderloins. Place under the broiler for 6 minutes. Turn the pork, brush with more oil and sprinkle with the remaining Canadian bacon bits. Place under the broiler 4 minutes longer.

■ Strain the pears and reserve the poaching liquid. In a skillet over medium heat, mix the honey and the remaining brown sugar. Add ¼ cup (59 ml) pear poaching liquid. Bring to a boil, then simmer until reduced to a thin glaze. Add the pears and coat with the glaze.

■ To Serve: Cut each tenderloin into ½ inch (1.5 cm) slices. Fan a quarter of the tenderloin on a plate and place a glazed pear half in the middle. Brush with the remaining glaze.

## Helpful Hints and Observations

TO BUTTERFLY PORK - Make an incision along the pork tenderloins, cutting lengthwise, not quite all the way through, and then open out — or ask your butcher to do this for you!

RE-USING THE SPICED VINEGAR - Simply pour the entire mixture into a sealable plastic bag or container and deep freeze for future use. Make sure you label it just in case you think it could be the fish fumet you made and froze and use it to poach scallops ... come to think of it, that could work !

BACON BITS SEND SIGNALS - I found that the bacon bits begin to explode on the tenderloin surface at just the stage when the meat is ready to be turned. Imagine that ... a natural timer !

## Unusual Ingredients

PEARS - I like Comice pears for this recipe. They're the chubby, roundish green pears that are rather sensitive to blemishes and bruise marks. At the store, choose pears that are firm but not hard. When are they ready? When the area around their stem gives just slightly under pressure. Remember, when you cook pears it might be better if they're slightly under-ripe.

VINEGARS - When you go to your supermarket, you should see quite an array of vinegars. These vinegar varieties vary distinctly in taste: rich, mellow or sharp. I prefer the fragrant, light, qualities of white wine vinegar in this recipe. Don't be alarmed if you take a wine vinegar home and over time see an eerie, cloudy residue. This is something all vinegars do, and for some obscure reason, it's called "mothering." A gentle shake and it's dispersed.

PORK TENDERLOIN - The fresh pork you buy in the store today is different - it's not as fatty! Pork breeders are actually feeding their pigs differently to get leaner meat. The tenderloin cut I use in this recipe is the tenderest part of the pork. At the supermarket, look for pork that is pink to pinkish-white and firm to the touch.

# HAWK'S PRAIRIE ENCHILADA

$\mathcal{C}$hef Richard Wright of the "Hawk's Prairie Inn," located just off Highway 5 near Olympia, Washington, has been creating special low-fat dishes for over ten years. I wanted to honor him and his work with a recipe made up from a list of his favorite ingredients.

Obviously this dish borrows from the Mexican style and so it helps to create an attractive, colorful setting. If you enjoy this type of dish, you could get some simple, bold, table top china to help in the celebration. Olé!

## Nutritional Profile

| PER SERVING | CLASSIC | MINIMAX |
|---|---|---|
| Calories | 685 | 532 |
| Fat (gm) | 35 | 17 |
| Calories From Fat | 46% | 28% |
| Cholesterol (mg) | 84 | 44 |
| Sodium (mg) | 2028 | 371 |
| Fiber (gm) | 11 | 9 |

■ *Classic Compared – Hawk's Prairie Enchilada*

## Time Estimate

| Hands On | | | | | | | | | |
|---|---|---|---|---|---|---|---|---|---|
| Unsupervised | | | | | | | | | |
| Hours | 1 | 2 | 3 | 4 | 5 | 6 | 7 | 8 | 9 |

## Cost Estimate

| | | | |
|---|---|---|---|
| Low | Medium | Medium High | Celebration |

*Serves 6*

## INGREDIENTS

4 tablespoons fresh chopped basil (60 ml)

¼ cup de-alcoholized chardonnay wine (59 ml)

1 cup strained yogurt (236 ml) (recipe page 210)

Freshly ground black pepper to taste

2 heads broccoli

1 pound smoked ham hocks (450 gm)

5½ cups water (1.3 L)

1 cup dried pinto beans  (236 ml)

1 cup wild rice  (236 ml)

1 teaspoon extra light olive oil with a dash of sesame oil (5 ml)

1 large red onion, peeled and cut in ¼ inch (.75 cm) cubes

2 jalapeño peppers, seeded and chopped

2 garlic cloves, peeled and chopped

6 Roma tomatoes, seeded and cut in ¼ inch (.75 cm) cubes

12 warm whole wheat tortillas

## FIRST PREPARE

■ For the Sauce:  Add half the basil and de-alcoholized chardonnay wine to the strained yogurt.  Season with pepper to taste and set aside.

■ Chop broccoli into individual florets.  Trim off the outer skin of the stalks and cut into small pieces.

## NOW COOK

■ In a pressure cooker, place the ham hocks and water.  Be sure the lid vent is clear of any food particles!  Pressure cook for 30 minutes.  Remove and discard the ham hocks, skim off the surface fats and add the pinto beans to the pressure cooker.  Bring it to the boil.  Put the lid on and when the top starts to flutter, begin timing for 5 minutes, then open, add the rice and cook 20 minutes more, for a total of 25 minutes.

■ In another casserole pan, heat the olive oil.  Add the onion, chopped broccoli stalks, jalapeño and garlic.  Cook until the onion is soft, about 5 minutes.

■ Add the chopped tomatoes and broccoli florets.  Cover and cook gently for 6 minutes.

■ Add the remaining basil to the cooking vegetables.

■ To Serve:  Spoon the rice and beans into a warm tortilla and roll.  Serve with the yogurt-wine sauce and the vegetables on the side.  You can add a spoonful of the yogurt-wine sauce to help combine the beans with the wild rice, but it isn't absolutely necessary.

### Helpful Hints and Observations

STRAINED YOGURT WINE SAUCE - This is a great idea!  I had been looking for an effective alternative to the standard dollop of sour cream and began with the strained yogurt concept adding the de-alcoholized wine and flavorings.  The result was excellent and it made me think of all kinds of sauces that could be developed in this manner.  Why not have a go at it yourself?

PRESSURE COOKING - I'm delighted to have found the HAWKIN'S® FUTURA™ Pressure Cooker.  It has removed all my old apprehensions about the method and it does make the full range of beans and "whole" rices much more attractive in this speed-conscious world.  Imagine:  25 minutes from scratch!

HAM HOCK STOCK - It's important to remember to skim the stock before using it to cook the beans and rice.  The flavor is wonderful but you really don't need the fats that are released in cooking.  You can shred the lean ham meat and add this to the dish.  Add another 20 calories per portion if you do.

### Unusual Ingredients

WILD RICE - See Unusual Ingredients, page 79.

JALAPEÑO PEPPERS - A variety of chili pepper that is the fruit of piquant types of Capsicums (Capsicum being the species name) native to the New World and first discovered by explorers some time in the 15th century.  There are many varieties, the most popular being the Jalepei and Anaheim.  When selecting a chili choose one that is firm and glossy.  Green in most cases means milder; red meants hotter.

HAM HOCKS - A smoked pork product found in the meat department.  When boiled, they lend their flavor to soups, stocks and bean dishes.

# LOBSCOUSE

*"Lob" means a piece of meat and "scouse" has come to mean an inhabitant of the city of Liverpool, England, where lobscouse is a well known meat and vegetable stew based on old clipper ship recipes of pickled pork and navy beans served with hard tack biscuits. Many changes have been made to this recipe but one thing remains the same: it's a wonderful rib-sticking family meal in the depths of winter!*

*This is another "food-of-the-people" dish that gets cooked all-at-once in one pot. You might like to add some freshly cooked, sweet green peas for added color but it isn't strictly necessary.*

## Nutritional Profile

| PER SERVING | CLASSIC | MINIMAX |
|---|---|---|
| Calories | 592 | 271 |
| Fat (gm) | 35 | 8 |
| Calories From Fat | 52% | 26% |
| Cholesterol (mg) | 78 | 32 |
| Sodium (mg) | 1116 | 253 |
| Fiber (gm) | 5 | 5 |

■ *Classic Compared – Creamed Pork & Peas*

## Time Estimate

| | | | | | | | | |
|---|---|---|---|---|---|---|---|---|
| Hands On | | | | | | | | |
| Unsupervised | | | | | | | | |

*Minutes*   10   20   30   40   50   60   70   80   90

## Cost Estimate

| | | | |
|---|---|---|---|
| Low | Medium | Medium High | Celebration |

*Serves 6*

## INGREDIENTS

1 tablespoon extra light olive oil with a dash of sesame oil (15 ml)

12 ounces lean pork shoulder (340 gm), cut into ½ inch (1.5 cm) cubes

1 large onion, peeled and diced

2 carrots, sliced

1½ pounds potatoes (680 gm), peeled and diced into 1 inch (2.5 cm) cubes

1 tablespoon fresh chopped mint (15 ml)

1 tablespoon fresh chopped thyme (15 ml)

½ teaspoon freshly ground salt (2.5 ml)

½ cup yellow split peas (118 ml)

½ cup green split peas (118 ml)

3 cups chicken stock (708 ml) (recipe page 210)

3 bay leaves

½ teaspoon freshly ground black pepper (2.5 ml)

1 cup celery leaves (236 ml)

## NOW COOK

■ In an ovenproof casserole pot, heat the oil and fry the pork until browned.

■ Scatter the onions over the pork; do not stir. This allows the pork to continue to brown on the bottom of the pot and the onions to steam.

■ Add the carrots and potatoes on top of the onions. Sprinkle in the mint, thyme and salt. Add the yellow and green peas and mix thoroughly, scraping the residue off of the bottom of the pan.

■ Pour in the stock, push the bay leaves under the surface and add pepper to taste. Bring to a boil, cover and simmer for 90 minutes.

■ Garnish with the celery leaves.

## Helpful Hints and Observations

THE DRY MEAT BENEFIT - It's always a good idea to dry surface juices off of meat, because it enhances the browning process.

## Unusual Ingredients

SPLIT PEAS - Split peas are a wonderful variation on the usual bean theme: you don't have to soak them before cooking. Simply simmer slowly for 40 or 50 minutes. Have you ever used the yellow split pea before? A refreshing color change, I think, especially in Spring, perhaps, in a kitchen filled with daffodils ...

MINT - Legend has it that mint was created when an envious Greek deity changed her rival into a plant so that mortals would tramp over her forever. Well I'm afraid that's backfired somewhat because mint is now a valued addition to many recipes. Fortunately, the cool, clean flavor of mint leaves can easily come from your garden. Indeed, mint grows like a weed. So if you haven't started your Minimax herb garden, yet, mint might be a marvelous one with which to start.

# TOLTOTT KAPOSZTA *(Hungarian Stuffed Cabbage)*

*This is Hungarian "food-of-the-people" fare. It's relatively simple to fix and makes an occasion out of very plain food. The center of the cabbage is relatively small so the rest of the filling winds up as a sauce.*

*I always take the whole cabbage to the table and cut wedges out of it, coating each slice with the meat sauce. Sour cream is traditionally served. I side stepped this with a cup (136 ml) of strained yogurt added to the sauce. How about whipped potatoes on the side? Or a hunk of dark rye bread?*

## Nutritional Profile

| PER SERVING | CLASSIC | MINIMAX |
|---|---|---|
| Calories | 372 | 226 |
| Fat (gm) | 26 | 5 |
| Calories From Fat | 62% | 22% |
| Cholesterol (mg) | 203 | 37 |
| Sodium (mg) | 727 | 295 |
| Fiber (gm) | 1 | 9 |

■  *Classic Compared – Stuffed Cabbage*

## Time Estimate

| | | | | | | | | | |
|---|---|---|---|---|---|---|---|---|---|
| Hands On | | | | | | | | | |
| Unsupervised | | | | | | | | | |

*Minutes*  10  20  30  40  50  60  70  80  90

## Cost Estimate

| | | | |
|---|---|---|---|
| | | | |

Low            Medium      Medium High    Celebration

*Serves 6*

## INGREDIENTS

12 ounces pork loin (340 gm), cut into 2 inch (5 cm) cubes

1 cup chopped onion (236 ml)

2 garlic cloves, peeled and chopped

8 ounces mushrooms (227 gm), coarsely chopped

1 cup chicken stock (236 ml) (recipe page 210)

¼ cup bulgur wheat (59 ml)

1 medium cabbage head, trimmed, with damaged leaves removed

1 tablespoon extra light olive oil with a dash of sesame oil (15 ml)

3 tablespoons low-salt tomato paste (45 ml)

1 tablespoon (15 ml) + 2 teaspoons (10 ml) paprika

½ teaspoon caraway seeds (2.5 ml)

⅛ teaspoon freshly ground salt (.6 ml)

¼ teaspoon freshly ground black pepper (1.25 ml)

¼ cup strained yogurt (59 ml) (recipe page 210)

1 tablespoon fresh chopped parsley (15 ml)

2 tablespoons cornstarch (30 ml) mixed with 2 tablespoons water (30 ml)

## FIRST PREPARE

■ Mince the pork, onion, garlic and mushrooms in a meat grinder (remember the bread trick on page 71!).

■ Bring the chicken stock to a boil, add the bulgur wheat and simmer 5 minutes. Remove from heat and set aside for later use in the sauce.

■ In a large saucepan, cover the whole cabbage with water, bring to a boil and cook for 30 minutes. Remove the cabbage from the pan and cool quickly with cold water. Drain.

## NOW COOK

■ Heat the olive oil in a medium-sized wok or large frypan and add the ground pork mixture. When there is no pink left in the pork meat, add the tomato paste. Sprinkle in 1 tablespoon (15 ml) of the paprika and caraway seeds. Remove from the heat, stir in the cooked bulgur and set aside.

■ Place the cabbage core-side down on a board. Peel back the leaves without pulling them off at the core. Pull back as many cooked leaves as possible leaving a round inner head about 4 inches (10 cm) in diameter. Hollow out the top of this inner head. Fill the hollow with a third of the pork filling or until packed solid. Set the leftover pork filling

aside. Carefully re-fold the cabbage leaves into their original order and position. Wrap securely in muslin or cheesecloth.

■ Place some marbles in the bottom of a Dutch oven or large covered casserole. Put a steamer insert on top of the marbles. Add water to just above the base of the steamer. Place the wrapped cabbage on the steamer and cover. Cook on high heat for 30 minutes. If you hear marbles clanking against the Dutch oven, you know it's time to add more water!

■ While the cabbage cooks, put the pork filling back on low heat, cover and simmer. Add additional stock if needed to keep it from sticking.

■ When the cabbage is done, lift it out of the pan with a couple of wooden spoons. Place it in a bowl just large enough to hold it, with the core facing upwards. Cut the muslin or cheesecloth away from the cabbage and fold it over the sides of the bowl. Cover the bowl with a plate and holding it firmly, turn it upside down. Remove the bowl, strip off the muslin or cheesecloth and you've got a big, steamed cabbage sitting right-side up!

■ Add the strained yogurt, the remaining paprika and parsley to the filling. Remove from the heat, stir in the cornstarch paste, return to the heat, bring to a boil and stir until thickened.

■ To Serve: Slice the cabbage in wedges like a cake and serve in a small pool of sauce. Garnish with parsley.

## Helpful Hints and Observations

THE STEAMER INSERT - By insert I mean one of those stainless steel, expanding steamers that open up their multiple leaves to just fit the pot. They stand on short legs and help to keep large re-heated dishes, like this one, off the bottom.

## Unusual Ingredients

CABBAGE - Talk about "foods-of-the-people," cabbage is eaten just about everywhere on earth! And why not? It's a good source of fiber, vitamin C and other vitamins and minerals. When you buy a cabbage, first get the feel of it in your hands. It should feel heavy. Now look at it: its leaves should be crisp and its color strong and unblemished. Kept in the refrigerator it should last about two weeks.

CARAWAY - This spice pervades the roof of your mouth with a cloud of freshness. A tiny, crescent-shaped speck, you've probably seen it scattered on top of breads and cakes.

# PANCIT LUGLUG PALABOK *(Pork & Shrimp in a Red Sauce with Rice Noodles)*

*This is a popular dish in the Philippines. It uses readily available ingredients and the simple two pan method is almost as quick as a stir-fry. I've added finely diced bell pepper and cilantro to help with the color and texture.*

*As with any noodle and sauce dish, the noodles are served in a deep bowl and the sauce placed on top. In the Philippines, the garnish is a salad of hard boiled egg, celery leaves, finely shredded lettuce and lemon wedges but I prefer to serve mine perfectly plain.*

## Nutritional Profile

| PER SERVING | CLASSIC | MINIMAX |
|---|---|---|
| Calories | 432 | 304 |
| Fat (gm) | 19 | 8 |
| Calories From Fat | 40% | 25% |
| Cholesterol (mg) | 143 | 89 |
| Sodium (mg) | 300 | 92 |
| Fiber (gm) | 2 | 1 |

■ *Classic Compared – Pancit Luglug Palabok*

## Time Estimate

| | | | | | | | | | |
|---|---|---|---|---|---|---|---|---|---|
| Hands On | | | | | | | | | |
| Unsupervised | | | | | | | | | |
| *Minutes* | 10 | 20 | 30 | 40 | 50 | 60 | 70 | 80 | 90 |

## Cost Estimate

| | | | |
|---|---|---|---|
| Low | Medium | Medium High | Celebration |

*Serves 6*

## INGREDIENTS

12 ounces raw shrimp (340 gm) (weight with shell on)

3 cups water (708 ml)

12 ounces boneless pork loin chop (340 gm), trimmed of all visible fat

1 teaspoon extra light olive oil with a dash of sesame oil (5 ml)

4 garlic cloves, peeled and chopped

1 teaspoon achiote powder (5 ml)

1 teaspoon fish sauce (5 ml)

2 tablespoons arrowroot (30 ml) mixed with 4 tablespoons water (60 ml)

2 green onions, chopped

1 red bell pepper, cored, seeded and finely chopped

1 tablespoon fresh chopped cilantro (15 ml)

8 ounces firm tofu (247 gm), cut into tiny dice

¼ teaspoon freshly ground black pepper (1.25 ml)

12 ounces rice noodles (Bijon) (340 gm)

## FIRST PREPARE

■ Pour the water into a medium saucepan and bring to a boil. Add the shrimp and simmer for 5 minutes. Strain, reserving the water. Plunge the shrimp into ice cold water, then peel. Put the shells back into the reserved water to make a stock. Simmer the shells for 15 minutes and then strain off 2 cups (472 ml) to use later. Coarsely grind the shrimp (don't forget the bread trick. page 71!).

■ Coarsely grind the pork loin chops.

## NOW COOK

■ Heat the oil in a large skillet or wok. Fry the garlic and pork quickly - about 2-3 minutes. Add the ground shrimp and fry until just warmed - about 1 minute.

■ Stir in the reserved shrimp stock, the achiote powder and the fish sauce. Remove the pan from the heat, stir in the arrowroot paste until thickened. Add the green onions, red pepper, cilantro, tofu and black pepper and heat through.

■ Cook the rice noodles in boiling water until soft - about 3 minutes. You should stir them once, at the beginning, the moment they become flexible. This will help to keep them separated during the cooking process. Drain well.

■ Serve the shrimp-pork mixture over the rice noodles.

## Helpful Hints and Observations

SHRIMP STOCK - There is a constant temptation to somehow leave stocks out of recipes. After all, they take time and in our modern lifestyles, time is so precious that something that appears so trivial can easily be replaced by tap water.

In my food style, water just won't cut the mustard (so to speak!). You see, I've already subtracted so much fat that it reduces the "depth" of taste. Stock is essential to give an added dimension to the taste, as well as aroma.

Less fat means less risk in recipes, but without creative alternative tastes, we are likely to be defeated before we start. So please, in both this and all other dishes, do try to make the stocks and don't forget to springboard by adding in your own thoughts and favorite ingredients. I'm absolutely delighted to be a catalyst for your new inventions.

P.S. - Let me know when you do — I'm eager to live on a two-way street and learn from you!

## Unusual Ingredients

ACHIOTE POWDER - Made from the small, reddish seeds of the annato tree, it gives a lovely color to many dishes. Don't hesitate to go into a Latin American or Philippino grocery and ask for it. It's pronounced "ah-chee-OH-tay".

FISH SAUCE - There's nothing fishy about its taste, despite the fact that its extracted from fish. Fish sauce is used as ubiquitously in Thailand as soy sauce is in China and Japan. You might want to sample several brands because they vary in saltiness. I recommend the Dek brand fish sauce from Thailand.

RICE NOODLES - These are noodles made from rice flour and water. Look for them in clear plastic packages in the oriental section of your food market. You might also see them under the name rice sticks or rice vermicelli.

*Pancit Luglug Palabok (Pork and Shrimp in a Red Sauce with Rice Noodles)* 121

# VEAL BUCO WITH RISOTTO

*H*ere it is: one of my all-time favorites. I can almost dream about it! I ate the classic "Osso Buco" with Risotto Milanese the other day and couldn't finish it — TOO RICH — wonderful to be sure, but much more than I can manage after a decade of change. So I made some alterations and dealt with my dreams.

The rice looks wonderful in a bright red bowl; the veal in a green casserole! No matter really, on the plate together they are handsome enough. Whole green beans or fresh asparagus goes well.

## Nutritional Profile

| PER SERVING | CLASSIC | MINIMAX |
|---|---|---|
| Calories | 1183 | 574 |
| Fat (gm) | 59 | 19 |
| Calories From Fat | 45% | 30% |
| Cholesterol (mg) | 312 | 135 |
| Sodium (mg) | 2283 | 959 |
| Fiber (gm) | 5 | 5 |

■ *Classic Compared – Osso Buco*

## Time Estimate

| Hands On | | | | | | | | | |
|---|---|---|---|---|---|---|---|---|---|
| Unsupervised | | | | | | | | | |

*Minutes*    10  20  30  40  50  60  70  80  90

## Cost Estimate

| | | | |
|---|---|---|---|
| Low | Medium | Medium High | Celebration |

*Serves 4*

## INGREDIENTS

1 tablespoon extra light olive oil with a dash of sesame oil (15 ml)

1 cup diced celery (236 ml)

1 cup diced carrot (236 ml)

2 garlic cloves, peeled and mashed

1 pound veal shank (450 gm), trimmed of fat and cut into 1 inch (2.5 cm) pieces

1¼ cups tomato puree (295 ml)

¼ cup de-alcoholized chardonnay wine (59 ml)

1 cup (236 ml) veal stock (recipe page 210)

¼ teaspoon freshly ground salt (1.25 ml)

¼ teaspoon freshly ground black pepper (1.25 ml)

8 ounces mushrooms (227 gm), quartered

½ teaspoon lemon zest (2.5 ml)

1 tablespoon fresh chopped parsley (15 ml)

1 tablespoon capers (15 ml)

¼ teaspoon baking powder (1.25 ml)

1 tablespoon arrowroot (15 ml) mixed with 2 tablespoons water (30 ml)

### BOUQUET GARNI

4 thyme sprigs

2 bay leaves

6 parsley stalks

### RISOTTO

1 tablespoon extra light olive oil with a dash of sesame oil (15 ml)

1 medium onion, peeled and very finely diced

1 cup uncooked arborio rice (236 ml)

1 pinch powdered saffron

2 cups chicken stock (472 ml) (recipe page 210)

½ cup de-alcoholized chardonnay wine (118 ml)

Freshly ground salt to taste

Freshly ground black pepper to taste

2 tablespoons finely chopped fresh parsley (30 ml)

2 ounces finely grated Parmesan cheese (57 gm)

## NOW COOK

■  In an ovenproof casserole, heat the olive oil and saute the celery, carrot and garlic for 5 minutes. Remove the cooked vegetables and set aside.

■  In the same casserole, increase the heat to high and add the meat one piece at a time. If you put all the meat in at once, liquid is released and the meat simmers instead of browning. Keep turning the meat until all surfaces are lightly browned. Browning adds more depth of flavor.

■  Return the cooked vegetables to the casserole and stir in the tomato puree. Add the bouquet garni, black pepper, wine and the veal stock and bring to a boil. Cover, reduce the heat and simmer gently for about 70 minutes.

■  The Risotto: In a large saucepan, heat the oil and saute the onions for 2 minutes. Add the rice, stirring until it's well coated. Scatter the saffron evenly over the rice and stir. In a small bowl, mix the chicken stock and wine. Pour in enough to just cover the rice and stir, over low heat, until it is absorbed. Continue to add the rest of the liquid, stirring until all of it has been absorbed. Remember, to achieve the proper creamy consistency, the rice must be stirred. Finally, fold in the salt, pepper, parsley and cheese.

■  After the veal is cooked, remove the bouquet garni, stir in the mushroom quarters and simmer uncovered for 5 minutes.

■  Just before serving, stir in the lemon zest, chopped parsley, capers and baking powder. Remove the casserole from the heat, add the arrowroot paste, return to the heat and stir until thickened.

## Helpful Hints and Observations

BONE OR NO BONE - The classic is made with sections of veal shin, the meat quite tender, and the bone filled with marrow - a highly saturated fat with ample cholesterol problems of its own! The shin meat can be cut off, the bones used for stock and the marrow discarded. The shin has good connective tissue content so it cooks well and becomes *almost* as succulent as the original. The result is easier to cook ... but Osso Buco it is *not*.

RISOTTO - Here is another problem child. The classic, made in the Milan style, is filled with butter and cheese ... very rich indeed! I've used the same Italian rice, arborio, with cheese, saffron, stock and wine. It's attractive and not as rich.

## Unusual Ingredients

SAFFRON - See Unusual Ingredients, page 61.

ARBORIO RICE - A short, roundish-grain rice from Northern Italy, opaque in the center and transparent around the edges, it is especially suited to risotto because, when properly cooked, it is neither too hard nor too soft. It will give your risotto both a creamy and slightly crunchy texture. You can generally find arborio rice in Italian markets as well as supermarkets. You can substitute a common, short-grain variety but beware: it's not the same texture, and you will have to decrease the amount of liquid added.

# VEAL HAMPSHIRE

*Treena and I visited the small Canadian city of Victoria on Vancouver Island off the west coast, and found a very pleasant little restaurant in Oak Bay called "The Hampshire Grill." This is one of their special dishes that we have since worked on together.*

*Add a sprig of fresh mint for garnish, especially if it's growing all over your garden patio, like mine!*

## Nutritional Profile

| PER SERVING | CLASSIC | MINIMAX |
|---|---|---|
| Calories | 473 | 386 |
| Fat (gm) | 22 | 12 |
| Calories From Fat | 41% | 28% |
| Cholesterol (mg) | 260 | 154 |
| Sodium (mg) | 531 | 450 |
| Fiber (gm) | 2 | 3 |

■ *Classic Compared – Veal Calvados*

## Time Estimate

| | | | | | | | | | |
|---|---|---|---|---|---|---|---|---|---|
| Hands On Unsupervised | | | | | | | | | |
| Minutes | 10 | 20 | 30 | 40 | 50 | 60 | 70 | 80 | 90 |

## Cost Estimate

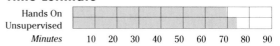

Low      Medium      Medium High      Celebration

*Serves 6*

## INGREDIENTS

3 pounds boneless veal loin (1.4 kg), cut slightly longer into the flap or skirt

STUFFING

1 onion, peeled and diced

1 green bell pepper, cored, seeded and diced

1 red bell pepper, cored, seeded and diced

1 cup chopped mushrooms (236 ml)

2 cups raw spinach leaves (472 ml)

1 tablespoon extra light olive oil with a dash of sesame oil (15 ml)

1 cup bread crumbs (236 ml)

1 tablespoon fresh thyme  (15 ml)

⅛ teaspoon freshly ground salt (.6 ml)

¼ teaspoon freshly ground black pepper (1.25 ml)

⅛ teaspoon allspice (.6 ml)

1 tablespoon Dijon mustard (15 ml)

1 ounce Canadian bacon (28 gm), cut into fine strips

½ medium apple, peeled, cored and sliced

FRUIT SAUCE

2 cups veal stock (472 ml) (recipe page 210)

1 tablespoon freshly squeezed orange juice (15 ml)

1 cup apple juice (236 ml)

1 tablespoon arrowroot (15 ml) mixed with 2 tablespoons water (30 ml)

⅛ teaspoon freshly ground black pepper (.6 ml)

## FIRST PREPARE

■  Butterfly and pound the veal until ½ inch (1.5 cm) thick.

■  The Stuffing:  Grind the onions, peppers and mushrooms through a meat grinder.  Drain to separate the juices from the vegetables, reserving the juice.  (I tried to use it as a super vitamin drink but it tasted awful - so it gets added to the stuffing later on!)

■  Steam the spinach for 2-3 minutes.  Put it into a cheesecloth, press out the excess juice and discard.

## NOW COOK

■  The Stuffing:  In a low-sided stewpot, heat the oil and fry the ground onions, peppers and mushrooms until the onions appear translucent. Add the bread crumbs and the reserved grinding juices, stirring constantly so that the ingredients bind together.  Add the thyme, salt, pepper and allspice.

■  Place the veal on a cutting board and spread with the mustard.  Spoon the cooked vegetables on top.  Next, lay the pressed spinach over the vegetables.  The Canadian bacon slices are next, topped with the apple slices.  Fold or roll the veal, so that the filling is encased by the meat.

■  Wrap the veal in butcher's net as described below.  Place the meat on a trivet in a roasting pan and roast at 375°F (190°C) for 1 hour.

■  The Sauce:  Drain off any surplus fats from the low-sided stewpot and blot the surface with a little paper towel.  Deglaze the stewpot with the veal stock.  Turn into a small saucepan along with the orange juice and apple juice and reduce by a third. Remove from the heat, add the arrowroot paste, return to the heat and stir until thickened.  Season with the pepper.

■  Remove the veal from the oven and let sit about 20 minutes.  Carve the veal into slices and serve on a pool of the fruit sauce.

## Helpful Hints and Observations

ELASTIC BUTCHER'S NET - This really is the easiest way to hold a rolled piece of meat or boned poultry (even baked double fillets of salmon) together.  It can be purchased from the meat department at your local supermarket.

The next time you use a 30 ounce (850 gm) can, simply cut off both ends, wash and dry it thoroughly and then brush it with oil and keep it in a large sealable plastic bag.

You slip the elastic net on one end, allowing two inches at either end beyond the piece you want to contain.  Slip the meat into the can and shake it through into the net.  It will come out the other end completely surrounded in the net.

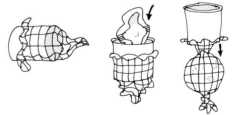

## Unusual Ingredients

SPINACH - Fresh spinach should look crisp and have unblemished green leaves.  Wash it several times as dirt seems to cling stubbornly to its stems.  It doesn't keep very well - about 2 to 4 days - so refrigerate it and use as soon as possible.

# VEAL SUTTON

*This was another of our very special "celebrity from the street" encounters, where we go out to find some real folks who are struggling with the whole food style issue. In New York, we found Brie Sutton and asked her to tell us her favorite foods. I created a dish using the ingredients she liked the most.*

*This is a very simple, yet almost tropical dish, served in a nest of rice. The papaya and avocado balls glisten under the slightly spicy curry sauce and go wonderfully with the veal — nice choices, Brie Sutton!*

## Nutritional Profile

| PER SERVING | CLASSIC | MINIMAX |
|---|---|---|
| Calories | 1384 | 521 |
| Fat (gm) | 134 | 18 |
| Calories From Fat | 87% | 30% |
| Cholesterol (mg) | 614 | 74 |
| Sodium (mg) | 1342 | 183 |
| Fiber (gm) | 3 | 8 |

■ *Classic Compared – Veal Savayarde*

## Time Estimate

| Hands On | | | | | | | | | |
|---|---|---|---|---|---|---|---|---|---|
| Unsupervised | | | | | | | | | |
| *Minutes* | 10 | 20 | 30 | 40 | 50 | 60 | 70 | 80 | 90 |

## Cost Estimate

| | | | |
|---|---|---|---|
| Low | Medium | Medium High | Celebration |

*Serves 4*

## INGREDIENTS

1 pound bottom round veal (450 gm), trimmed

1 papaya, halved lengthwise and seeded

1 avocado, halved and the pit removed

4 tablespoons freshly squeezed lime juice (60 ml)

1 tablespoon fresh chopped cilantro (15 ml)

2½ cups beef stock (590 ml) (recipe page 210)

¼ cup wild rice (59 ml)

1 cup uncooked long grain rice (236 ml)

2 tablespoons garam masala (30 ml)

½ cup chopped onion (118 ml)

1 tablespoon (15 ml) + 1 teaspoon (5 ml) extra light olive oil with a dash of sesame oil

⅛ teaspoon freshly ground salt (.6 ml)

¼ teaspoon freshly ground black pepper (1.25 ml)

2 shallots, peeled and finely sliced

2 teaspoons curry powder (10 ml)

1 cup papaya nectar (236 ml)

¼ cup water (59 ml)

1 tablespoon cornstarch (15 ml) mixed with 2 tablespoons papaya nectar (30 ml)

GARNISH

4 sprigs of fresh cilantro

## FIRST PREPARE

■ Carefully remove any silver skin from the veal. Cut the veal across the grain at a 45 degree angle, into 10 (¼ inch or .75 cm) slices. Tenderize and pound the veal to increase the size of each piece by about one third.

■ Scoop the papaya and avocado into small balls using a melon baller. Place in a bowl and stir in the lime juice and cilantro.

## NOW COOK

■ Put the beef stock in a large pot and bring to a boil. Add the rices, garam masala and chopped onion and return to the boil. Turn the heat to the lowest possible point and cook, covered, until all the water has been absorbed by the rice. Test the rice after 15 minutes - if it's soft but not mushy, turn off the heat and let the rice sit, covered, for 5 more minutes.

■ Pour 1 tablespoon (15 ml) of the olive oil on a plate. Rub the veal slices in oil on each side and sprinkle with the salt and pepper.

■ In a large skillet, heat the remaining olive oil and saute the shallots and the curry powder.

Add the papaya nectar, pour into a small bowl and set aside.

■ Rinse the skillet and place back on the burner over medium heat. Place as many veal slices as will fit without overlapping. Brown the veal and set aside. Continue browning the rest of the veal slices in this manner. Depending on your skillet size, it may take 2 or 3 lots.

■ Add the water to the same skillet and drop in the papaya and avocado balls. Pour the curried papaya nectar through a sieve and into the skillet. Add the veal. Gradually stir in the cornstarch paste, bring to a boil and stir until thickened.

■ To Serve: Put 1 cup (236 ml) of the rice on each plate and spoon over the veal and sauce. Garnish with a cilantro sprig.

## Helpful Hints and Observations

THIN SLICES ... SMALL PANS - Very thin slices of meat, poultry or fish cook rapidly, but are seldom used because people say, "I don't have a large enough pan." Indeed, veal slices, like the ones used in this dish, usually take up half a regular skillet.

I have found the perfect cooking method for these thin slices is to cook them a few pieces at a time, without crowding the pan, about 30 seconds on each side, and then set aside. Just before serving, you can return them to a skillet sauce to heat through.

This is such an easy and interesting way to cook that I hope you'll give it a go and then make up a dish with a few of your own favorite foods.

## Unusual Ingredients

SHALLOTS - See Unusual Ingredients, page 57.

PAPAYA - Walking down the supermarket aisle you might not look twice at this large, pear shaped fruit. Green with overtones of yellow and orange, papaya might not look exciting on the outside, but just under its skin lurks a source of hidden power — it's loaded with Vitamins A and C, and potassium! A ripe papaya should feel just slightly yielding when pressed. It will last about a week if you store it in the refrigerator.

AVOCADO - With a green, leathery hide, this small oval fruit looks most like an alligator egg! But like papaya, under the skin an avocado hides its treasure: creamy smooth, nutty flesh. Choose avocados that feel heavy in your hand and have no blemishes. You'll know they're ripe when they yield gently to pressure. If you buy them very hard, put them in a paper bag, and they'll ripen beautifully.

# VEAL WEYERHAEUSER

$\mathcal{I}$'ve grown increasingly disenchanted with the idea of snow white veal, called provimi or milk-fed veal. It seems to me that the color benefit is far outweighed by the apparent suffering caused these young animals. This recipe shows that grass-fed veal can work just as well!

This is an elegant dish that rivals Chinese techniques for last minute speed cooking. Crisp cooked, bright green snow peas are wonderful on the side.

## Nutritional Profile

| PER SERVING | CLASSIC | MINIMAX |
|---|---|---|
| Calories | 1384 | 455 |
| Fat (gm) | 134 | 15 |
| Calories From Fat | 87% | 31% |
| Cholesterol (mg) | 614 | 76 |
| Sodium (mg) | 1342 | 277 |
| Fiber (gm) | 3 | 4 |

■ *Classic Compared – Veal Savayarde*

## Time Estimate

| Hands On | | | | | | | | | |
|---|---|---|---|---|---|---|---|---|---|
| Unsupervised | | | | | | | | | |
| *Minutes* | 10 | 20 | 30 | 40 | 50 | 60 | 70 | 80 | 90 |

## Cost Estimate

| Low | Medium | Medium High | Celebration |
|---|---|---|---|

*Serves 4*

## INGREDIENTS

MIXED RICE PILAF

1 tablespoon extra light olive oil with a dash of sesame oil (15 ml)

1 large yellow onion, peeled and chopped

1 cup uncooked mixed rice (236 ml)
(see Helpful Hints)

1 good size garlic clove, peeled and chopped

2 cups chicken stock (472 ml) (recipe page 210)

2 bay leaves

1 sprig of fresh thyme

1 sprig of fresh parsley

4 ounces small green peas (113 gm)

4 ounces large mushrooms (113 gm), cut into
½ inch (1.5 cm) slices

VEAL AND SAUCE

1¼ pounds grass-fed veal loin (560 gm), yielding 1 pound (450 gm) boned and trimmed meat

2 tablespoons extra light olive oil with a dash of sesame oil (30 ml)

1 green bell pepper, cored, seeded and finely chopped

1 red bell pepper, cored, seeded and finely chopped

1 yellow bell pepper, cored, seeded and finely chopped

1 cup veal stock (236 ml) (recipe page 210)

2 tablespoons cornstarch (30 ml)

¼ cup de-alcoholized dry white wine (59 ml)

¼ cup evaporated skim milk (59 ml)

Freshly ground black pepper

¼ teaspoon freshly ground salt (1.25 ml)

1 tablespoon fresh chopped basil (15 ml)

## FIRST PREPARE THE MIXED RICE PILAF

■ Heat the oil in a casserole pan and fry the onions and garlic until the onions are translucent. Add the rice and stir until well coated. Add the stock and lay the herbs on top. Cook uncovered in a 375°F (190°C) oven for 30 minutes. When it's done, remove the herbs, stir in the peas and the mushrooms and return to the oven to heat through - about 5 minutes.

## NOW COOK THE VEAL

■ Trim all visible fat and silver skin from the veal. You can use the bones to make the veal stock for this recipe (see Helpful Hints). Cut the trimmed veal into 20 even sized pieces, just over ¼ inch (.75 cm) thick.

■ Heat half of the oil in a large frypan and quickly fry the veal pieces for about 30 seconds on each side. Place the cooked veal on a plate and keep warm while cooking the remaining pieces.

■ Put the remaining oil into the same frypan and fry the peppers for 1 minute. Add the veal stock and bring quickly to a boil. Scrape the meat residues off the bottom of the pan in order to blend all the flavors. Remove the pan from the heat.

■ In a small bowl, mix together the cornstarch, wine and evaporated milk. Add to the veal, bring to a boil and stir until thickened.

■ Add the cooked veal to the sauce and heat through. Season with the pepper, salt and basil. Serve with the Mixed Rice Pilaf.

## Helpful Hints and Observations

THE PERFECT PILAF MIX - I recommend ½ cup (118 ml) Lundberg mixed long grain rice, ¼ cup (59 ml) pearl barley and ¼ cup (59 ml) wild rice.

VEAL STOCK - Since you will pay quite a price for the veal I suggest you ask your butcher for some veal bones to make the stock.

# SWEDISH MEATBALLS

The classic version is almost irresistible - until you add up the fat! "Well," you might argue, "it's a matter of tradition ... er ... it's our cultural heritage!" So rather than chuck it all out I tried to put three and three and three together and came up with nine meat balls coated in cream sauce ... that are not all they seem to be!

This dish must take the prize for plate appeal: the wreath of red cabbage filled with cream-coated potatoes, mushrooms and meatballs. Nothing else is needed.

## Nutritional Profile

| PER SERVING | CLASSIC | MINIMAX |
|---|---|---|
| Calories | 707 | 489 |
| Fat (gm) | 51 | 11 |
| Calories From Fat | 65% | 21% |
| Cholesterol (mg) | 197 | 39 |
| Sodium (mg) | 900 | 370 |
| Fiber (gm) | 4 | 18 |

■ *Classic Compared – Swedish Meatballs*

## Time Estimate

| | | | | | | | | | |
|---|---|---|---|---|---|---|---|---|---|
| Hands On | | | | | | | | | |
| Unsupervised | | | | | | | | | |
| *Minutes* | 10 | 20 | 30 | 40 | 50 | 60 | 70 | 80 | 90 |

## Cost Estimate

| | | | |
|---|---|---|---|
| Low | Medium | Medium High | Celebration |

*Serves 6*

## INGREDIENTS

MEATBALLS

1¼ cups boiling water (295 ml)

½ cup bulgur wheat (118 ml)

6 ounces lean veal shoulder (170 gm)

6 ounces lean pork shoulder (170 gm)

3 cups water (708 ml)

18 small, red, new potatoes

8 ounces mushrooms (227 gm) 1 inch (2.5 cm) long (about the same size as the potatoes and meatballs)

4½ teaspoons extra light olive oil with a dash of sesame oil (22.5 ml)

¼ cup finely chopped shallots (59 ml)

1 tablespoon fresh chopped dill (15 ml)

¼ teaspoon freshly ground nutmeg (1.25 ml)

1 egg white

½ teaspoon freshly ground salt (2.5 ml)

¼ cup de-alcoholized white wine (59 ml)

1 medium onion, peeled and finely sliced

5 cups finely sliced red cabbage (1.2 L)

1 cup canned pickled beets (236 ml), drained and julienned with the juice reserved

¼ teaspoon freshly ground black pepper (1.25 ml)

3 tablespoons fresh chopped parsley (45 ml)

SAUCE

2 tablespoons cornstarch (30 ml)

1 cup strained yogurt (236 ml) (recipe page 210)

1 cup canned low-salt chicken broth (236 ml)

1 tablespoon fresh chopped dill (15 ml)

¼ teaspoon cayenne pepper (1.25 ml)

GARNISH

Fresh chopped parsley

## FIRST PREPARE

■ For the Meatballs: Pour the boiling water on top of the bulgur and let stand for 15 minutes. Strain and set aside. Put the veal and pork through a fine blade grinder into a large bowl (see page 71 for the bread trick).

■ Put a steamer platform in a large pot and bring the 3 cups (708 ml) of water to a boil. Put the potatoes on the platform, cover and steam for 20 minutes. Add the mushrooms, cover and steam for 4 minutes more.

■ For the Sauce: In a medium sized bowl, mix the cornstarch and strained yogurt. Stir in the chicken broth, dill and cayenne pepper with a wire whisk until all the lumps are gone.

## NOW COOK

■ The Meatballs: In a small pan heat ½ teaspoon (2.5 ml) of the oil and saute the shallots until slightly translucent.

■ In a large bowl combined the cooked shallots with the cooked bulgur, dill, nutmeg and ground meat. Stir in the egg white and half of the salt. Using one rounded tablespoonful (15 ml), make the meatballs by squeezing and rolling the mixture between lightly water-moistened hands. You should have 18.

■ In a large non-stick skillet, heat 3 teaspoons (15 ml) of the oil and brown the meatballs, shaking the skillet frequently to prevent them from sticking. Cook for approximately 10 minutes.

■ Add the steamed potatoes and mushrooms, pour in the wine and chicken stock-yogurt sauce, bring to a boil and stir until thickened.

■ In another skillet, heat the remaining oil and fry the onions and cabbage until the onions are slightly translucent. Add ½ cup (118 ml) of the reserved beet juice, the remaining salt and the pepper. Cover and cook for 10 minutes. Sprinkle with the parsley.

■ To Serve: Make a wreath of the cabbage mixture on each individual plate, garnished with the strips of pickled beets. Into the center spoon 3 meatballs, 3 potatoes and 3 mushrooms. Coat with the sauce and garnish with chopped parsley.

## Helpful Hints and Observations

APPEARANCES ARE IMPORTANT! - Somehow a serving of only 3 small meatballs per head sends the wrong visual signal. Moderation is wonderful but — ONLY THREE MEATBALLS?

In this case we supplemented "the meat in a minor key" with the same sized potatoes and button mushrooms. Even though they are obviously not meatballs their number and shape lends enough support and frankly, they make a delicious combination of flavors, especially with the beets and cabbage.

# VENISON WITH SPICED PEARS

𝒱enison comes from the hunter's bag or a properly regulated game farm. It is hard to say which is more expensive when you add in all the trappings enjoyed by the modern hunter. Whichever, it isn't cheap, but it's extra lean and very tasty. This recipe can be made using well trimmed pork loin as a delicious alternative.

Serve with boiled potatoes, dusted with fresh mint and a little parsley, small green peas with a touch of brown sugar and half a small, baked sweet potato, served perfectly plain - sounds great, doesn't it?

## Nutritional Profile

| PER SERVING | CLASSIC | MINIMAX |
|---|---|---|
| Calories | 421 | 152 |
| Fat (gm) | 17 | 3 |
| Calories From Fat | 37% | 15% |
| Cholesterol (mg) | 132 | 59 |
| Sodium (mg) | 253 | 100 |
| Fiber (gm) | 3 | 3 |

■ *Classic Compared – Marinaded Saddle of Venison*

## Time Estimate

| Hands On | | | | | | | | | |
|---|---|---|---|---|---|---|---|---|---|
| Unsupervised | | | | 3 Hours, 30 Minutes | | | | | |

Minutes  10  20  30  40  50  60  70  80  90

## Cost Estimate

| Low | Medium | Medium High | Celebration |
|---|---|---|---|

## INGREDIENTS

VENISON

1¼ pounds venison loin (560 gm)

1 teaspoon extra light olive oil with a dash of sesame oil (5 ml)

3 tablespoons tomato paste (45 ml)

2 large carrots, peeled and chopped into 1 inch (2.5 cm) chunks

2 medium leeks, cleaned and chopped into 1 inch (2.5 cm) chunks

1 tablespoon fresh thyme (15 ml)

1 cup de-alcoholized red wine (236 ml)

1 sprig fresh rosemary

8 juniper berries

1 tablespoon arrowroot (15 ml) mixed with 2 tablespoons water (30 ml)

MARINADE

½ cup de-alcoholized red wine (118 ml)

½ cup cider vinegar (118 ml)

4 sprigs fresh rosemary

GARNISH

Sprigs of fresh rosemary

PEAR POACHING LIQUID

½ cup de-alcoholized red wine (118 ml)

½ cup cider vinegar (118 ml)

6 whole cloves, freshly ground

6 allspice berries

1 (3 inch) cinnamon stick (8 cm)

2 pears, peeled, halved and cored

1 cup water (236 ml), or amount needed to cover

## FIRST PREPARE

■ Trim away the excess fat and silver skin from the venison. Mix the marinade ingredients together in a glass or ceramic bowl. Place the trimmed venison in the marinade and marinate overnight in the refrigerator.

■ Remove the venison from the marinade and blot dry with paper towels. Reserve the marinade. Wrap the venison in butcher's net, as described on page 125.

## NOW COOK

■ Preheat the oven to 375°F (190°C). Pour the reserved marinade into a small saucepan, bring to a boil and set aside.

■ The Poaching Liquid: In a medium sized saucepan, heat the wine and vinegar. Mix in the cloves, allspice berries and the cinnamon stick. Add the pear halves, cover with the water and poach for approximately 30 minutes.

■ Heat the oil in a low sided casserole pan and fry the tomato paste, carrots and leeks until the tomato darkens in color. Put the wrapped venison into the pan and brown, rolling to brown the entire outer surface. Add the thyme and wine.

■ Pour the boiled marinade over the venison. Add the rosemary sprig and juniper berries and cover. Put in the preheated oven to braise for 40 minutes.

■ Transfer the cooked venison onto a cutting board. Pour the casserole juices through a strainer into a small heated saucepan. Remove the saucepan from the heat, add the arrowroot paste, return to the heat and stir until thickened.

■ Cut the butcher's net away from the venison and discard. Slice the meat into ¼ inch (.75 cm) slices. Arrange the slices in the center of a serving tray and surround with the pear halves. Pour the thickened sauce over the venison and garnish with rosemary sprigs.

## Helpful Hints and Observations

MARINADE - A marinade is a great flavor booster but it can also be a trap for bacteria! I always bring marinades to the boil to kill off these unfriendly fellows before adding the strained mixture to the cooking liquid for an added bite.

COATING SAUCE BEFORE SERVING - Sometimes sauce is best poured onto a plate first and then the meat set on top. In this case it is reversed. Venison tends to look dry and needs the glossy arrowroot sauce to appear as succulent as it is!

## Unusual Ingredients

VENISON - The venison available in markets is from deer raised on game farms. The deer are fed a special diet to promote growth and health. In many countries it is illegal to purchase wild game because it is not inspected for disease. Farm raising these animals ensures both quality and availability.

JUNIPER BERRIES - These "berries" are actually a cone from an evergreen tree than can grow up to 40 feet (12 m) in height and is found in all temperate zones, from Africa to North America. Juniper berries (cones) take two years to ripen, changing color from light green to a deep purple blue. They are used to impart their flavorful perfume in the making of gin.

# MINIMAX SEED BREAD

$\mathcal{T}$his is a robust bread: full of flavor and texture and good nutrient density. It toasts well and makes excellent sandwiches. If that isn't enough, it only needs one proofing and very little kneading!

Serve toasted Minimax Seed Bread with "proper tea!" To make tea properly, pour boiling water into your china tea pot, just to warm it, then pour it out. I like Earl Grey tea, and usually put two tea bags in the pot. Pour boiling water on whatever tea bags suit your fancy. The boiling water brings out the tea's volatile oils.

## Nutritional Profile

| PER SERVING | CLASSIC | MINIMAX |
|---|---|---|
| Calories | 187 | 183 |
| Fat (gm) | 3 | 6 |
| Calories From Fat | 15% | 29% |
| Cholesterol (mg) | 8 | 0 |
| Sodium (mg) | 833 | 245 |
| Fiber (gm) | 2 | 5 |

■ *Classic Compared – Flower Pot Bread*

## Time Estimate

| Hands On | | | | | | | | | |
|---|---|---|---|---|---|---|---|---|---|
| Unsupervised | | | | 2 Hours | | | | | |
| *Minutes* | 10 | 20 | 30 | 40 | 50 | 60 | 70 | 80 | 90 |

## Cost Estimate

| | | | |
|---|---|---|---|
| Low | Medium | Medium High | Celebration |

*Makes One 18 – 20 Slice Loaf*

## INGREDIENTS

Extra light olive oil with a dash of sesame oil (for the pan)

3 cups 100% whole wheat flour (708 ml)

1 envelope active dry yeast

1 tablespoon sugar (15 ml)

2¼ cups warm (105°F, 41°C) water (531 ml)

1 teaspoon salt (5 ml)

¾ cup Minimax Seed Mix (157 ml) (See Unusual Ingredients, page 205) very coarsely cracked in an electric coffee grinder

## FIRST PREPARE

■ Make sure all ingredients are warm. Put the flour in a large bowl in a 100°F (38°C) oven with all your utensils and keep the door open.

■ Use a piece of paper towel dipped in the olive oil mixture to grease a 10 x 5 x 4 inch (25 x 13 x 10 cm) loaf pan.

## NOW COOK

■ Dissolve the active dry yeast and sugar in ½ cup (118 ml) of the warm water. Measure the temperature with a cooking thermometer to ensure the best results. Stir well and let the mixture rest in the warm oven about 10 minutes to develop a froth.

■ In a large bowl, mix the flour, salt and Minimax Seeds. Add the frothy yeast and start kneading with an electric dough hook or by hand. Swish 1¾ cups (413 ml) of the warm water around the now empty yeast bowl, and add it to the dough. This water will contain any remaining yeast. Knead until the dough is silky - about 3 minutes.

■ Transfer the dough to the prepared loaf pan and cover loosely with plastic wrap. Let it rise, or "proof", for about 1 hour in a warm place. It will rise only slightly.

■ Pre-heat oven to 400°F (205°C). Bake the bread on the middle rack for 35 - 40 minutes.

■ After 35 minutes take the pan out of the oven and remove the loaf. Return bread to the oven rack upside-down. Bake for another 10 minutes to crisp the bottom. It should sound hollow when tapped.

■ Please note that this recipe does not produce a "tall" loaf. It never rises above the level of the loaf pan. Place the loaf on a wire rack and let it cool completely before slicing.

## Helpful Hints and Observations

OUR DAILY BREAD - Once a known commodity, a staple, attractive, homely thing upon which we could rely. We can now expect our daily bread to be treated to an incredible barrage of chemical manipulation. We can assume that the following list has  been applied: preservatives, added nutrients, antisprouting, coloring, flavoring, bleaches, texture enhancers, emulsifiers, softeners, acidifiers, sweeteners, anti-foamers, dough conditioners. The reason for their addition is logical enough: they reduce the effect of human error on the eventual product. Note please that it permits the error to continue, but it fixes up the mistakes. What man lacks in genuine honest skill he makes up for with chemical manipulation! The best comment I ever heard about bread sums up the whole thing wonderfully: "If mold won't grow on it, neither will you." So now it's up to you. Either find a quality source of bread or summon up all your creative resolve and try mine - with proper tea, of course!

# BANANA SPICE BREAD

*H*ere's another well known favorite where our standards have been set by wonderful, thick, fragrant, spicy slabs of melting, soft, fruit bread. No need for added butter ... it's built in! Can it be done another way? Well yes, but our standards need to change. This isn't fat on fat on sugar, but it is thick, fragrant and spicy!

You may want a "touch" of whipped butter or extra light margarine on the Banana Spice Bread, but please, don't undo all we've tried to achieve: a snacking bread that doesn't bite first ... especially where it shows!

## Nutritional Profile

| PER SERVING | CLASSIC | MINIMAX |
|---|---|---|
| Calories | 489 | 187 |
| Fat (gm) | 25 | 5 |
| Calories From Fat | 47% | 26% |
| Cholesterol (mg) | 71 | 18 |
| Sodium (mg) | 338 | 157 |
| Fiber (gm) | 2 | 3 |

■ *Classic Compared – Kona Inn Banana Bread*

## Time Estimate

| | | |
|---|---|---|
| Hands On | | |
| Unsupervised | | |
| *Minutes* | 10  20  30  40  50  60  70  80  90 | |

## Cost Estimate

| | | | |
|---|---|---|---|
| Low | Medium | Medium High | Celebration |

*Serves 12*

## INGREDIENTS

¼ cup (59 ml) + ⅛ teaspoon (.6 ml) margarine

1 cup (236 ml) + 1 teaspoon (5 ml) all-purpose flour, sifted

1 cup whole wheat flour (236 ml), sifted

2 teaspoons baking soda (10 ml)

2 ounces sun-dried whole bananas, or sun-dried papaya chunks (57 gm)

5 tablespoons light brown sugar (75 ml)

1 egg

½ cup buttermilk (118 ml)

3 ripe bananas, mashed

1 teaspoon vanilla (5 ml)

1 teaspoon cinnamon (5 ml)

1 teaspoon allspice (5 ml)

2 tablespoons sliced almonds (30 ml)

## FIRST PREPARE

■ Preheat oven to 350°F (180°C).

■ Grease a 9x5x3 inch (23x13x8 cm) loaf pan with ⅛ teaspoon (.6 ml) of the margarine. Dust with 1 teaspoon (5 ml) of the flour and shake out the surplus.

■ Into a large bowl, sift 1 cup (236 ml) of the all-purpose and the whole wheat flour and the baking soda.

■ Cut the bananas (or papaya) into ¼ inch (.6 cm) chunks. Toss them in the flour, making sure all the chunks are completely separate and well coated.

## NOW COOK

■ In a large bowl, cream the brown sugar and ¼ cup (59 ml) of the margarine. Beat in the egg and buttermilk. Add the mashed bananas, vanilla, cinnamon and allspice. Beat with an electric mixer on low speed until all the ingredients are combined.

■ Gradually beat in the flour mixture with the electric mixer on low - don't overwork it please!

■ Spread the batter into the greased and floured loaf pan. Drop the pan onto the counter top to remove any excess air bubbles. Sprinkle sliced almonds over the top, and poke them under the surface.

■ Pop in the oven for about 1 hour.

■ Remove when a thin bladed knife inserted into the middle of the loaf comes out clean. Cool on a baking rack.

## Helpful Hints and Observations

THE WET AND THE DRY - Try to see the two mixtures as importantly different tasks.

WET - Always start by dissolving the sugar in the fat. This is called "creaming" and it's essential. An electric mixer helps but it can be done by hand with a wooden spoon. Just beat until the mixture lightens in color and the sugar loses some of its grittiness. It takes longer with brown sugar, but you get more flavor.

Then whisk in the egg until it has absorbed the sweetened fat. Now you can add the remaining wet items just as you please. Finally, pop in the only dry ingredients — the spices.

DRY - You have two flours: For added nutrition and texture they must be double sifted along with the baking soda (and a ½ teaspoon (2.5 ml) of salt, if you feel you really must).

WET MEETS DRY - Always tip the flours into the smooth batter using a dough hook or spoon rather than a whisk (it clogs up!!).

## Unusual Ingredients

SUN-DRIED BANANAS - Not the prettiest of fruit, but the taste is unbeatable! Look for these in the dried fruit section of your grocery store. The dried banana is different from banana chips, which are fried in oil. When you bite one you'll see how densely the banana taste has been concentrated by drying. It's interesting to note that the nutrient value of the banana isn't affected by the drying process.

BROWN SUGAR - Simply made by adding a small amount of molasses to refined white sugar, it is about 96 percent sucrose.

# SMOKED CHICKEN PASTA JACKIE

*Here's* another dish created for "a celebrity from the street." This time we asked Jackie Bylund from Bellevue, Washington, for a list of her favorite foods. It included Fettucine Alfredo (a very rich pasta concoction with egg yolks, cream and cheese), smoked chicken and sweet red peppers (pimentos). Now you can see how this dish got its name!

Typically, it's a simple matter of serving the pasta, topped with chicken and sauce, in a large soup bowl with a good salad on the side and a hunk of crusty bread to give the pasta a nudge ... if it's being difficult!

## Nutritional Profile

| PER SERVING | CLASSIC | MINIMAX |
|---|---|---|
| Calories | 668 | 506 |
| Fat (gm) | 39 | 9 |
| Calories From Fat | 53 | 15% |
| Cholesterol (mg) | 201 | 134 |
| Sodium (mg) | 881 | 233 |
| Fiber (gm) | 3 | 5 |

■ *Classic Compared – Fettucine Alfredo with Chicken*

## Time Estimate

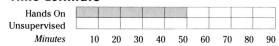

| Hands On | | | | | | | | | |
|---|---|---|---|---|---|---|---|---|---|
| Unsupervised | | | | | | | | | |
| *Minutes* | 10 | 20 | 30 | 40 | 50 | 60 | 70 | 80 | 90 |

## Cost Estimate

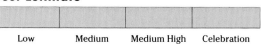

| Low | Medium | Medium High | Celebration |
|---|---|---|---|

*Serves 4*

## INGREDIENTS

### HERB POWDER

1 tablespoon fresh rosemary (15 ml)

1 tablespoon fresh thyme (15 ml)

3 large sage leaves, roughly chopped

12 black peppercorns

⅛ teaspoon freshly ground salt (.6 ml)

### SMOKE

2 tablespoons brown rice (30 ml)

1 Earl Grey tea bag

1 tablespoon brown sugar (15 ml)

4 whole cloves

1 teaspoon extra light olive oil with a dash of sesame oil (5 ml)

2 (1 pound) whole skinless and boneless chicken breasts (450 gm each)

12 ounces fettucini noodles (340 gm)

2 tablespoons freshly grated Parmesan cheese (30 ml)

### SAUCE

1 cup strained yogurt (236 ml) (recipe page 210)

4 ounces whole pimento (113 gm)

½ cup chicken stock (118 ml) (recipe page 210)

½ cup de-alcoholized white wine (118 ml)

2 tablespoons cornstarch (30 ml) mixed with 4 tablespoons de-alcoholized white wine (60 ml)

1 tablespoon fresh chives (15 ml)

1 tablespoon fresh parsley (15 ml)

2 ounces pimento (57 gm), diced

## FIRST PREPARE

■ For Herb Powder: Put all the herbs and spices in a small coffee mill or grinder and whiz until it forms a powder. Set aside.

## NOW COOK

■ For Smoke: Fold several layers of aluminum foil into a platform that will hold the smoke ingredients about 1 inch off the bottom of a solid cast aluminum or cast iron Dutch oven. Place the ingredients on the platform in the bottom of the pot. Cover tightly (see Helpful Hints) and allow the smoke to build up heat for 3-5 minutes.

■ Pour the oil on a plate and sprinkle with the herb powder mix. Wipe the chicken in the oil and herbs so that both sides are evenly coated. Arrange the chicken on a stainless steel, expanding steamer platform. Place carefully in the Dutch oven, over the smoke mixture, cover tightly and smoke for 10 minutes. Remove the chicken. (Hint: Wrap the smoke mixture in its foil saucer, pop it into a bag and put it outside in the trash as soon as possible. This will prevent smoke from filling your kitchen!)

■ For the Sauce: Puree the strained yogurt, whole pimento, chicken stock and wine in a food processor or blender. Pour into a saucepan and bring to a boil. Stir in the cornstarch paste, chives, parsley and diced pimento, bring to a boil and stir until thickened.

■ Cook the pasta in boiling water, about 2 minutes if the pasta is fresh, about 11 minutes if it is dried. Drain in a colander set over a large serving bowl. When the hot water has warmed the bowl, discard the water.

■ Pour half the sauce into the heated bowl. Stir in the pasta and Parmesan cheese. Place a portion of the sauced pasta on a plate and top with half a chicken breast sliced diagonally into thick chunks. Serve the remaining sauce on the side.

## Helpful Hints and Observations

TIGHT LIDS OR SMOKE ALARM! - I have perfectly fitted, heavy, glass lids on my SCANPAN 2001+ cookware. If you are using a large pot without such a good lid, you'll need to find a way to create a good seal. This can be done with a large, damp, piece of old toweling, aluminum foil, or even some flour and water mixed to a stiff dough and made into a long sausage, to be squeezed between the lid and pan after the early smoke has been created.

## Unusual Ingredients

PIMENTO - You can call this red pepper or (if you really want to dazzle your grocer) "capsicum fruescens!" The term, pimento, usually refers to cooked, fully ripened, sweet red peppers. You've probably used pimento in one of its dried and powdered forms: cayenne pepper, chili powder, paprika and red pepper. Look for bottled pimentos in the condiment section of your grocery. If you can't find bottled pimentos, roasted red peppers are a fine substitute.

# PASTA MARINARA

There is so much truly excellent dried and freshly made pasta on the market that it might not seem necessary to make your own. However, for some wonderful reason, there are people who love to do it for themselves and who gain a great deal by converting their energy into a skilled gift of love. So for all you "make it from scratch" people out there, here's a recipe for your very own Minimax pasta in a simple sauce.

I enjoy tossing my pasta in the sauce and serving it in a deep pasta bowl. Because of the fat factor, I seldom serve the classic bowl of grated Parmesan cheese on the side.

## Nutritional Profile

| PER SERVING | CLASSIC | MINIMAX |
|---|---|---|
| Calories | 983 | 452 |
| Fat (gm) | 44 | 6 |
| Calories From Fat | 40% | 12% |
| Cholesterol (mg) | 822 | 107 |
| Sodium (mg) | 1743 | 189 |
| Fiber (gm) | 4 | 8 |

■ *Classic Compared – Tortellini*

## Time Estimate

Hands On
Unsupervised

Minutes    10  20  30  40  50  60  70  80  90

## Cost Estimate

Low        Medium      Medium High   Celebration

*Serves 4*

## INGREDIENTS

PASTA

1½ cups all-purpose flour (354 ml)

1½ cups semolina flour (354 ml)

2 large eggs

¼ teaspoon salt (1.25 ml)

7 tablespoons water (105 ml)

½ cup of loosely packed, fresh herb leaves (118 ml)
(Use your favorite. I recommend oregano. Also,
use more or less depending on your taste.)

SAUCE

1 teaspoon extra light olive oil with a dash of
sesame oil (5 ml)

1 medium onion, peeled and finely sliced

1 garlic clove, peeled and chopped

1 tablespoon fresh oregano leaves (15 ml)

1 (28 ounce) can of whole Roma tomatoes
(794 gm), peeled and seeded

1 tablespoon cornstarch (15 ml) mixed with
2 tablespoons water (30 ml)

## FIRST PREPARE THE PASTA

■ In a food processor combine the 2 flours, eggs
and salt. Process at high speed, gradually incorporating the water. When slightly tacky, remove the
dough and put it on a smooth surface.

■ Knead the dough until it becomes very smooth -
about 2 to 3 minutes. Roll the dough into a 6 inch
long (15 cm) cylinder shape and let rest for 30
minutes.

■ Cut the dough into quarters and using a rolling
pin or pasta machine, roll each piece into very a
thin sheet. You should be able to see the shadow
of your hand through the thin dough. Cut sheets
into manageable working pieces - about 12 to
15 inches long (30 to 38 cm).

■ Fold the sheets of pasta in half lengthwise,
creasing the folded edge to mark the center, then
open the pasta sheet again. Line one side of the
sheet with the herb leaves. Fold the pasta back
along the crease, covering the herbs. Using a
rolling pin or pasta machine, seal the two sides.

■ Cut the pasta into bite size pieces, incorporating an herb leaf in each piece. You could also
leave them in sheets and use them for lasagna,
ravioli or tortellini!

## NOW COOK THE SAUCE

■ In a medium saucepan on medium heat, add
the olive oil, onions and garlic. Sweat these
ingredients until the onion is translucent and
they've released their volatile oils.

■ Add the oregano and cook for 1 minute to
incorporate its flavor. Add the tomatoes and cook
for 5 minutes more. Pour into a blender and whiz
until it's reached a thick consistency.

■ Return the sauce to the saucepan and re-heat.
When it's hot, add the cornstarch paste, bring to
a boil and stir constantly until thickened - about
1 minute.

■ Add the pasta to a large pot of boiling water
and cook for 2 to 3 minutes. Strain and serve
tossed with the sauce!

## Helpful Hints and Observations

ALL THAT GLISTENS ISN'T FAT! - When you
remove fat from a sauce you lessen the sparkle.
The pasta starch seems to take over and cloud
the sauce. Therefore, I always add either cornstarch for opaque or dairy sauces, or arrowroot
for totally clear sauces and gravies. In either
case, the proportion is 1 tablespoon (15 ml) starch
mixed to a creamy consistency with 2 tablespoons
(30 ml) of cold liquid to thicken 1 cup (236 ml) of
thin liquid. When these starches clear, they
produce a glistening surface on the sauce that
looks like a rich fatty gloss.

Now here's a look at this year's Designer Pasta...

DESIGNER PASTA? - The idea of putting fresh
herbs into pasta is perfect justification for making
your own from scratch - it really is different and
delicious!

# SPAGHETTI CARBONARA

$\mathcal{M}$y first brush with this great classic "food-of-the-people" was appropriately in Rome. It was served in the "Golden Room" at the Hosteria Dell 'Orso, and prepared on a golden lamp, with golden spoon and fork ... well ... you've got the picture.

I've left the flavors intact and want you to sample what is a great supper dish, made in 10 minutes, enjoyed for years.

Since this is a supper dish, it really needs nothing more than a good heel of well made bread. Have fun and don't forget the candle in the chianti bottle and a red checked table cloth!

If you really want to reduce your cholesterol levels, it will help to use an egg substitute, which will reduce the cholesterol to 17 mg!

## Nutritional Profile

| PER SERVING | CLASSIC | MINIMAX |
|---|---|---|
| Calories | 900 | 413 |
| Fat (gm) | 38 | 13 |
| Calories From Fat | 38% | 28% |
| Cholesterol (mg) | 379 | 124 |
| Sodium (mg) | 1399 | 632 |
| Fiber (gm) | 5 | 5 |

■ *Classic Compared – Spaghetti Carbonara*

## Time Estimate

| Hands On | | | | | | | | | |
|---|---|---|---|---|---|---|---|---|---|
| Unsupervised | | | | | | | | | |
| *Minutes* | 10 | 20 | 30 | 40 | 50 | 60 | 70 | 80 | 90 |

## Cost Estimate

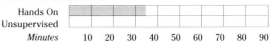

| Low | Medium | Medium High | Celebration |
|---|---|---|---|

*Serves 4*

## INGREDIENTS

2 eggs or the equivalent in egg substitute

⅛ teaspoon freshly ground salt (.6 ml)

¼ teaspoon freshly ground black pepper (1.25 ml)

8 ounces spaghetti (227 gm)

3 teaspoons extra light olive oil with a dash of sesame oil (15 ml)

4 ounces Canadian bacon (113 gm), diced

⅛ cup pine nuts (30 ml)

2 tablespoons fresh chopped parsley (30 ml)

2 tablespoons fresh snipped chives (30 ml)

¼ cup freshly grated Parmesan cheese (59 ml)

3 sun-dried tomato halves, ground to yield 1 tablespoon (15 ml)

## NOW COOK

■ Break the eggs lightly with a fork. Sprinkle with the freshly ground salt and pepper.

■ Drop the spaghetti into boiling water and cook 10 minutes until al dente. Drain in a colander set over a large serving bowl. Pour the water out of the bowl, leaving it nicely heated.

■ While the spaghetti is cooking, heat one teaspoon (5 ml) of the oil in a large skillet. Add the Canadian bacon and the pine nuts. Saute until lightly browned, then transfer into the heated bowl.

■ Add the remaining oil to the heated skillet. Scrape the residue off the bottom of the pan and pour into the heated bowl.

■ Stir the beaten eggs, parsley, chives, cheese and sun-dried tomatoes into the bowl. Add the spaghetti and toss to cover with the egg mixture, which will be cooked by the spaghetti's heat. Season with additional salt and pepper to taste.

## Helpful Hints and Observations

A DASH OF SESAME? - You might easily wonder what quantity constitutes a dash. We make up our special signature oil with 16 parts Bertolli's extra light olive oil to 1 part toasted sesame seed oil, and store it in the refrigerator. If you don't make it in bulk, we suggest a dash. I think the nutty aroma of the sesame imparts a hint of butter to the otherwise highly scented olive oil.

By the way, "extra light" refers to the aroma, not the fat content, which is the same as in any other olive oil.

TO GRIND DRIED TOMATOES - Put them through a clean coffee grinder or a mini-mill.

CHOPPED PARSLEY - To produce freshly cleaned, beautifully colored parsley, simply wrap the chopped herb in the corner of a towel, rinse under cold water and wring it out.

IN THE PINK? - According to Jane Brody, nitrates and nitrites have been used as curing agents for meat for more than 2,000 years. Why? Primarily for the pink color they add to things like ham and hot dogs. Unfortunately when you cook the meat, a cancer-causing chemical can be formed. This is a controversial issue, of course. But if you think (like me), "why expose myself to unnecessary risk," then read your meat label before buying. Nitrates and nitrites must be listed if they are present. I do, on occasion, use very small amounts of Canadian bacon and ham hocks for their essential flavor, largely because I'm against outright exclusion. But note: in very small amounts ... occasionally.

## Unusual Ingredients

PARMESAN CHEESE - If you want to get the extra zest from this cheese, you must buy it in hard wedges and grate it yourself. Natives of Parma, Italy, where this cheese originated, will also add that only the green grass of Parma, eaten by  the cows of Parma, can produce the true flavor of Parmesan cheese. In any case, only grate as much as you'll use for the recipe and store the rest in an airtight plastic bag or container in the refrigerator.

# RADIATORE

*𝓜ost people think a radiatore is the "thing-a-ma-jig" in between the head lights of their car! But it's actually an unusual, spiral pasta, cooked here in a remarkable way. Instead of hurling it into massive amounts of water, the pasta is cooked from its raw state in its finishing sauce — a most extraordinary taste and texture!*

*Like most pasta, this is really good served "as is." You may want to add a few pieces of freshly stir-fried chicken if you absolutely must get your teeth into something fleshy.*

## Nutritional Profile

| PER SERVING | CLASSIC | MINIMAX |
|---|---|---|
| Calories | 1122 | 378 |
| Fat (gm) | 59 | 9 |
| Calories From Fat | 47% | 20% |
| Cholesterol (mg) | 165 | 7 |
| Sodium (mg) | 1562 | 76 |
| Fiber (gm) | 7 | 7 |

■ *Classic Compared – Spaghetti Kareena*

## Time Estimate

| | | | | | | | | | |
|---|---|---|---|---|---|---|---|---|---|
| Hands On | | | | | | | | | |
| Unsupervised | | | | | | | | | |
| *Minutes* | 10 | 20 | 30 | 40 | 50 | 60 | 70 | 80 | 90 |

## Cost Estimate

| | | | |
|---|---|---|---|
| Low | Medium | Medium High | Celebration |

*Serves 4*

## INGREDIENTS

10 Roma tomatoes

1 cup water (236 ml)

1 tablespoon extra light olive oil with a dash of sesame oil (15 ml)

1 red bell pepper, seeded and chopped

2 garlic cloves, peeled and chopped

1 cup de-alcoholized white wine (236 ml)

1 branch of fresh basil (at least 6 leaves)

8 ounces radiatore (227 gm)

1 tablespoon fresh chopped oregano (15 ml)

1 tablespoon fresh chopped parsley (15 ml)

4 tablespoons grated dry Monterey Jack cheese (60 ml)

4 teaspoons pine nuts (20 ml)

## FIRST PREPARE

■ Use one of the following two methods to make a tomato puree: Using the traditional method, remove the stalk end and then drop the tomatoes into a pot of boiling water. In a few moments, you'll see the skins start to peel back. Drain the tomatoes and plunge them into cold water. You should be able to pick them up quite easily. Peel off the skin and cut out the seeds, reserving the seeds and skins. Take the tomato meat and put it into the work bowl of your food processor. Use the pulse switch and process into a smooth puree. See Helpful Hints and Observations, for a quicker way.

## NOW COOK

■ In a small saucepan add the water to the tomato skins and seeds and bring to a boil.

■ Drain the tomato skins and seeds into a small strainer. Press out all the juice you can. This gives you an extra taste of the tomatoes. Set the liquid aside. And don't throw those skins out yet! Pour them into your potted plants (not over them, that would look sordid, but under, to enrich the soil).

■ In a large saucepan, heat the olive oil with the chopped peppers and garlic.

■ To the frying garlic and peppers add the tomato puree, tomato skin water, de-alcoholized wine and the branch of fresh basil. Stir in the radiatore.

■ Turn the heat to low and put the lid on the saucepan. Cook for 4 minutes if you have fresh pasta, 8 minutes for dried pasta. This will cook the pasta "verde verde", or just a little bit less than "al dente." You'll see that most of the sauce is absorbed into the radiatore.

■ Remove the basil branch. Add the oregano and parsley and stir.

■ Place in a serving bowl and sprinkle with the grated cheese and pine nuts.

## Helpful Hints and Observation

MORE THAN ONE WAY OF SKINNING A TOMATO! - A new machine, called a "Tomato Press," makes this quite a bit simpler. Quarter the tomatoes and hurl them into a saucepan on medium heat until they're just heated through - just a few minutes. Then pour them into the top of the press. When you turn the handle, the tomatoes will be processed so that the skin and seeds come out one end and the tomato puree comes out the other! Not only is this method much less time consuming than the old-fashioned way — it is also a good aerobic activity!

## Unusual Ingredients

RADIATORE - A dry pasta shaped like an old-fashioned radiator. The wonderful shape, all the ins and outs, holds the sauce and keeps it on the pasta, not the plate. You can find this pasta boxed at your local supermarket.

PINE NUTS - Also called pignoli in Italian, pine nuts are actually the seeds of certain pine trees. The most prized are grown in Portugal. These pine cones are harvested, then dried to crack and separate the scales. The hard shell is then cracked and the seed is released. Raw pine nuts have a "piney" flavor and some cooks say a turpentine smell. They are wonderful roasted. Place them on a baking sheet at 400°F (205°C) for 6-8 minutes. Look for pine nuts near the baking needs in your local supermarket. For the best value, purchase them in bulk and store them airtight in the refrigerator.

# TORTELLINI IN BUTTER BEAN SAUCE

*My favorite pasta suddenly got better! I'm really delighted with this recipe which has only one real drawback: it takes time to make the little pasta packages, unless you press the entire family into service! Of course, then it's not only easy, it's fun!*

*This dish is wonderful garnished with 2 table-spoons (30 ml) of freshly grated Parmesan cheese and a tablespoon (15 ml) of fresh snipped chives. Serve with a colorful herbed salad in the summer (or in a well-heated winter home!), or perhaps freshly cooked green beans seasoned with a touch of fresh garlic and nutmeg.*

## Nutritional Profile

| PER SERVING | CLASSIC | MINIMAX |
|---|---|---|
| Calories | 983 | 566 |
| Fat (gm) | 44 | 7 |
| Calories From Fat | 40% | 11% |
| Cholesterol (mg) | 822 | 146 |
| Sodium (mg) | 1743 | 520 |
| Fiber (gm) | 4 | 8 |

■ *Classic Compared – Tortellini*

## Time Estimate

| Hands On | | 3 Hours | | | | | | | |
|---|---|---|---|---|---|---|---|---|---|
| Unsupervised | | | | | | | | | |
| *Minutes* | 10 | 20 | 30 | 40 | 50 | 60 | 70 | 80 | 90 |

## Cost Estimate

| Low | Medium | Medium High | Celebration |
|---|---|---|---|

*Serves 4 as Main Course*

## INGREDIENTS

FILLING

8 ounces boneless, skinless, turkey thighs (227 gm), fat trimmed

1 ounce Canadian bacon (28 gm)

5 large sage leaves

¼ teaspoon freshly ground black pepper (1.25 ml)

⅛ teaspoon freshly ground salt (.6 ml)

PASTA

1½ cups all-purpose flour (354 ml)

1½ cups semolina flour (354 ml)

2 eggs

7 tablespoons water (105 ml)

¼ teaspoon freshly ground salt (1.25 ml)

4 quarts water (3.8 L)

SAUCE

¾ cup whey from strained yogurt (177 ml) (recipe page 210)

1½ cups butter beans (354 ml) (from a 15 ounce or 425 gm can), drained

½ cup evaporated skim milk (118 ml)

2 cups chicken stock (472 ml) (recipe page 210)

1 teaspoon fresh chopped tarragon (5 ml)

1 teaspoon fresh chopped sage (5 ml)

½ teaspoon cayenne pepper (2.5 ml)

⅛ teaspoon freshly ground salt (.6 ml)

1 tablespoon cornstarch (15 ml) mixed with 2 tablespoons evaporated skim milk (30 ml)

## FIRST PREPARE THE FILLING

■ In a meat grinder, coarsely grind the turkey breast and Canadian bacon, ending with 1 slice of whole wheat bread. When you see the bread come through the grinder you know you've ground all the turkey (the bread is not part of the filling!). Spread the meat over a cutting board and sprinkle with the seasonings. Scrape and smooth together to combine all the ingredients, form into a ball and set aside.

## PREPARE THE PASTA

■ In a food processor combine the flours, eggs and salt. Process at high speed, gradually incorporating the water. When slightly tacky, remove the dough and put it on a smooth surface.

■ Knead the dough until it becomes very smooth - about 2 to 3 minutes. Roll the dough into a 6 inch long (15 cm) cylinder shape and let rest for 30 minutes.

■ Cut the dough into quarters and using a rolling pin or pasta machine, roll each piece into a very thin sheet. You should be able to see the shadow of your hand through the thin dough. Cut the sheets into manageable working pieces - about 12 to 15 inches long (30 to 38 cm).

■ Working with 1 sheet at a time, lay it on a cutting board. Cut out 2 inch (5 cm) diameter circles. You should have 48 circles from this recipe. Cover them with a damp cloth, as they should not dry out before they are molded.

■ Using a small pastry brush, lightly brush the pasta circles with water. Put a ¼ teaspoon (1.25 ml) of the filling in the center of each circle - don't overfill. Fold the pasta in half, in the shape of a half moon. Crimp the folded-over edge tightly so it's completely sealed. Fold the half moon ends over towards each other, slightly twisting one end under the other in a graceful swirl (it's supposed to look like a navel!). Set aside on a plate with a little semolina flour underneath to keep them separate.

## NOW COOK THE SAUCE

■ In a food processor, puree the yogurt whey, butter beans, chicken stock and skim milk until smooth. Pour into a large non-stick wok or high-sided frypan. The pan needs to be large because you will be tossing the tortellini in the sauce. Add the cayenne pepper, salt, sage and tarragon. Bring to a boil and simmer until it has a thin consistency.

■ Just before adding the tortellini, stir in the cornstarch paste, bring to a boil and stir until thickened.

## COOK THE TORTELLINI

■ Put the water in a large pot and bring to a boil. Toss in the tortellini and boil until al dente, or just tender to the tooth - about 3 minutes. Taste to see if the texture suits your palate.

■ Drain the cooked tortellini in a colander. Spoon them into the sauce and toss until well coated. (You can then freeze the stock to use again.)

■ Bring to the table and dazzle your dinner guests!

## Helpful Hints and Observations

BUTTER BEAN SAUCE - See Helpful Hints, page 45.

# TORTELLINI METROPOLITAN

$\mathcal{I}$ must admit to being a tortellini fan. It began, for me, in Bologna, when I first ate these little pasta parcels bathed in a cream sauce with sliced white truffles!

Recently I ate tortellini at the extraordinarily creative "Metropolitan Diner" in Victoria, British Columbia, owned and run by brothers Ford and Matt MacDonald with the able assistance of their mother, Leslie. It's well worth a special visit.

At the "Metropolitan Diner" they serve this as an appetizer, but I've tweaked it to go the distance as a main dish. Chef McDonald and I have also collaborated to bring the nutritional numbers into line for special needs. It's still a lovely dish!

## Nutritional Profile

| PER SERVING | CLASSIC | MINIMAX |
|---|---|---|
| Calories | 508 | 311 |
| Fat (gm) | 32 | 10 |
| Calories From Fat | 56% | 28% |
| Cholesterol (mg) | 164 | 58 |
| Sodium (mg) | 303 | 679 |
| Fiber (gm) | 3 | 3 |

■ *Classic Compared – Spinach Tortellini*

## Time Estimate

| Hands On Unsupervised | | | | | | | | |
|---|---|---|---|---|---|---|---|---|
| Minutes | 10 | 20 | 30 | 40 | 50 | 60 | 70 | 80 | 90 |

## Cost Estimate

| Low | Medium | Medium High | Celebration |
|---|---|---|---|

*Serves 4*

## INGREDIENTS

4 quarts water (3.8 L)

2 (9 ounce) packages Spinach Tortellini with cheese filling (255 gm)

SAUCE

1 teaspoon extra light olive oil with a dash of sesame oil (5 ml)

1 tablespoon finely chopped onion (15 ml)

1 teaspoon minced garlic (5 ml)

3 tablespoons cornstarch (45 ml)

1 cup strained yogurt (236 ml) (recipe page 210)

8 ounces evaporated skim milk (227 gm)

¼ cup de-alcoholized white wine (59 ml) (I prefer a somewhat sweet variety and recommend Ariel Blanc, see page 31.)

¼ cup shredded Swiss cheese (59 ml)

1 tablespoon freshly grated Parmesan cheese (15 ml)

1 teaspoon fresh chopped tarragon (5 ml)

1 tablespoon toasted cashew pieces (15 ml)

GARNISH

1 tablespoon freshly squeezed lime juice (15 ml)

1 tablespoon toasted cashew pieces (15 ml)

1 teaspoon tarragon (5 ml)

1 teaspoon fresh chopped chives (5 ml)

⅛ teaspoon freshly ground salt (.6 ml)

## NOW COOK

■ Bring the water to a boil, add the spinach tortellini, bring back to a boil and cook for 8 minutes. Drain the tortellini and set aside.

■ Heat the olive oil in a saucepan and saute the onion and garlic.

■ In a bowl, combine the cornstarch with the strained yogurt. Add the evaporated milk and the wine.

■ Remove the saucepan from the heat and add the cornstarch-yogurt mixture. Return to the heat, bring to a boil and stir until thickened.

■ Add the Swiss and Parmesan cheese, tarragon and cashews to the sauce.

■ Pour the sauce into a large skillet. Add the tortellini and toss until well coated.

■ Spoon the tortellini onto a plate and garnish with the lime juice, toasted cashews, tarragon, and chives.

## Helpful Hints and Observations

THE SAUCE IS CONTROVERSIAL! - Some of the world's most popular sauces are those that have a dense, white, creamy finish (Alfredo sauce is a good example). Unfortunately they are also loaded with saturated fat and impossible to recreate Minimax style without adding strange, reconstructed non-fat emulsions.

This sauce recipe is the best I've been able to design. It retains some of the characteristics of the original, but with much less fat - a drop of 20 grams of saturated fat per serving. The most important issue here is, "Do I like it?", and not, "How does it compare to my Fettucini Alfredo!!"

## Unusual Ingredients

CASHEWS - If you saw a cashew tree, would you know where to find the nuts? Cashew trees have a red and yellow fruit, and the cashews grow on the bottom. But nut pluckers beware: cashew shells have two layers and between them is a caustic black liquid that can cause skin blisters if you try to crack the shell by hand.

Shoppers buying cashews in their local market should be wary for another reason. Read the label of commercially toasted cashews: very high in oil, salt, sugar, and preservatives. I recommend buying them raw and toasting them at home. Stored in a tightly covered container they will keep in the refrigerator for up to 6 months.

TARRAGON - Described as sweet, clean, bold and full-bodied when used fresh, it's been used for years by chefs in the classic French sauces, such as bernaise and hollandaise. It seems to have a natural ability to enhance strong-flavored foods such as duck, lamb, seafood, beets, greens and mushrooms. If you must use dried tarragon, be careful: the drying process emphasizes tarragon's licorice taste while suppressing its other more subtle aromas. This hardy perennial herb is a good one to grow in your garden. Make sure you get French tarragon (this is one place the Russian tarragon can't compete).

# HARD HAT PIZZA

Scott Keck was minding his own business and hard at work on the construction of a new building when our cameras caught him! His favorite foods were: beef, tomato, sweet potato and crisp greens. I put them together into a crustless pizza and put him on the spot to taste it publicly on the television show.

He liked it! And once again the old adage was proven wrong: men aren't simply meat and potato eaters to the exclusion of every new idea!

This is another all-in-one meal. One quarter slice is ample with the sauce served on the side.

## Nutritional Profile

| PER SERVING | CLASSIC | MINIMAX |
|---|---|---|
| Calories | 814 | 316 |
| Fat (gm) | 53 | 9 |
| Calories From Fat | 58% | 25% |
| Cholesterol (mg) | 187 | 57 |
| Sodium (mg) | 417 | 107 |
| Fiber (gm) | 3 | 7 |

■ *Classic Compared – Steak & Fries*

## Time Estimate

| | | | | | | | | | |
|---|---|---|---|---|---|---|---|---|---|
| Hands On | | | | | | | | | |
| Unsupervised | | | | | | | | | |

Minutes   10   20   30   40   50   60   70   80   90

## Cost Estimate

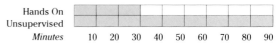

Low     Medium     Medium High     Celebration

*Serves 4*

## INGREDIENTS

8 ounces beef bottom round (227 gm)

1½ large yams (preferably garnet yams)

10 large savoy cabbage leaves, core removed

¼ teaspoon freshly grated nutmeg (1.25 ml)

¼ teaspoon freshly ground black pepper (1.25 ml)

4 Roma tomatoes, sliced lengthwise

4 basil leaves, thinly sliced

Freshly ground salt and pepper to taste

SAUCE

1 teaspoon extra light olive oil with a dash of sesame oil (5 ml)

1 garlic clove, peeled and chopped

8 ounces no-salt tomato sauce (227 gm)

1 tablespoon fresh chopped basil leaves (15 ml)

1 tablespoon fresh chopped parsley stalks (15 ml)

⅛ teaspoon freshly grated nutmeg (.6 ml)

¼ teaspoon freshly ground black pepper (1.25 ml)

½ cup de-alcoholized white wine (118 ml)

1 tablespoon arrowroot (15 ml) mixed with
2 tablespoons de-alcoholized white wine (30 ml)

1 Roma tomato, finely diced

½ teaspoon baking powder (2.5 ml)

1 tablespoon fresh chopped parsley (15 ml)

½ teaspoon horseradish (2.5 ml)

## FIRST PREPARE

■ Roast the beef at 350°F (180°C) for 25 minutes. The meat thermometer should measure 140°F (60°C). Remove the roast from the oven, let it cool for 15 minutes and then slice it into fine strips.

## FOR THE PIZZA

■ Bake the yams for 1 hour at 350°F (180°C). Remove from the oven, allow to cool and slice 1 inch (2.5 cm) thick.

■ Place the cabbage leaves in a steamer and steam for 2-3 minutes. Make a bed of 5 leaves on a large oven proof plate. The leaves should fully cover the base of the plate and have a slight overhang.

■ Lay the yam slices over the leaves, sprinkle with the nutmeg and pepper and cover with 2 cabbage leaves.

■ Layer tomatoes slices on top of the cabbage and sprinkle with the basil, salt and pepper. Cover with the remaining cabbage leaves.

■ Trim the overhanging leaves and place an inverted ovenproof plate on top. Your pizza is now ready to go into the oven!

■ Place the covered pizza in the oven and cook at 350°F (180°C) for 20 minutes.

■ While the pizza cooks, make the sauce: Heat the oil in a large saucepan and cook the garlic, tomato sauce, basil, parsley stalks, nutmeg and pepper. Add the wine and cook for 15 minutes over medium heat.

■ Remove from the heat, add the arrowroot paste, put back on the heat and add the diced tomato and strips of beef. Stir in the baking powder, parsley and horseradish.

■ When the pizza is cooked, remove from the oven and flip the top plate. Firmly lift the plates into a vertical position and squeeze them together so that most of the flavorful pizza juices drizzle into the sauce. Stir the sauce to mix thoroughly.

■ To Serve: Slice the pizza into quarters and serve on individual plates. Spoon a quarter of the sauce onto each serving.

## Unusual Ingredients

SAVOY CABBAGE - Next to the pale green, flat leaves of the common domestic cabbage, savoy is the fancy cousin: yellowish-green, loose crinkly leaves. It is not as strong tasting as the domestic. At the supermarket, look for fresh, crisp leaves. Stay away from wilted or thin leaved cabbage.

# PIZZA POLESE

*Incredibly popular, the classic pizza has an almost no-fault crust, especially when compared to the rich, fatty, pie crust used for quiche and some fruit pies. Instead, it's the pizza toppings that can go overboard - our version tries to keep you in the boat!*

*Slice as you would any pizza. I love to serve a colorful salad, including, if possible, some arugula (rocket).*

## Nutritional Profile

| PER SERVING | CLASSIC | MINIMAX |
|---|---|---|
| Calories | 419 | 271 |
| Fat (gm) | 26 | 10 |
| Calories From Fat | 57% | 32% |
| Cholesterol (mg) | 47 | 68 |
| Sodium (mg) | 1356 | 240 |
| Fiber (gm) | 3 | 3 |

■ *Classic Compared – Pepperoni Pizza*

## Time Estimate

| | | | | | | | | | |
|---|---|---|---|---|---|---|---|---|---|
| Hands On | | | | | | | | | |
| Unsupervised | | | | | | | | | |
| *Minutes* | 10 | 20 | 30 | 40 | 50 | 60 | 70 | 80 | 90 |

## Cost Estimate

| Low | Medium | Medium High | Celebration |
|---|---|---|---|

*Serves 6*

## INGREDIENTS

CRUST

1½ cups all purpose flour (354 ml)

1 egg

¼ cup water (59 ml)

1 tablespoon extra light olive oil with a dash of sesame oil (15 ml)

1 teaspoon salt (5 ml)

1 clove garlic

2 loosely-packed tablespoons oregano leaves (30 ml)

1 tablespoon packed rosemary leaves (15 ml)

½ ounce compressed yeast (14 gm)

1 tablespoon hot water to blend yeast (15 ml)

TOPPING

2 (4 ounce) skinless and boneless chicken breasts (113 gm each)

1 red bell pepper, cored, seeded and finely diced

1½ cups seeded and diced Roma tomatoes (356 ml)

1 tablespoon fresh chopped oregano leaves (15 ml)

1 tablespoon fresh chopped parsley (15 ml)

½ teaspoon freshly ground black pepper (2.5 ml)

4 teaspoons capers (20 ml)

6 (⅛ inch) slices of mozzarella cheese (.5 cm)

4 good quality anchovy fillets, soaked in a little milk to remove the saltiness, soaking milk reserved, quartered lengthwise

## PREPARE THE CRUST

■ Put the garlic, oregano and rosemary into a small food grinder or pepper mill and process to a fine, moist "dust."

■ Pre-heat the oven to 500°F (260°C). Put the flour in a large bowl. Make a well in the center and pour in the egg, water, oil and ground herb mixture. In another small bowl, break the compressed yeast into small pieces, add the hot water and stir until completely dissolved. Pour into the flour well.

■ Gradually start incorporating the flour and egg mixture together. Stir gently up against the sides of the well, mixing in a little flour at a time. The dough will be fairly stiff. When it's hard to stir, use your hands to form the dough into a ball. Turn it out onto a board and continue kneading until the dough feels springy. It will be slightly tacky but should come off your hands after you press into it.

Form it into a ball, put it back in the bowl, cover it with a towel and leave it in a warm place for 30 minutes, or until doubled in size.

■ Turn the proved dough out onto a board. Knead it just a couple more times then roll it out to fit a 14 inch (35 cm) pizza pan. The dough should be fairly thin, about ⅛ inch (.5 cm) thick.

■ Prepare the pizza pan with a light dusting of semolina flour. Press the dough to fit the shape of the pan and let it sit for 15 minutes before baking. Bake in the preheated oven for 8 minutes or until light brown.

## PREPARE THE TOPPING

■ On the coarsest setting, grind the chicken.

■ In a small bowl, mix the ground chicken, red pepper, tomatoes, oregano, parsley, black pepper and 3 teaspoons (15 ml) of the capers.

■ Flip your cooked pizza crust over so that the browned, crisp side is now on the bottom. Spread the filling over the crust, leaving a ½ inch (1.5 cm) crust edge.

■ Place the mozzarella slices around the edge of the filling. Sprinkle the remaining capers on top and decorate with a criss-cross of anchovy fillets.

■ Bake in the preheated oven for 8 more minutes.

■ When the pizza comes out of the oven, brush the exposed crust very lightly with the reserved anchovy soaking milk.

### Helpful Hints and Observations

SEASONED PIZZA DOUGH - Whenever you move in to take fat out of a dish it really does help to make every attempt to replace the taste loss with aroma, color and texture (A.C.T.). In this case, I added some classic Mediterranean herbs (oregano and rosemary) to the dough.

THIN CRUST - OVERTURNED - I prefer a crust on the thin side (even though the classic pizza crust from Napoli is quite thick). The overturning technique allows for a pre-bake, after which the crusted bottom becomes the top and the layers of garnish don't prevent the surface from cooking.

### Unusual Ingredients

ANCHOVY - Oh, come on, try them just once! You will be in for a marvelous, salty, tangy tidbit with every bite.

CAPERS - See Unusual Ingredients, page 59.

# GHIVETCH

*In Romania, this meatless vegetable dish is often used to celebrate the arrival of the summer vegetables. I use it as a "vegetables only" dish to alternate with meat proteins. It keeps well in the refrigerator for four to five days and can be served hot or cold.*

*I like to serve Ghivetch as a "wedge of salad", ice cold in summer with cold meats - it really is wonderful! You can, by the way, serve it hot, as is, by the glorious spoonful, directly from the bowl. As a first course, Ghivetch can be served as a "terrine of vegetables" with whole wheat toast and a little of Treena's vinaigrette sauce on the side (recipe page 39).*

## Nutritional Profile

| PER SERVING | CLASSIC | MINIMAX |
|---|---|---|
| Calories | 278 | 298 |
| Fat (gm) | 13 | 7 |
| Calories From Fat | 41% | 21% |
| Cholesterol (mg) | 0 | 0 |
| Sodium (mg) | 229 | 211 |
| Fiber (gm) | 11 | 14 |

■ *Classic Compared – Ghivetch*

## Time Estimate

| Hands On Unsupervised | | | | 4 Hours, 30 Minutes | | | | | |
|---|---|---|---|---|---|---|---|---|---|
| *Minutes* | 10 | 20 | 30 | 40 | 50 | 60 | 70 | 80 | 90 |

## Cost Estimate

| Low | Medium | Medium High | Celebration |
|---|---|---|---|

*Serves 8*

## INGREDIENTS

2 cups boiling water (472 ml)

¼ teaspoon baking soda (1.25 ml)

1 bunch spinach, washed and stemmed (winter "savoy" cabbage can be used in the fall season)

2 cups boiling chicken stock (472 ml)

1 cup bulgur wheat (236 ml)

FIRST LOT

1 tablespoon extra light olive oil with a dash of sesame oil (15 ml)

1 garlic clove, peeled and chopped

1 onion, peeled and chopped

1 large carrot, peeled and sliced on the diagonal, ⅛ inch thick (.5 cm)

1 green pepper, seeded and chopped

1 tablespoon freshly squeezed lemon juice (15 ml)

SECOND LOT

2 tablespoons extra light olive oil with a dash of sesame oil (30 ml)

1 large potato, peeled and cut into ½ inch (1.5 cm) cubes

1 pound eggplant (500 gm), cut into ½ inch (1.5 cm) cubes

1 acorn squash, peeled and cut into ½ inch (1.5 cm) cubes

1 tablespoon fresh chopped dill (15 ml)

Juice of ½ lemon

½ teaspoon cracked black peppercorns (2.5 ml)

¼ teaspoon nutmeg (1.25 ml)

1 tablespoon fresh chopped chives (15 ml)

2 tablespoons fresh chopped parsley (30 ml)

¾ cups green beans (177 ml), topped and tailed

1 teaspoon salt (5 ml)

THIRD LOT

1½ cups peas (354 ml)

1 pound tomatoes (450 gm), seeded and diced

2 tablespoons fresh chopped basil (30 ml)

1 cup mushrooms (236 ml), quartered

SAUCE

1 cup chicken stock (236 ml)

Zest of 1 lemon

2 tablespoons freshly squeezed lemon juice (30 ml)

¼ teaspoon turmeric (1.25 ml)

1 tablespoon arrowroot (15 ml) mixed with 1 tablespoon water (15 ml)

1 teaspoon fresh chopped dill (5 ml)

## FIRST PREPARE

■ In a large saucepan add the baking soda to the boiling water followed by the spinach leaves. Blanch for a moment then plunge the leaves immediately into iced water. When they are bright green, remove the leaves, line a large serving bowl with them and set aside.

■ In a large saucepan, add the boiling chicken stock to the bulgur and let stand for 5 minutes.

## NOW COOK

■ For the First Lot: Heat the olive oil in a large, heavy fry pan. Add the remaining First Lot ingredients and cook about 2 minutes. Turn into a Dutch oven or pot large enough to hold all 3 lots of vegetables.

■ For the Second Lot: In the empty fry pan, heat half the olive oil. Add the potato and acorn squash and fry until brown on the edges. Add to the vegetables in the Dutch oven and stir together. Pour the remaining oil into the empty pan followed by the remaining Second Lot ingredients and the cooked bulgur. Cover and simmer for 35 minutes. Add more chicken stock as necessary to keep the mixture moist and avoid "catching" the wheat. Tip the contents into the Dutch oven.

■ For the Third Lot: Add the Third Lot ingredients to the vegetables in the Dutch oven. Fill the large, spinach leaf-lined bowl with the vegetable mixture. Press down firmly. Place a plate over the top and push down hard. Remove any extra liquid that comes into the plate. Chill the ghivetch.

■ For the Sauce: In a small saucepan, mix the chicken stock, lemon zest, lemon juice and turmeric. Stir the arrowroot paste into the sauce to thicken. Add dill and set aside.

■ Unmold the vegetables on a platter and serve the sauce on the side.

## Helpful Hints and Observations

ALTERNATE DAYS OF VEGETABLES - See Helpful Hints, page 157.

OVEN COOKING - The classic Ghivetch is often cooked in an oven, uncovered, for at least 1½ hours. We've reduced the time by two thirds in an effort to preserve color, texture and nutrition. Do watch the stove top heat. Keep it low, stir well and use a heavy based, well covered pot.

## Unusual Ingredients

BULGUR WHEAT - See Unusual Ingredients, page 103.

TURMERIC - See Unusual Ingredients, page 15.

# GOLDEN THREADS SQUASH

*Just for the record, this dish is the brain child of my Senior Food Associate, Robert Prince. Since it was his own from concept, I wanted to make sure he got the credit for at least this, his first step, in a hopefully long, creative journey as part of our team.*

*What a great natural invention: the so-called spaghetti squash has a unique internal thread-like structure — and bright golden color! The classic uses a sausage filling, but we've kept the meat out for another wonderful vegetable dish. With one brimming cup per head it will serve six. We like some freshly steamed broccoli on the side.*

## Nutritional Profile

| PER SERVING | CLASSIC | MINIMAX |
|---|---|---|
| Calories | 192 | 194 |
| Fat (gm) | 12 | 6 |
| Calories From Fat | 57% | 27% |
| Cholesterol (mg) | 31 | 3 |
| Sodium (mg) | 474 | 258 |
| Fiber (gm) | 4 | 10 |

■ *Classic Compared – Sausage and Squash Bake*

## Time Estimate

| | | | | | | | | | |
|---|---|---|---|---|---|---|---|---|---|
| Hands On | | | | | | | | | |
| Unsupervised | | | | | | | | | |

*Minutes*   10   20   30   40   50   60   70   80   90

## Cost Estimate

| Low | Medium | Medium High | Celebration |
|---|---|---|---|

*Serves 6*

## INGREDIENTS

1 (4½ pound) spaghetti squash (2 kg)

1 tablespoon extra light olive oil with a dash of sesame oil (15 ml)

2 garlic cloves, peeled and crushed

2 medium carrots, peeled and cut into matchsticks

1 red bell pepper, seeded and cut into matchsticks

1 green pepper, seeded and cut into matchsticks

¼ cup chicken stock (59 ml) (recipe page 210)

1½ tablespoons finely chopped fresh basil (22 ml)

4 tablespoons freshly grated Parmesan cheese (60 ml)

Freshly ground black pepper

1 tablespoon arrowroot (15 ml) mixed with 2 tablespoons chicken stock (30 ml)

GARNISH

1 sprig of fresh basil

½ ounce cracked filberts (14 gm)

## FIRST PREPARE

■ Prick the squash on one side, allowing it to "breathe". Place it on a baking sheet and bake at 325°F (165°C) for 80 minutes. Remove and dip it in an ice water bath to prevent it from overcooking by retained heat.

■ Put the squash on one side and cut a long lid. Remove the lid and scoop out the seeds, carefully scraping the spaghetti-like threads out of the shell. Put these golden threads on a plate and set aside.

■ Put the empty squash shell on a serving platter. If the shell won't stay in place, scoop out some of the pulp from the sides, and put in on the plate as a base to hold the shell stable.

## NOW COOK

■ Heat the olive oil in a wok and fry the crushed garlic.

■ Add the carrots, peppers and chicken stock, then gradually stir in the golden threads of reserved spaghetti squash.

■ Sprinkle with the basil and half of the grated cheese and stir lightly to mix.

■ Add some freshly ground pepper. Now remove from the heat and add the arrowroot paste. Return the wok to the heat and stir until thickened.

■ Tip the mixture into the squash shell and garnish with the remaining cheese, the filberts, and the basil sprig.

## Helpful Hints and Observations

PRICK IT OR STAND BACK! - There are stories of this kind of baked squash building a moist heat internally in the seed cavity and suddenly blowing up - a sort of "smart squash" bomb? A couple of vent holes will completely cure this problem.

ALTERNATE "VEGETABLES ONLY" DAYS - Just another reminder of how an attractive "vegetables only" dish can replace the traditional flesh protein foods on an occasional basis. Not only is this a healthy idea, reducing calories, fat, and cholesterol, it also saves you money on your food budget and tastes delicious! At one time Treena and I used to alternate one day on, one day off, beginning with Monday for vegetables and allowing the weekend to be "fleshy" days. Don't be too rigid on this ... keep variety coming and the family reception will be increasingly flexible and appreciative.

## Unusual Ingredients

SPAGHETTI SQUASH - You can't miss it (or ignore it) at the grocery: a big, egg shaped, yellow-skinned presence amongst the other vegetables. Make sure that its skin is hard, with no soft spots, decay, cracks, or bore holes. It should keep for about a month at room temperature. And by the way, do try the "golden threads" as a substitute for pasta with your favorite spaghetti sauce — it's delicious!

FILBERTS - or hazelnuts! Buy them in the shell or not in the shell: your goal is the same, a wonderful, sweet-tasting nut meat. Do watch out for commercially roasted filberts that could contain high amounts of salt, fat, etc. If you want your filberts roasted, just buy them raw, throw them on a cookie sheet and bake at 350°F (180°C), 5 to 10 minutes if shelled; 20 - 25 minutes if still in the shell.

ARROWROOT - There is a legend that this name originated because the Indians considered the sap obtained from the roots capable of healing wounds caused by arrows. The fact is that arrowroot's name is from the American Indian word for flour-root, araruta. In any case, this versatile starch is leached from the tubers of several kinds of tropical plants, refined and packaged. It is a lot less expensive when you buy it by the pound from a natural food outlet. Easily digestible, arrowroot can be used as a thickener in many soups, sauces, puddings and numerous sweet dishes. I usually keep it for clear or dark sauces, soups and gravies. Dairy products thicken better with cornstarch used in the same way.

# PANJABI KALI DAL

The "New Dehli Restaurant" must be spelled, rather than spoken, otherwise it sounds like a "new deli" and that doesn't do justice to this exotic San Francisco eatery. Treena and I have never had such delicious dal (lentil stew) and we've eaten Indian food on four continents.

Dal is usually served as a side dish with either poultry or meat and sometimes as an appetizer. It is full of flavor and even though it doesn't look wonderful, it is extremely nutritious.

## Nutritional Profile

| PER SERVING | CLASSIC | MINIMAX |
|---|---|---|
| Calories | 156 | 93 |
| Fat (gm) | 11 | 5 |
| Calories From Fat | 62 | 48% |
| Cholesterol (mg) | 0 | 0 |
| Sodium (mg) | 139 | 13 |
| Fiber (gm) | 3 | 2 |

■ Classic Compared – Panjabi Kali Dal

## Time Estimate

| Hands On | | | | | | | | |
|---|---|---|---|---|---|---|---|---|
| Unsupervised | | | 2 Hours, 30 Minutes | | | | | |
| *Minutes* | 10  20 | 30  40 | 50 | 60 | 70 | 80 | 90 |

## Cost Estimate

| Low | Medium | Medium High | Celebration |
|---|---|---|---|

*Serves 6*

## INGREDIENTS

¼ cup dried kidney beans (rajmah) (59 ml)

¼ cup yellow split peas (split bengal gram or chana dal) (59 ml)

½ cup garbanzo beans (black gram) (118 ml)

2 tablespoons extra light olive oil with a dash of sesame oil (30 ml)

1 teaspoon garam masala (5 ml)

½ teaspoon cayenne pepper (2.5 ml)

1 teaspoon paprika (5 ml)

½ teaspoon turmeric (2.5 ml)

1 teaspoon coriander (5 ml)

1 teaspoon freshly grated ginger root (5 ml)

2 garlic cloves, peeled and finely diced

1 tablespoon fresh chopped cilantro (15 ml)

¼ cup strained yogurt (59 ml) (recipe page 210)

1 tablespoon freshly squeezed lemon juice (15 ml)

BOUQUET GARNI

4 bay leaves

4 pieces whole green cardamom

2 pieces whole black cardamom

1 (2 inch) cinnamon stick (5 cm)

4 whole cloves

1 teaspoon whole cumin seed (5 ml)

GARNISH

Fresh cilantro

## NOW COOK

■ Pour the kidney beans, yellow split peas and garbanzo beans into a large stock pot. Just cover with water, bring to a boil and simmer for 2 minutes. Remove from the heat, cover and let stand 1 hour. Drain and rinse well.

■ In a small, high-sided casserole, heat half the olive oil. Add the garam masala, cayenne, paprika, turmeric and coriander. Mix to make a curry paste.

■ Stir the strained beans and lentils into the curry paste. Add 3 cups (708 ml) of water and the bouquet garni. Bring to a boil, cover and simmer for one hour. Remove the bouquet garni.

■ In a small saute pan, heat the remaining olive oil and saute the ginger and garlic. Combine with the beans and stir in the cilantro.

■ Take out a third of the beans and set aside. Scoop the rest into a food processor and puree. Mix the whole beans back into the puree. Add the strained yogurt and lemon juice.

■ Garnish with a sprig of cilantro and serve with pita bread.

## Helpful Hints and Observations

WASH WELL! - In many western nations we are so used to clean food in ultra-sealed containers that we sometimes doubt instructions that say "wash several times." It is a very wise precaution to do this when using beans and lentils. You might also want to pick over these legumes and discard any that look tight and shriveled. Some might even be stones!

## Unusual Ingredients

SPLIT BENGAL GRAM - Lentils, split peas or legumes are called "dals" in Hindustani. There are all sorts of varieties and colors. Split Bengal Gram are yellow split peas. Split peas, like lentils, are one of the easiest legumes to use because they do not require pre-soaking. Keep them in an air tight container - they will last indefinitely.

BLACK AND GREEN WHOLE CARDAMOM - These ingredients are seed pods belonging to the ginger family. The seeds in the pods are where the aroma comes from. Ground cardamom in the bottle is not as aromatic because the ground seeds are mixed with ground pod. Look for them in the spice department of your supermarket or in a specialty food shop.

# STIR-FRIED SALAD VINAIGRETTE

*I* often suggest you add a crisp, well-dressed herbal salad as a side dish, so I thought it was time that I gave you an example. Several years ago I invented an idea called a split salad and we've used it ever since as it avoids overuse of dressing and slimy greens!

This idea can be used with many, many variations. Do try to fix it with your own favorite vegetables and herbs.

## Nutritional Profile

| PER SERVING | CLASSIC | MINIMAX |
|---|---|---|
| Calories | 263 | 141 |
| Fat (gm) | 27 | 5 |
| Calories From Fat | 93% | 34% |
| Cholesterol (mg) | 0 | 0 |
| Sodium (mg) | 73 | 57 |
| Fiber (gm) | 2 | 5 |

■ *Classic Compared – Vinaigrette Sauce*

## Time Estimate

| Hands On Unsupervised | | | | | | | | | |
|---|---|---|---|---|---|---|---|---|---|
| Minutes | 10 | 20 | 30 | 40 | 50 | 60 | 70 | 80 | 90 |

4 Hours

## Cost Estimate

| | | | |
|---|---|---|---|
| Low | Medium | Medium High | Celebration |

*Serves 4*

## INGREDIENTS

VINAIGRETTE DRESSING

½ cup rice wine vinegar (118 ml)

¼ cup extra light olive oil with a dash of sesame oil (59 ml)

2 tablespoons brown sugar (30 ml)

¼ teaspoon cayenne pepper (1.25 ml)

2 tablespoons freshly squeezed lime juice (30 ml)

3 thin "quarter" sized slices of fresh ginger root

2 garlic cloves, finely chopped

6 fresh basil leaves, finely sliced

6 fresh mint leaves, finely sliced

12 leaves of assorted salad greens, rinsed and dried with paper towels or a salad spinner

SALAD

1 tablespoon extra light olive oil with a dash of sesame oil (15 ml)

½ small yellow onion, peeled and finely sliced

1 garlic clove, peeled and finely chopped

2 large carrots, sliced diagonally

5 green onions, sliced

4 ounces green beans (113 gm), sliced in half lengthwise

2 ounces fennel bulb (57 gm), finely sliced

4 thin "quarter" sized slices of fresh ginger root, finely chopped

4 ounces red bell pepper (113 gm), cored, seeded and cut into fine matchsticks

4 ounces green bell pepper (113 gm), cored, seeded and cut into fine matchsticks

2 stalks celery, sliced diagonally

4 ounces jicama (113 gm)

4 ounces cucumber (113 gm), finely sliced

## VINAIGRETTE

■ In a blender combine the vinegar, olive oil, brown sugar and cayenne pepper. Add the lime juice, ginger, garlic, basil and mint and mix on high speed for 45 seconds. Strain into a bowl.

## SALAD

■ Heat the olive oil in a medium sized casserole and fry the yellow onion, garlic and carrots. Add the green onions, green beans, fennel, ginger, peppers, celery and jicama and cook until just warmed through.

■ Remove the warmed vegetables and place in a large bowl. Add the cucumbers and set aside.

■ Pour the vinaigrette into the casserole, dredging the residue from the bottom and edges. Heat the vinaigrette slightly and then pour over the vegetables. Marinate for about 4 hours.

■ Strain the vegetables over a bowl, catching the excess vinaigrette. You should have about ½ cup (118 ml) of excess vinaigrette.

■ Place the salad greens in a bowl, pour in the excess vinaigrette and toss well. Add the marinated vegetables and serve!

## Helpful Hints and Observations

STIR-FRIED SALAD? - It must seem rather odd to toss the hard salad items in oil, but I do this to get the maximum flavor from the volatile oils of the vegetables which can only be fully released at frying temperatures.

## Unusual Ingredients

ASSORTED SALAD GREENS - The class of vegetable called "greens" is not only a festival of greens, blues, whites, and reds, it's also loaded with Vitamins A and C. And some greens - like collards, mustard, turnips and kale - are thought to be cancer-preventers. Take your time at the market and look at the varieties available. Select greens that have fresh, vibrant colors. The leaves should not look wilted or have blemish spots. Since greens grow so close to the ground, wash them well.

CELERY - Long, green stalks of celery are a familiar sight in the produce section of any supermarket. The stalks are usually harvested from year old plants. If the plants are allowed to grow for two years they go to seed, which is where we get the spice celery seed. Choose celery that is firm, with no yellow or wilted leaves. If you store it in an air tight container it will stay fresh for up to two weeks. But don't separate the stalks until you're ready to use them - once separated they wilt more quickly. If your celery is a bit soft, cutting off the stalks and putting them in a jug of cold water set in the refrigerator will restore their crispness.

GINGER - If you haven't already, you should add this ingredient to your Minimax larder! Fresh ginger is a tan, knobby, underground stem that can be found in most supermarkets. Its taste is completely different from that of powdered ginger. It adds zest, zing and zoom to your dishes. Fresh ginger should be hard and its skin tight. If the skin is shriveled, the flavor of the ginger will be weakened. Most recipes call for you to peel ginger before using it. In the orient, they just slice off the scarred tips and use it skin and all! Fresh ginger keeps very well in the refrigerator, in a dry, air-tight plastic bag.

# MUESLI & KERRMUSH

*I have been eating these cereals since 1978. I alternate between the Kerrmush and the Muesli, according to either the weather or boredom! My Welsh "dinner" guest on television was terrorized by porridge as a child — this recipe helped to change his mind. If it changes yours, you will have taken the largest single step toward a more creative food-style. Most breakfasts are either smothered in fat or don't exist at all. Kerrmush and Muesli are low in fat and provide lots of good energy all morning.*

*Muesli must be served cold and the surface scattered with fresh fruit, such as straw-berries, blue-berries or even slices of kiwi.*

*One bowlful with a toasted whole wheat muffin does the trick for me until lunchtime.*

## MUESLI

*Serves 1*

### INGREDIENTS

2 tablespoons rolled oats (30 ml)
1 tablespoon dark raisins (15 ml)
½ Granny Smith apple, grated
1 tablespoon freshly squeezed lemon juice (15 ml)
1 tablespoon honey (15 ml), Fireweed if possible
2 tablespoons plain, non-fat yogurt (30 ml)
1 tablespoon Minimax Seed Mixture (15 ml)
(see Unusual Ingredients, page 205) ground
until just broken
Fruit of choice

### FIRST PREPARE

■ Soak the oats and raisins in water overnight.

### NOW COOK

■ Drain the oats and raisins.
■ Mix the grated apple with the lemon juice, oats and raisins.
■ Mix together the honey and yogurt, and stir into the oat mixture.
■ Sprinkle with Minimax Seed Mix, garnish with small pieces of bright fruit, and serve.

### Nutritional Profile

| PER SERVING | CLASSIC | MINIMAX |
|---|---|---|
| Calories | 186 | 278 |
| Fat (gm) | 7 | 5 |
| Calories From Fat | 33% | 16% |
| Cholesterol (mg) | 15 | 1 |
| Sodium (mg) | 238 | 58 |
| Fiber (gm) | 3 | 5 |

■ *Classic Compared – Muesli*

### Time Estimate

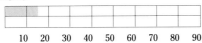

```
        10  20  30  40  50  60  70  80  90
```

### Cost Estimate

```
   Low      Medium    Medium High   Celebration
```

## KERRMUSH

*Serves 4*

### INGREDIENTS

1 cup rolled oats (236 ml)
4 tablespoons dark raisins (60 ml)
2⅔ cups non-fat milk (629 ml)
4 tablespoons Minimax Seed Mix (60 ml)
(See Unusual Ingredients, page 205)
4 teaspoons honey (20 ml), Fireweed if possible

### NOW COOK

■ Simmer the oats, raisins and milk until just cooked - about 10 minutes. Stir and remove from the heat.
■ Sprinkle with the Minimax Seed Mix, either whole, partly or fully ground. I use a small electric coffee bean grinder to do this fresh each day.
■ Drizzle the honey on top and serve hot.

### Unusual Ingredients

ROLLED OATS - This grain is oat groats that have been heated to soften then rolled or literally flattened. Rolled oats will cook more quickly than oat groats, which can take up to 2 hours.

### Nutritional Profile

| PER SERVING | CLASSIC | MINIMAX |
|---|---|---|
| Calories | 211 | 248 |
| Fat (gm) | 9 | 5 |
| Calories From Fat | 37% | 19% |
| Cholesterol (mg) | 28 | 3 |
| Sodium (mg) | 281 | 92 |
| Fiber (gm) | 2 | 3 |

■ *Classic Compared – Oatmeal*

### Time Estimate

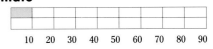

```
        10  20  30  40  50  60  70  80  90
```

### Cost Estimate

```
   Low       Medium    Medium High   Celebration
```

# CREMPOG *(Welsh Pancakes)*

*I*n Wales there is a charming seasonal custom of cooking Crempog (pancakes) for the children who go from house to house in search of the best buttered, best sugared, softest fudge syruped ... well ... it's charming!

My changes have kept the Welsh styled soft soda pancake and used the seasonal apples and plums of the area to make a most unusual dessert. No cream needed: this is full of its own flavors.

## Nutritional Profile

| PER SERVING | CLASSIC | MINIMAX |
|---|---|---|
| Calories | 885 | 271 |
| Fat (gm) | 49 | 3 |
| Calories From Fat | 50% | 9% |
| Cholesterol (mg) | 180 | 37 |
| Sodium (mg) | 590 | 196 |
| Fiber (gm) | 2 | 3 |

■ *Classic Compared – Crempog*

## Time Estimate

| | | |
|---|---|---|
| Hands On | | |
| Unsupervised | | |
| *Minutes* | 10  20  30  40  50  60  70  80  90 | |

## Cost Estimate

| Low | Medium | Medium High | Celebration |
|---|---|---|---|

*Serves 4*

## INGREDIENTS

PANCAKE BATTER

1½ cups all-purpose flour (354 ml)

1 egg, lightly beaten

¾ cup non-fat plain yogurt (177 ml)

1 cup non-fat milk (236 ml)

1 teaspoon baking soda (5 ml)

1 teaspoon cider vinegar (5 ml)

1 teaspoon extra light olive oil with a dash of sesame oil (5 ml)

SYRUP

1 cup water (236 ml)

1 cup cranberry juice (236 ml)

2 tablespoons brown sugar (30 ml)

1 (3 inch) cinnamon stick (8 cm)

8 whole cloves

⅛ teaspoon freshly grated nutmeg (.6 ml)

4 allspice berries

1 large Granny Smith apple, peeled and cored, but left whole

3 large red plums

2 tablespoons arrowroot (30 ml) mixed with 4 tablespoons water (60 ml)

## FIRST PREPARE

■ Sift the flour into a bowl, make a well in the center and pour in the lightly beaten egg, yogurt and ¾ cup (177 ml) of the milk. Beat until smooth. The batter should be thick. Cover and let rest for 1 hour.

■ Cut the apple into 4 thick slices. The slices should look like flat donuts. Cut one plum in half and remove the stone.

## NOW COOK

■ The Syrup: Put the water, cranberry juice, brown sugar, cinnamon stick, cloves, nutmeg and allspice berries into a saucepan and bring to a boil. Add the apple slices, the whole plums and the plum halves and poach for 2 minutes or until the fruit is soft.

■ Remove the apple slices and whole plums, leaving the 2 plum halves. Remove the skins from the whole plums and cut them in half.

■ Reduce the syrup to 1 cup (236 ml). Strain and transfer to a clean saucepan. Stir in the arrowroot paste and stir until thickened.

■ Mix the baking soda and vinegar together and stir into the batter.

■ Before you cook the pancakes, adjust the batter's consistency by adding the remaining milk (up to ¼ cup) until the batter runs smoothly off the ladle.

■ Heat an 8 inch (20 cm) saute pan and brush with oil. Ladle ¼ cup (59 ml) of the batter into the prepared pan and cook until bubbles appear and burst on the surface - about 1 minute. Turn the pancake over and cook another minute. Remove and cool on a wire rack. Repeat with the remaining batter. You need 8 pancakes for this recipe.

■ Trim the pancakes into even circles (see Helpful Hints). Place one pancake on a serving plate and set a poached apple slice on top. Top with a second pancake, so that you have an apple sandwich. Top with a plum half and drizzle with the syrup.

## Helpful Hints and Observations

THE SPICED FRUIT SYRUP - Sugar and fat seem naturally made for each other: one begs for the other. When you try to separate them, it's difficult!

One method, used here, is to develop an aromatic smoke screen of spices. I made up a simple syrup with only 2 tablespoons (30 ml) of brown sugar (a more complex flavor than white sugar) in place of the classic 12 tablespoons (180 ml) and none of the 12 tablespoons (180 ml) of butter!

The spices do the trick but the syrup needs flavor more from the fruit than the brief poaching time would bring out. Therefore, I added an extra plum to the reduction process, giving me more body, color and flavor in the syrup.

PERFECTLY TRIMMED PANCAKES - Cut them with a 4 inch (10 cm) round cookie cutter.

## Unusual Ingredients

ALLSPICE BERRIES - You might think that this is a combination of several spices. But the name, allspice, comes from the fact that these berries are said to smell like a mixture of cloves, cinnamon and nutmeg. Allspice is a native of Central America and the West Indies, where it is harvested from a slender evergreen tree. The fruit of this tree is a juicy berry that ripens from shiny green to a dark purple. The berry is gathered by hand and dried until the seeds rattle inside.

PLUMS - Do try to get fresh plums - the canned ones just aren't big enough. We made this for the television show in the dead of winter, with plums that were available in the grocery store from South America! So it is possible to find fresh ones, even out of the normal plum season.

# DUTCH PANCAKES

*I*'ve always had great fun with this dish. It began in Amsterdam, back in the early 70s, when I ate it with gusto (not a side dish!). Recently my recipe has changed, and when once you master the idea it's even more fun to fix - with much less risk!

This is basically a pancake and ham sandwich with glazed apples on top and a maple flavored custard sauce. I serve it as an unusual breakfast for a crowd. Everyone seems to have a good time!

## Nutritional Profile

| PER SERVING | CLASSIC | MINIMAX |
|---|---|---|
| Calories | 1068 | 493 |
| Fat (gm) | 60 | 10 |
| Calories From Fat | 50% | 19% |
| Cholesterol (mg) | 580 | 128 |
| Sodium (mg) | 716 | 627 |
| Fiber (gm) | 4 | 3 |

■ *Classic Compared – Dutch Pancakes*

## Time Estimate

| Hands On | | | | | | | | | |
|---|---|---|---|---|---|---|---|---|---|
| Unsupervised | | | | | | | | | |
| *Minutes* | 10 | 20 | 30 | 40 | 50 | 60 | 70 | 80 | 90 |

## Cost Estimate

| Low | Medium | Medium High | Celebration |
|---|---|---|---|

*Serves 2*

## INGREDIENTS

*Please Note: This pancake recipe makes 4 pancakes, but you only need 2 for your finished dish. That leaves 2 pancakes for your children to try their hand with!*

PANCAKE

1 whole egg

1 egg yolk

1¼ cups 2% milk (295 ml)

1 cup all-purpose flour (236 ml)

¼ teaspoon freshly ground salt (1.25 ml)

¼ teaspoon freshly ground white pepper (1.25 ml)

1 tablespoon extra light olive oil with a dash of sesame oil (15 ml)

SAUCE

¼ cup unsweetened evaporated skim milk (59 ml)

¼ cup real maple syrup (59 ml)

1 tablespoon cornstarch (15 ml)

2 tablespoons water (30 ml)

½ cup strained yogurt (recipe page 210)

FILLING

4 slices (2 ounces) Canadian bacon (57 gm)

1 Granny Smith apple, peeled, cored and sliced

1 teaspoon brown sugar for dusting (5 ml)

¼ teaspoon ground cinnamon (1.25 ml)

## FIRST PREPARE THE PANCAKES

■ In a small bowl, mix the egg, egg yolk and milk. Sift the flour, salt and pepper into a medium bowl and make a well in the center. Pour the egg mixture into the well and gradually stir it together with the flour until fully incorporated with no lumps. Set the batter aside in a cool place to rest for 30 minutes. The resting will relax the starch cells and provide a more delicately finished pancake.

■ Heat a 10 inch (25 cm) non-stick fry pan to medium. Pour the olive oil into the pan, coat well, then pour the oil into the pancake batter. Mix thoroughly. This will help make the pancake self-releasing.

■ Pour one ladle (½ cup or 118 ml) of pancake batter onto the heated fry pan. Rotate the pan until the entire surface is covered.

■ When the edges of the pancake start curling up and the top looks waxy, flip the pancake over. Cook the other side until it's light brown - just a minute or two - and turn out onto a dish. Finish cooking the rest of the pancakes.

## NOW COOK THE SAUCE

■ In a small saucepan, over medium heat, combine the evaporated skim milk and maple syrup. Cook until hot, but not boiling.

■ In a small bowl, dissolve the cornstarch in the water. Stir into the milk mixture, bring to a boil and stir until thickened. It will have the consistency of whipped honey. Remove from the heat and let cool.

■ To finish the sauce, stir in the strained yogurt and return to lowest heat, stirring occasionally to keep the sauce from sticking.

## TO ASSEMBLE

■ Put 1 pancake on an individual, oven-proof serving plate. Place the Canadian bacon on top of the pancake.

■ Arrange the oven rack 3 inches (8 cm) from the broiler element and broil the pancake until just brown, approximately 2½ minutes.

■ Remove from the broiler, cover with another pancake and arrange the apple slices around the edge in two concentric circles: one circle around the outside edge and one in the middle. Extend the slices just over the edge of the pancake so the delicate edge doesn't burn.

■ Dust with a scattering of cinnamon, sprinkle with brown sugar and pop back under the broiler until the apples are just brown on the edges and glazed.

■ Serve warm, with the sauce.

### Helpful Hints and Observations

SKIM MILK - See Helpful Hints, page 203.

### Unusual Ingredients

MAPLE SYRUP - One of the sweet fruits of spring, when it is collected in the form of sap from holes drilled into maple trees, its unique flavor is the result of trace amounts of minerals, sugars and other substances in the sap: a combination that is very difficult to manufacture artifically. I use it as a personal "signature" item that adds character to sweetened dishes and helps me to reduce the total sugars added.

EVAPORATED SKIM MILK - See Unusual Ingredients, page 197.

# WAFFLES WITH APPLE BUTTER

*C*reating this recipe I faced the biggest gastronomic hurdle of my culinary life: could I find a creative alternative to waffles, dripping with butter and syrup which could please the most discerning eleven year old boy, Chris Cashman, otherwise known as, "The Waffle Master?"

Let's just say that the only word uttered after "The Waffle Master" tasted this recipe was "Awesome!"

Minimax Waffles with Apple Butter are a crisp, crunchy wholesome food for a special breakfast. A variation on the apple butter can be made by combining it with a little strained yogurt. You'll be delighted with the resulting whipped cream-like mixture. And never forget the sweet pleasures of ripe, sliced fruit on a steaming waffle!

## Nutritional Profile

| PER SERVING | CLASSIC | MINIMAX |
|---|---|---|
| Calories | 1069 | 460 |
| Fat (gm) | 35 | 9 |
| Calories From Fat | 29% | 18% |
| Cholesterol (mg) | 199 | 55 |
| Sodium (mg) | 916 | 412 |
| Fiber (gm) | 3 | 4 |

■ *Classic Compared – Waffles with Syrup*

## Time Estimate

Hands On
Unsupervised
*Minutes*   10   20   30   40   50   60   70   80   90

## Cost Estimate

Low          Medium     Medium High   Celebration

*Serves 4*

## INGREDIENTS

APPLE BUTTER

3 sweet cooking apples, washed, cored and sliced

¼ cup clear, unsweetened apple juice (59 ml)

¼ cup water (59 ml)

⅛ cup dark raisins (30 ml) (without sulfites)

¼ cup brown sugar (59 ml)

⅛ teaspoon cinnamon (.6 ml)

Dash of ground cloves

Dash of ground allspice

¼ teaspoon freshly grated nutmeg (1.25 ml)

1 teaspoon grated lemon rind (5 ml)

WAFFLES

1¾ cups all-purpose flour (413 ml)

1 tablespoon baking powder (15 ml)

Pinch of salt

1 tablespoon sugar (15 ml)

2 cups non-fat milk (472 ml)

1 egg

2 tablespoons extra light olive oil with a dash of sesame oil (30 ml)

3 egg whites

## FIRST PREPARE THE APPLE BUTTER

■ Put the apples, apple juice, water and raisins in a saucepan and bring to a boil. Cover, reduce the heat and simmer until the apples are soft - about 20 minutes.

■ Press the fruit through a sieve, or whiz at high speed in a food processor until smooth then return to the saucepan. Continue to simmer, uncovered, on very low heat, or in a 300°F (150°C) oven. Add the brown sugar, spices and lemon zest. Cook for another 30 minutes until very thick and a lovely dark brown.

■ Apple butter can be eaten right away or preserved by the usual bottling methods.

## NOW COOK THE WAFFLES

■ In a medium sized mixing bowl, stir together the flour, baking powder, salt and sugar. In another bowl combine the milk, whole egg and oil. Stir the wet ingredients into the dry ones and blend until smooth and creamy.

■ Just before cooking the waffles, in a copper bowl, beat the egg whites until they form soft peaks. Gently fold the beaten egg whites into the waffle batter, one third at a time.

■ Preheat the waffle iron according to the manufacturer's directions, or until a drop of water sizzles and bounces when dropped onto the hot iron.

■ Brush the waffle iron lightly with canola oil, then pour approximately ½ cup (118 ml) batter per waffle square or enough to fill the entire waffle iron. Cook for 3 minutes and serve immediately with apple butter.

## Helpful Hints and Observations

THE LIMP WAFFLE SOLUTION - If you are cooking a batch of waffles for the family, never stack them. Stacking causes waffles to go limp! Instead, preheat the oven to 300°F (150°C) and slip them onto the racks, leaving the door slightly open. They will stay crisp for at least 30 minutes.

FRESH AND FRAGRANT - If you have the time, always use freshly ground spices - you will have a wonderfully fragrant experience.

IF YOU LIKE THE APPLE BUTTER - There is just enough volume in this recipe for you to make a small experimental batch. If you like it, simply multiply the amount and invite your friends to an apple butter production party, which is the way it is done in the Pennsylvania Dutch communities.

## Unusual Ingredients

APPLES - Apples are the world's most common fruit. There are over 7,000 varieties, but only about 25 types make it to our commercial market. Of those, I feel the following make the best apple butter: Winesap, Rome Beauty, Granny Smith, McIntosh or Jonathan. All of these varieties are readily available. If you want your apples at their peak of flavor, buy them in late summer or autumn, when they are being harvested.

# ARNOLD BENNETT OMELET

$\mathcal{T}$here are very few classical exceptions to the rule, "savory omelets are solid in texture and sweet omelets are fluffy," but having said this, I can fully endorse the Arnold Bennett Omelet as super! However, the method of egg yolk reduction that I've used here only works when you boost the basic one yolk with all the added seasonings.

Whole wheat rolls or whole wheat toast with a light margarine and a well herbed green salad go very nicely.

## Nutritional Profile

| PER SERVING | CLASSIC | MINIMAX |
|---|---|---|
| Calories | 239 | 182 |
| Fat (gm) | 18 | 9 |
| Calories From Fat | 67% | 43% |
| Cholesterol (mg) | 260 | 130 |
| Sodium (mg) | 501 | 786 |
| Fiber (gm) | 0 | 1 |

■ *Classic Compared – Arnold Bennett Omelet*

## Time Estimate

| | | | | | | | | | |
|---|---|---|---|---|---|---|---|---|---|
| Hands On | | | | | | | | | |
| Unsupervised | | | | | | | | | |

*Minutes*  10  20  30  40  50  60  70  80  90

## Cost Estimate

| Low | Medium | Medium High | Celebration |
|---|---|---|---|

*Serves 2*

## INGREDIENTS

4 ½ ounces smoked black cod or other moist, tender smoked fish fillet (128 gm) (1 cup (236 ml) when flaked)

Enough non-fat milk to cover the fish

3 tablespoons sun-dried tomatoes (45 ml)

4 egg whites*

1 teaspoon cold water (5 ml)

⅛ teaspoon salt (.6 ml)

1 egg yolk

¼ teaspoon freshly ground black pepper (1.25 ml)

1 teaspoon fresh finely chopped cilantro (5 ml)

¼ teaspoon freshly grated nutmeg (1.25 ml)

1 good pinch of saffron threads (or ¼ teaspoon (1.25 ml) powdered saffron)

2 tablespoons finely chopped green onions (30 ml)

1 teaspoon butter (5 ml)

1 tablespoon grated dry Monterey Jack cheese (15 ml)

1 tablespoon fresh finely chopped chives (15 ml)

*\* The extra egg yolks can be frozen and added to the dog food. Dogs don't have a problem with cholesterol.*

## FIRST PREPARE

■ Cover smoked fish in milk, soak for 1 hour, drain and pat dry. Remove the black skin and flake the fish into a bowl.

■ Soak the dried tomatoes in boiling water 10 minutes to soften. Thinly slice.

■ Whip the egg whites with the cold water and salt until they just peak.

■ Place the yolk in a 10 inch (25 cm) diameter mixing bowl. Beat with the freshly ground pepper, cilantro, 1 tablespoon (15 ml) of the sun-dried tomatoes, the nutmeg and saffron. This forms the essential flavor base; if you skimp on these flavors, the volume of the egg whites will turn the omelet into latex!

■ Combine the flaked fish with the chopped green onions and the remaining sun-dried tomatoes.

■ Immediately before making the omelet, stir one third of the beaten egg whites into the seasoned yolk mixture. You can make a thorough job of this so as to lighten the flavor base. Now pour the base into the remaining whites and fold together carefully; don't beat it - just fold until the yolk has evenly colored the whites.

■ Preheat the broiler and set the rack 4 to 5 inches (10 to 13 cm) from the heating element.

## NOW COOK

■ Set a pan over medium heat and, when hot, add the butter. Wait until edges of the butter froth and brown. Add the egg mixture all at once and stir quickly, using a spatula and making a figure eight motion. This helps to expose the eggs to the bottom heat. Bang the pan on the heating element a couple of times to settle the mixture. Smooth the surface with a knife. Scatter the cheese and the onion/fish/tomato mixture over the top.

■ Slide the whole pan immediately under the pre-heated broiler and cook until small, brown bubbles appear, the level has risen, the cheese has melted and the omelet is golden brown.

■ Loosen the edges and carefully shake it out of the pan with a spatula onto a serving dish. Dust with finely chopped fresh chives and serve.

### Helpful Hints & Observations

EGGS IN YOUR LIFE? - The problem with eggs is that they are perhaps the most perfect convenience food, an excellent source of protein, easily digested, extremely varied in use, universally enjoyed and reasonably inexpensive - but they have this problem with cholesterol. The American Heart Association has suggested, within their conservative guidelines, that we consume no more than three to four eggs per week, and then only if we are in good health and at no apparent risk of heart disease. If problems do exist, then it's no more than two, and some people I know, like my wife, Treena, are off them altogether with only an occasional "reminder." (We will not call it a "treat" because that means to avoid them is a continued denial that can build up into a rebellion binge, and that can cause a great deal of harm.) This omelet is designed to meet your needs for a pleasant reminder.

### Unusual Ingredients

SMOKED BLACK COD - A moist, oily, smoked fish with a rich flavor, black cod is easily available on the west coast of the U.S. If you can't find it where you live, substitute salmon, haddock or whitefish. Remember, smoked fish should smell smokey, not fishy. Select whole pieces that are more dry than slimy on the exterior.

SAFFRON THREADS - See Unusual Ingredients, page 61.

# FU YUNG GAI *(Chinese Chicken Omelet)*

*A*re you a tofu fan yet? When I made this dish for the television program, most of the people in our studio audience were quite hesitant! But once they had dabbed a bit of fresh ginger and oyster sauce behind their ears, they were ready for anything! Maybe all you'll need to do is taste this dish's unique combination of textures and flavors to become a true tofu connoisseur!

## Nutritional Profile

| PER SERVING | CLASSIC | MINIMAX |
|---|---|---|
| Calories | 421 | 398 |
| Fat (gm) | 30 | 10 |
| Calories From Fat | 64% | 23% |
| Cholesterol (mg) | 562 | 189 |
| Sodium (mg) | 791 | 437 |
| Fiber (gm) | .3 | 2 |

■ *Classic Compared – Fu Yung Gai*

## Time Estimate

| Hands On Unsupervised | | | | | | | | | |
|---|---|---|---|---|---|---|---|---|---|
| *Minutes* | 10 | 20 | 30 | 40 | 50 | 60 | 70 | 80 | 90 |

## Cost Estimate

| Low | Medium | Medium High | Celebration |
|---|---|---|---|

*Serves 4*

## INGREDIENTS

OMELET

6 ounces boneless chicken breast (170 gm),
finely diced

4 teaspoons freshly squeezed lemon juice (20 ml)

4 teaspoons rice wine vinegar (20 ml)

½ teaspoon freshly grated ginger root (2.5 ml)

2 green onions, chopped

¼ teaspoon freshly ground white pepper (1.25 ml)

3 ounces tofu (85 gm), finely diced

1 teaspoon extra light olive oil with a dash of
sesame oil (5 ml)

½ ounce butter (14 gm)

3 large eggs, beaten

1 tablespoon fresh chopped cilantro (15 ml)

4 cups steamed rice (944 ml)

SAUCE

½ cup chicken stock (118 ml) (recipe page 210)

2 tablespoons oyster sauce (30 ml)

2 teaspoons freshly squeezed lemon juice (10 ml)

1 teaspoon arrowroot (5 ml) mixed with
1 teaspoon water (5 ml)

## FIRST PREPARE

■ Marinate the diced chicken in 3 teaspoons
(15 ml) of the lemon juice, 3 teaspoons (15 ml) of
the rice wine vinegar, the green onions, ginger and
freshly ground white pepper for 20 minutes. (Do
try freshly grinding your pepper ... it is a remarkable experience for your olfactory sense!) Strain
out the chicken and set aside.

■ Marinate the tofu for 30 minutes in the remaining lemon juice and rice wine vinegar. Strain out
the tofu and set aside.

## NOW COOK

■ To make the sauce, heat the chicken stock,
oyster sauce and lemon juice in a small pan.
Remove the pan from the heat, add the arrowroot
paste, return to the heat and stir until thickened.
Set aside and keep warm.

■ To make the omelet, heat the olive oil in a non-
stick pan and quickly fry the marinated chicken
until white — about 1-2 minutes. Add the tofu
pieces so the flavors can mingle. Because the
pieces are the same size, the tofu will give you the
feeling of a lot more chicken. Cook just about a
minute, then remove the pan from the heat and
turn the chicken and tofu out onto a plate.

■ Wipe the pan, add the butter and heat until it
just begins to turn brown - this is the correct time
to add the eggs! Pour the beaten eggs into the pan
and stir quickly, spreading the eggs to cover the
entire pan (stirring will bring the butter taste into
the omelet).

■ When the eggs look fairly set, sprinkle the
chicken and tofu on top in a vertical line down the
center of the pan. Fold over each side as for a
regular omelet.

■ To Serve: Heat a plate in your oven. Gently
shake the omelet out of the pan onto the warmed
plate so that the fold is on the bottom and the egg
completely covers it. Pour your warm coating
sauce over the top and sprinkle with fresh cilantro.
What color! What aroma! Rice is the perfect
accompaniment to sop up every drop!

## Unusual Ingredients

TOFU - Did you know that for much of their history,
Asian people didn't use butter or cheese? Soybean
products have traditionally taken the place of dairy
foods in their diet (soybean milk is quite similar to
cow's milk).

If you're wondering where the connection to
tofu is in all this, tofu is really soybean curd. Yes,
I know, the thought of soybean curd as a substitute
for meat or dairy products takes some getting used
to. But tofu is inexpensive, high in protein, low in
saturated fats - and definitely worth the effort!

Tofu is available in two basic textures: hard
and soft. Pick the one that suits your fancy and
you're off - on a new minimax food adventure!

OYSTER SAUCE - Fu Yung Gai is really the dish
for excitement! First tofu and now oyster sauce!
Don't hesitate for even a moment: oyster sauce is
dark, tangy, mysterious ... well, almost inscrutable!
You'll want to add it as a seasoning to all sorts of
stir-fries and other dishes. Buy it in the bottle
from the Oriental section of your supermarket.

# QUICHE KIRKLAND

Depending, of course, upon how deep the quiche is, the nutrition risk often comes as much from the crust as from the filling.

In a classic, butter-made crust, there are about 21 grams of saturated fat, which runs about 63 percent of calories derived from fat. That really isn't good news for pie fanciers (like me!). However, here is an unusually tasty crust that goes a long way toward making this recipe an acceptable alternative: it's actually made from rice!

I always serve quiche with an attractive salad. (See Helpful Hints for the Split Salad recipe.)

## Nutritional Profile

| PER SERVING | CLASSIC | MINIMAX |
|---|---|---|
| Calories | 464 | 195 |
| Fat (gm) | 33 | 5 |
| Calories From Fat | 63% | 21% |
| Cholesterol (mg) | 122 | 44 |
| Sodium (mg) | 637 | 607 |
| Fiber (gm) | 1 | 2 |

■ *Classic Compared – Quiche a la Lorraine*

## Time Estimate

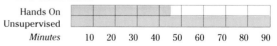

| Hands On | | | | | | | | |
|---|---|---|---|---|---|---|---|---|
| Unsupervised | | | | | | | | |

*Minutes*   10   20   30   40   50   60   70   80   90

## Cost Estimate

Low          Medium          Medium High          Celebration

*Serves 6*

## INGREDIENTS

PARMESAN RICE CRUST

2 cups cooked long grain rice (472 ml)

½ teaspoon salt (2.5 ml)

1 egg white, beaten

1 teaspoon low-salt soy sauce (5 ml)

¼ cup freshly grated Parmesan cheese (59 ml)

Freshly ground black pepper to taste

QUICHE FILLING

7 sun-dried tomato halves

½ cup matchstick-sliced Canadian bacon (118 ml)

1⅓ cups thinly sliced mushrooms (314 ml)

¼ cup diced green pepper (59 ml)

¼ cup diced red pepper (59 ml)

1 tablespoon fresh thyme leaves (15 ml)

1 tablespoon fresh chopped basil leaves (15 ml)

¼ teaspoon freshly grated nutmeg (1.25 ml)

Freshly ground black pepper to taste

¼ cup freshly grated Parmesan cheese (59 ml)

1 whole egg

4 egg whites

1½ cups skim milk (354 ml)

GARNISH

½ tablespoon fresh chopped basil (7 ml)

½ tablespoon fresh chopped parsley (7 ml)

Pinch of cayenne pepper

## PARMESAN RICE CRUST

■ In a medium bowl, mix together all the ingredients. Press into a 9 inch (23 cm) non-stick pie pan. Bake at 375°F (190°C) for 25 minutes, until it looks dry and just golden brown around the edges.

## QUICHE FILLING

■ Preheat the oven to 400°F (205°C).

■ Soak the sun-dried tomatoes in warm water until plump - about 10-15 minutes. Drain and finely dice.

■ In a medium skillet, saute the Canadian bacon, mushrooms, peppers and sundried tomatoes. Notice the great colors! Sprinkle with the thyme leaves, basil, nutmeg and black pepper. Cook the vegetables until they are just tender and their flavors blended - about 5 minutes.

■ Turn the cooked vegetables into a fine mesh strainer and drain any excess liquids. Turn them into the cooked pie crust and sprinkle with half of the Parmesan cheese.

■ In a medium bowl, beat together the egg yolk, egg whites and milk. Pour the custard on top of the vegetables. It should just cover them. Sprinkle with the remaining Parmesan cheese.

■ Bake at 400°F (205°C) for 25 minutes, or until the custard is set.

■ To Serve: Sprinkle the completed quiche with fresh basil, parsley and cayenne pepper. Cut into wedges and delight your guests!

## Helpful Hints and Observations

SPLIT SALAD - One hidden source of fat is salad dressings. The Split Salad method allows the dressing flavor to marinate the vegetables while lowering the calorie count.

A mixed salad can be broken down into two kinds of components: hard and soft. For the hard vegetables, include celery, tomatoes, sweet onion, radishes and carrots. Place the finely sliced hard vegetables in a bowl, add a dressing and marinate in the refrigerator for at least 3 hours or even overnight. When you are ready to make the salad, pour off the excess dressing (which can be saved and re-used, providing it is kept under refrigeration), add the marinated hard vegetables to the fresh greens and toss.

This method substantially lowers fat and restricts the more liberal use of thin dressings for a zesty, flavorful, salad!

CHEESE ... FRESHLY GRATED - I'm trying to reduce, but never eliminate, the fabulous taste of cheese which contains a high percentage of saturated fat, from some of my favorite dishes. I'm especially fond of the classic Parmesan cheese from Reggio Emilia, Italy, and its quite different American counterpart, Monterey Jack, from California. For the best taste, both must be grated as needed, and for this purpose, I use either the old fashioned, hand-cranked, rotary Mouli, from France or the "new" hand held cheese stroker (as I call it).

STICKY FINGERS - When preparing the rice crust, it helps to have a small bowl of cold water to moisten your fingers and avoid stickiness.

# FRENCH RAREBIT

*C*heese on toast? Well, not really! The Welsh make fine cheese and, like every cheese-producing area, they developed their own bread and cheese idea (Welsh Rarebit): a little beer, some mustard, a slice of toast. I've springboarded on this classic to produce my own recipe.

This is really a snack food for Fall or Winter weather: a firm "welcome home" when it's raw outside and the family has been burning energy. I've dropped the calories from 529 to 235 with only 6 grams of fat ... so it's within the limit!

## Nutritional Profile

| PER SERVING | CLASSIC | MINIMAX |
|---|---|---|
| Calories | 529 | 235 |
| Fat (gm) | 39 | 6 |
| Calories From Fat | 66% | 24% |
| Cholesterol (mg) | 170 | 19 |
| Sodium (mg) | 747 | 366 |
| Fiber (gm) | 1 | 2 |

■ *Classic Compared – Welsh Rarebit*

## Time Estimate

| | | | | | | | | | |
|---|---|---|---|---|---|---|---|---|---|
| Hands On | | | | | | | | | |
| Unsupervised | | | | | | | | | |
| *Minutes* | 10 | 20 | 30 | 40 | 50 | 60 | 70 | 80 | 90 |

## Cost Estimate

| Low | Medium | Medium High | Celebration |
|---|---|---|---|
| | | | |

*Serves 6*

## INGREDIENTS

1½ pounds yellow new potatoes (700 gm)
(the Yukon Gold variety is preferable)

¼ cup skim milk (59 ml)

¼ teaspoon freshly ground white pepper (1.25 ml)

¼ teaspoon freshly grated nutmeg (1.25 ml)

2 tablespoons white wine Worcestershire sauce (30 ml)

½ cup de-alcoholized beer (118 ml)

1 teaspoon dry mustard (5 ml)

1 cup dry Monterey Jack cheese (or another good grating cheese) (236 ml), finely grated

1 French baguette loaf (about 15 inches (38 cm) long), sliced in half horizontally, doughy center scooped out

Paprika

Fresh chopped parsley

## FIRST PREPARE

■ Bake the potatoes at 375°F (190°C) for 1 hour. Wrap them in a towel and gently squeeze from all sides to break up the flesh but taking care not to rupture the skin. Spoon the potato out of the skin and into a medium size mixing bowl and mash well. Save the skins for use in Cynthia's Skins (see Helpful Hints).

## NOW COOK

■ Return the hot potato to a warm saucepan over medium heat. Add the milk, white pepper and nutmeg and beat well to cream. (This is, by the way, the best way to make mashed potatoes. You may need ⅛ teaspoon (.6 ml) of salt, but you don't need added butter or fat.)

■ Now stir in the Worcestershire sauce, beer, dry mustard and finally ¾ cup (177 ml) of the cheese - mix well and taste it!

■ Pour the cheese sauce into the hollowed out baguette. Dust with the remaining cheese and a little paprika.

■ Broil until dappled brown. Dust with parsley and cut it in front of the gang!

## Helpful Hints and Observations

CYNTHIA'S SKINS - Cynthia is my food associate: the one who keeps tabs on how long everything takes to cook, how much it costs, and she knows, because she hunts down the best suppliers for all the produce we need.

During this simple test she suggested an idea with the leftover potato skins. We tried it and it worked so well we named it after her!

The recipe is as follows:

*Brush the leftover potato skins with a little beaten egg white and put them on a baking sheet. Sprinkle them with cayenne pepper to taste, and about 2 tablespoons (30 ml) of your favorite grated or crumbled cheese. Pop them under the broiler for 4 minutes and serve.*

## Unusual Ingredients

WHITE PEPPER - This was first used by Hippocrates in his prescriptions and was one of the first spices to be introduced into Europe. There are two kinds of pepper in commerce today: black and white. They are both fruit of the pepper plant. Black pepper is the result of drying the pepper berries, and has a greenish-black, wrinkled surface. White pepper is produced from the same seed, but the berries are immersed in water for several weeks, then freed from the skin and the fleshy part of the fruit. It is less pungent than black pepper.

YELLOW FINNISH POTATOES - "Yukon Gold": A king among A.C.T. potatoes! A hybrid developed and grown in the world-famous town of Wapato, Washington, this potato has a creamy, butter-flavored flesh. Use any potato available to you, but do ask your produce manager about getting this beauty. The Yellow Finnish Potato is just now starting to be available throughout the United States.

WHITE WINE WORCESTERSHIRE SAUCE - "Oh," with a sigh you say, "The yuppies of the world have finally triumphed!" "Oh," I reply, "not entirely!" This white wine version was not created so that yuppies could nip at cool canapes while tinkling glasses at power parties. It was actually created by Lee & Perrins because they felt the public was becoming more health conscious and needed a sauce to use with fish, chicken and pasta. "Well," you repeat, "isn't that yuppy style?" "O.K.," I shrug, quite happy to be associated with young upwardly mobile professionals at the age of 57!

# PEARS ROVER

My good friend Chef de Cuisine, Thierry Rautureau, chef/owner of "Rovers" in Seattle, Washington, worked with me to develop this idea. We "spring-boarded" off the famous French Bavarois dessert: a rich, egg yolk, heavy cream custard with a wonderful texture and taste. Our dish begins by using strained yogurt in place of the cream! It's a good dessert for a hot summer evening.

## Nutritional Profile

| PER SERVING | CLASSIC | MINIMAX |
|---|---|---|
| Calories | 299 | 225 |
| Fat (gm) | 16 | 1 |
| Calories From Fat | 47% | 5% |
| Cholesterol (mg) | 39 | 3 |
| Sodium (mg) | 148 | 94 |
| Fiber (gm) | 1 | 7 |

■ *Classic Compared – Pears Rover*

## Time Estimate

| Hands On | | | | | | | | | |
|---|---|---|---|---|---|---|---|---|---|
| Unsupervised | | | | 7 Hours | | | | | |
| *Minutes* | 10 | 20 | 30 | 40 | 50 | 60 | 70 | 80 | 90 |

## Cost Estimate

| Low | Medium | Medium High | Celebration |
|---|---|---|---|
| | | | |

*Serves 4*

## INGREDIENTS

4 sweet D'Anjou pears
2 egg whites
1¼ cups (295 ml) + ¼ teaspoon (1.25 ml) water
Dash of salt
1 envelope unflavored gelatin
1¼ cups strained yogurt (295 ml) (recipe page 210)
1 tablespoon Fireweed honey (15 ml)
1½ cups de-alcoholized white wine (354 ml)
Raspberry puree for garnish (optional)

## FIRST PREPARE

■ Peel and core pears, but leave them whole. Save peel and cores. Cover the pears with water into which you've squeezed a few drops of lemon juice, to prevent browning.

■ In a large bowl, mix egg whites with ¼ teaspoon (1.25 ml) water and a dash of salt (to help them hold their texture). Beat until just firm.

■ Sprinkle the gelatin on top of ¼ cup (59 ml) of water and dissolve for 3 minutes. Individual granules will soften. Stir into the yogurt and honey.

■ Lightly grease 4 individual dessert molds with oil.

## NOW COOK

■ Put the pear peels and cores in 1 cup (236 ml) of water. Bring to a boil and reduce to ½ cup (228 ml). Mash and strain, saving the pear juice.

■ Add the wine to the whole pears along with the strained pear juice and gently poach the pears until tender, about 20 to 30 minutes.

■ Remove the pears, strain the liquid and cook the juice down until you have ¼ cup (59 ml) pear "nectar". Stir into the strained yogurt.

■ Fold the whipped egg whites gently into the strained yogurt mixture.

■ Spoon 1 tablespoon (15 ml) yogurt mixture into each dessert mold.

■ Cut your perfectly poached pears into small pieces. Continue filling the molds by putting a layer of diced pears, topped with a last layer of the yogurt mixture.

■ Put in the refrigerator to chill.

■ Unmold on a serving plate by submerging the mold in boiling water for a few seconds. Invert on plate.

■ You can serve your Pears Rovers encircled in a ring of bright, red hearts! Simply beat some strained yogurt until thin. Pour a small amount in a ring around each individual serving. With an eye dropper, take some raspberry puree and squeeze small drops, evenly spaced, on top of the yogurt. Now take a toothpick or knife tip and drag it lightly through the center of the raspberry dots. You'll create small heart shapes: a good-hearted garnish!

## Helpful Hints and Observations

GELATIN - While preparing this recipe I really learned a lesson about gelatin and its qualities that I'd like to pass on here in detail. First of all, it's a natural protein found in young bones and connective tissues. The gelatin we use comes from pig skin (it's either that or gloves!). One envelope of gelatin equals 1 tablespoon (15 ml) (or four leaf gelatin). This will set 2 cups (472 ml) of liquid. Some fruit will stop the setting process and should be pre-cooked: kiwi, papaya and pineapple, for example. Essential Hint: Always sprinkle each envelope of gelatin on about ¼ cup (59 ml) cold water to soften before adding to hot liquids. Stir rapidly and don't ever allow it to boil. The moment it boils its setting quality is seriously reduced. When the liquid is totally clear (no flecks left) it is ready to add to your recipe and have the desired effect. P.S. Don't add too much unless you want to bounce the dessert on to your guests!

## Unusual Ingredients

PEARS - Did you know this fruit is a member of the rose family, along with apples, peaches, plums and cherries? There are several thousand varieties known, but only about one hundred grown commercially. The most common variety is the yellow bartlett, followed by bosc, and

D'anjou. Select pears that are just slightly soft. Pears are picked green and ripen off the tree.

# BREAD & BUTTER PUDDING

*B*read and Butter pudding is a British standard and many farmers have family recipes. Because of the lush pastures and temperate climate you get "cows upon cows". So it isn't surprising that buttered homemade bread is drowned in cream and eggs. I've tried hard to keep the "feelings" alive but reduce the fat. See what you think for yourself!

The big problem with desserts is that we insist upon whipped toppings, cream, or ice cream as garnish. This simply increases the fat problem (and our waistline) and sometimes covers the essential flavors and textures of an otherwise great idea. My suggestion is to leave it alone. Let it be. The custard gives it built-in moisture.

## Nutritional Profile

| PER SERVING | CLASSIC | MINIMAX |
|---|---|---|
| Calories | 600 | 191 |
| Fat (gm) | 26 | 4 |
| Calories From Fat | 38% | 19% |
| Cholesterol (mg) | 208 | 79 |
| Sodium (mg) | 564 | 159 |
| Fiber (gm) | 5 | 3 |

■ *Classic Compared – Bread & Butter Pudding*

## Time Estimate

| | | | | | | | | |
|---|---|---|---|---|---|---|---|---|
| Hands On | | | | | | | | |
| Unsupervised | | | | | | | | |

Minutes   10   20   30   40   50   60   70   80   90

## Cost Estimate

| | | | |
|---|---|---|---|
| Low | Medium | Medium High | Celebration |

*Serves 6*

## INGREDIENTS

8 tablespoons raisins (120 ml)

¼ cup wheat germ (59 ml)

2 large eggs

2 tablespoons brown sugar (30 ml)

Grated rind of 1 lemon

2 cups 2% milk (590 ml)

4 (1 ounce) (28 gm) slices whole wheat bread

4 (1 ounce) (28 gm) slices white bread

1 whole cinnamon stick, about 1½ inches (4.5 cm)
(½ teaspoon grated (2.5 ml))

## FIRST PREPARE

■ Wash the raisins and then toss with the wheat germ. Sprinkle half this mixture evenly into a shallow, 3 cup (708 ml) capacity, ovenproof baking or pie dish.

■ Make an egg custard: beat the eggs, 1 tablespoon (15 ml) of the brown sugar, milk and lemon rind together.

■ (With apologies to my homeland) Leave the crust on the bread and cut it in half diagonally.

■ Arrange the bread slices in the baking dish so that they overlap. Press down to mold into the dish and then carefully pour the egg custard so that it soaks into the bread.

■ Grate the whole cinnamon and sprinkle it over the top. I use a small coffee mill to finely powder a cinnamon stick.

■ Finally, sprinkle with remaining raisins and brown sugar.

## NOW COOK

■ Place the baking pan in a bain-marie and bake uncovered in a 350°F (180°C) oven for 30 to 35 minutes or until set. Serve warm.

## Helpful Hints and Observations

COATING THE RAISINS - I wanted to boost the nutritional value of the bread by adding ¼ cup (59 ml) of wheat germ and found that it's better when "stuck" to the damp raisins by tossing them together.

BAIN-MARIE - This is simply a baking dish half filled with water into which the bread pudding dish can fit. This water "jacket" protects the egg custard from curdling in the hot oven.

CRUSTS ON OR OFF? - The British have traditionally cut the crusts off their bread. This might have started as a means of cutting away mold, or removing travel soil. Whatever the reason, it doesn't make sense to throw out such good food, especially since it helps to provide added texture. So, I left them on and crouch under the table awaiting the mail!

BROWN OR WHITE BREAD? - Obviously, for best nutrition whole wheat bread is the right choice. However, it isn't as luscious as the white. So we compromised and went half and half but tossed in the wheat germ to compensate.

## Unusual Ingredients

WHEAT GERM - The heart of the wheat berry, the germinating center for the wheat plant. The best source of wheat germ is in whole wheat products, such as bulgur or flour. Wheat germ has a very high oil content and can become rancid quickly. It is best to purchase untoasted wheat germ and keep it refrigerated in an airtight container. Wheat germ also freezes well and can be bought in larger quantities this way. Eat wheat germ sprinkled on your breakfast cereal or use it as a flour extender in any recipe for making whole wheat bread. Try replacing half the flour with wheat germ when making breadings for chicken.

# JOYCE BROTHERS' COMFORT CUP

$\mathcal{D}$r. Joyce Brothers has provided all of us with a great deal of good advice and comfort over the years. I created this dish as a comfort to her, based on a list of her favorite foods. The result: a very successful dessert for a smashing lady who, incidentally, is extremely interested in eating Minimax style.

Serve in tall glasses with long spoons, or wide glass coupe dishes and short spoons! Your choice!

## Nutritional Profile

| PER SERVING | CLASSIC | MINIMAX |
|---|---|---|
| Calories | 316 | 243 |
| Fat (gm) | 19 | 0.3 |
| Calories From Fat | 53% | 1% |
| Cholesterol (mg) | 65 | 0 |
| Sodium (mg) | 126 | 65 |
| Fiber (gm) | 0.2 | 2 |

■ *Classic Compared – Rice Pudding*

## Time Estimate

| | | |
|---|---|---|
| Hands On | | |
| Unsupervised | 2 Hours | |
| *Minutes* | 10  20  30  40  50  60  70  80  90 | |

## Cost Estimate

| Low | Medium | Medium High | Celebration |
|---|---|---|---|

*Serves 6*

## INGREDIENTS

3 cups (708 ml) + 2 tablespoons (30 ml) mango nectar

4 ounces dried mango slices (113 gm), finely diced

1 tablespoon cornstarch (15 ml)

1 cup uncooked short grain pearl rice (236 ml)

3 cups water (708 ml)

⅜ teaspoon freshly ground nutmeg (2 ml)

¾ cup liquid egg substitute (177 ml) (I prefer Fleischmann's Egg Beaters)

¼ cup castor sugar (59 ml)

## FIRST PREPARE

■ Heat 1 cup (236 ml) of the mango nectar, pour it over the diced mango and soak for 2 hours. Strain, reserving the mango pieces and soaking liquid separately.

■ Stir the cornstarch and 2 tablespoons (30 ml) of the mango nectar together to make a paste.

## NOW COOK

■ Place the rice, 2 cups (472 ml) of the water and 1 cup (236 ml) of the mango nectar in a pressure cooker. Stir in ¼ teaspoon (1.25 ml) of the nutmeg, put the lid on and cook for 8 minutes from the time it begins to steam.

If you don't have a pressure cooker, put the rice, 2 cups (472 ml) of the water and 1 cup (236 ml) of the mango nectar in a saucepan, bring to a boil, reduce heat and simmer until the rice is cooked through - about 25 minutes.

■ In a medium sized saucepan, bring the remaining water to a boil. Set a round copper bowl in the saucepan, giving a double-boiler effect. Now pour in the egg substitute, the remaining mango nectar and the sugar. Beat until the consistency is thick and creamy, like a custard.

■ Slowly whisk the cornstarch paste into the mango custard, bring to a boil and stir until thickened. Add ⅛ teaspoon (.6 ml) of the nutmeg.

■ Spoon the cooked rice mixture into a large measuring cup. Add the custard and half of the soaked and drained mango pieces.

■ To Serve: Pour the custard into six (6 ounce or 170 gm) glasses. Top with the remaining mango pieces and 2 tablespoons (30 ml) of the reserved mango soaking liquid. Sprinkle with the remaining nutmeg and enjoy!

## Helpful Hints and Observations

COPPER AND ITS EFFECT ON EGG SUBSTITUTE - I feel that a good 10 inch (25 cm) copper bowl is an essential Minimax kitchen tool because I use egg whites so often to give added volume and texture - without a gram of fat!

The reason why copper works so well with liquid egg substitutes is because they are made predominantly of egg white. In this recipe I used a copper bowl over hot water as a double boiler, in which I had the space to use a whisk, and it worked wonderfully.

Also, please try to use Fleischmann's Egg Beaters. We did some comparative tests with other yolkless products and didn't think they were nearly as good.

## Unusual Ingredients

MANGOES - Now here's a powerful fruit for your Minimax A.C.T. (aroma, color and texture): not only do mangoes provide a gorgeous, orange color for your dishes, but few fruits provide more Vitamin A per serving. In fact fresh mangoes provide 30 percent of the Recommended Dietary Allowance of Vitamin A, along with the full allowance of Vitamin C! Dried mangoes will give you the same nutritional punch.

At the supermarket you'll know the ripe mango by its color: deep green with touches of yellow and red. It should also yield just lightly to the touch.

Mango nectar is available canned.

WHOLE NUTMEG - Don't miss the olfactory (and taste) satisfaction that comes from grating whole fresh nutmeg into your dishes! The small nut is quite easily ground if you buy a small instrument that looks a lot like a pepper grinder - just a twist, and you'll be able to enjoy its full, luxurious flavor. As you'll see throughout this book, I use freshly grated nutmeg often, even in my mashed potatoes!

CASTOR SUGAR - See Unusual Ingredients, page 193.

# GINGER PUMPKIN CUPS

This delicious dessert is the perfect accompaniment to the special *Thanksgiving Turkey & Stuffing Pie* that you'll find the recipe for on page 80.

But don't be restricted to enjoying Ginger Pumpkin Cups just one day a year - they're great any time!

good, aren't they? I saw them on graham kerr...

## Nutritional Profile

| PER SERVING | CLASSIC | MINIMAX |
|---|---|---|
| Calories | 417 | 107 |
| Fat (gm) | 18 | 2 |
| Calories From Fat | 39% | 13% |
| Cholesterol (mg) | 99 | 18 |
| Sodium (mg) | 276 | 87 |
| Fiber (gm) | 4 | 1 |

■ *Classic Compared – Pumpkin Pie*

## Time Estimate

| Hands On Unsupervised | | | | | | | | | |
|---|---|---|---|---|---|---|---|---|---|
| *Minutes* | 10 | 20 | 30 | 40 | 50 | 60 | 70 | 80 | 90 |

## Cost Estimate

| Low | Medium | Medium High | Celebration |
|---|---|---|---|

## INGREDIENTS

1 package filo dough
Extra light olive oil with a dash of sesame oil
¼ cup brown sugar (59 ml)
1 cup non-fat milk (236 ml)
1 envelope unflavored gelatin
1 teaspoon ginger (5 ml)
1 large egg yolk
1 (1 pound) can solid-pack pumpkin (450 gm)
½ teaspoon freshly grated cinnamon (2.5 ml)
½ teaspoon freshly grated nutmeg (2.5 ml)
3 large egg whites
¼ cup granulated sugar (59 ml)

## FIRST PREPARE THE FILO CUPS

■ Lay one sheet of filo dough out flat on a cutting board and brush with oil. Cover with a second, third and fourth sheet, brushing each layer with oil.

■ Cut the layered dough into 12 (4 inch or 10 cm) circles. Gently brush the top layer with oil.

■ Fit the layered filo dough circles, oiled-side down, into muffin tins to form cups. Gently brush again with oil.

## NOW COOK

■ Preheat the oven to 400°F (250°C). Bake the filo cups in the preheated oven until browned - about 10 minutes. Remove from tins and cool on a wire rack. These should be baked as close as possible to the serving time as filo has a tendency to soften with time.

■ In a small saucepan, combine the brown sugar and ¼ cup (59 ml) of the milk. Sprinkle the gelatin and ginger evenly over the surface and let soften for 5 minutes. Put the saucepan on low heat and cook, stirring constantly, for 5 to 6 minutes or until the gelatin and sugar dissolve. Remove from the heat.

■ In a small bowl, beat the egg yolk and remaining milk together. Slowly whisk in the hot gelatin mixture then pour it back into the saucepan. Stir over low heat for 2 to 3 minutes or until slightly thickened. Be careful not to let the mixture boil or it will curdle.

■ Transfer to a large bowl. Blend in the pumpkin, cinnamon and nutmeg. Cover and refrigerate for 20 to 30 minutes, stirring occasionally, until the mixture mounds slightly when dropped from a spoon.

■ In a large bowl, beat the egg whites at moderate speed until foamy. Slowly beat in the granulated sugar. Beat at moderately high speed until the whites hold soft peaks. Fold the egg whites into the pumpkin mixture and refrigerate for 30 minutes.

■ Not more than 1 hour ahead of serving time, spoon the ginger pumpkin filling into the filo cups (because of the pastry's tendency to soften). Refrigerate until ready to serve.

## Unusual Ingredients

FILO DOUGH - This pastry is the result of combining flour and water and kneading, resting and stretching it in such a way that it becomes tissue-thin. The result, when you use it in your cooking, is flaky and delicious. Fortunately, you don't have to make filo dough yourself. The thin sheets are available packaged in the fresh or frozen section of your supermarket. It might also be named fillo, phyllo, yukka, brik or malsouka. Don't put off trying it - filo dough is so easy to use that you'll find yourself inventing many recipes to include it!

# LONG WHITE CLOUD *(New Zealand Christmas Pudding)*

*C*hristmas Day in New Zealand can be really hot, with a temperature of 90°F (32°C) on occasions. It is, after all, their summer. When Treena and I lived there (from 1958 to 1966) we had midwinter traditions in a midsummer climate. So we changed our Christmas Pudding to Long White Cloud, which is part of the English translation of the native Maori word for New Zealand, Aotearoa - the land of the long white cloud!

This recipe is a very lean edition of the British classic, which combines dried fruit with beef suet (the creamy fat that surrounds the kidney), brandy, heavy beer and eggs!

It is essential to let the pudding steam through on a very hot platter. We usually serve the apricot sauce warm, from a sauce boat at the table.

## Nutritional Profile

| PER SERVING | CLASSIC | MINIMAX |
|---|---|---|
| Calories | 1189 | 245 |
| Fat (gm) | 56 | 2 |
| Calories From Fat | 43% | 8% |
| Cholesterol (mg) | 145 | 2 |
| Sodium (mg) | 483 | 86 |
| Fiber (gm) | 7 | 4 |

■ *Classic Compared – Plum Pudding*

## Time Estimate

| Hands On Unsupervised | | | | | | 10 Hours | | | | |
|---|---|---|---|---|---|---|---|---|---|---|
| Minutes | 10 | 20 | 30 | 40 | 50 | 60 | 70 | 80 | 90 |

## Cost Estimate

| | | | |
|---|---|---|---|
| Low | Medium | Medium High | Celebration |

*Serves 12*

## INGREDIENTS

PUDDING

½ cup minced dried apricots (118 ml)

½ cup minced dried peaches (118 ml)

½ cup minced raisins (118 ml) (I prefer the "flame" variety)

½ cup minced dried figs (118 ml)

1 (16 ounce) can plums (454 gm) syrup packed

⅓ cup sliced almonds (78 ml)

1 large Granny Smith Apple, peeled, cored and finely chopped

2 tablespoons molasses (30 ml)

½ teaspoon freshly ground cloves (2.5 ml)

½ teaspoon freshly ground mace (2.5 ml)

½ teaspoon freshly ground cinnamon (2.5 ml)

2 teaspoons baking powder (10 ml)

½ cup all-purpose flour (118 ml)

⅛ teaspoon extra light olive oil with a dash of sesame oil (.6 ml)

TOPPING

1 pint frozen non-fat vanilla yogurt (472 ml)

2 (16 ounce) cans apricot halves (454 gm each)

¼ teaspoon freshly grated nutmeg (1.25 ml)

1 teaspoon arrowroot (5 ml)

## NOW COOK ON CHRISTMAS EVE

■ Combine the apricots, peaches, raisins and figs. It's really important to get them completely mixed up. Drain the can of plums, reserving the syrup. Add the almonds and plums to the dried fruit.

■ Stir in the apples, molasses and the spices. Shape into a ball and put the mixture onto a board.

■ In a small bowl, sift the baking powder and flour together, then sift again over the fruit mixture. Chop it all together with a broad knife or scraper, until it's thoroughly combined. Now drizzle in the reserved plum syrup, chopping as you go.

■ Scoop the pudding mixture into a slightly oiled bowl that will fit into the pan you use for steaming. Press down lightly, allowing some room for the baking powder to expand.

■ Place wax paper covered with a light cotton towel over the top of the bowl. Tie this down with string. Now tie the tails of the cotton material over the top of the bowl to give you a nice handle!

■ Put the bowl in a Dutch oven, or any heavy saucepan with a lid. Add water to reach half-way up the sides of the bowl. Drop a dozen marbles in

the water and put the lid on. Turn the heat to high and cook for 2 hours. If the water boils away, the marbles will start to clatter, giving you a noisy reminder to add more water!

■ Spoon the hot, cooked pudding mixture into a lightly oiled 9½ x 5 inch (24 x 13 cm) loaf pan. Press the mixture down into the pan, cover with plastic wrap and refrigerate overnight.

■ In another loaf pan of the same size, pack the frozen yogurt until it's a layer 1 inch (2.5 cm) thick. Put the pan in the freezer. The pudding and its topping are now the same size.

## BEFORE SERVING ON CHRISTMAS DAY

■ Drain the apricot syrup into a small bowl. Puree the apricots in a food processor, or blender, reserving 5 halves for garnish. Pour the puree and syrup into a medium sized saucepan set over medium heat. Stir in the nutmeg.

■ Make a paste of the arrowroot with 2 teaspoons (10 ml) of the apricot syrup and stir into the sauce. Bring to a boil, stirring until the sauce thickens. Remove from the heat.

■ The pudding must warm before serving. Heat an ovenproof serving platter in a 500°F (260°C) oven for 10 minutes. Remove and put on a baking rack on top of the stove burner on medium heat.

■ Unmold the pudding onto the hot serving platter. Unmold the frozen yogurt and place it on top of the pudding. Garnish or decorate with the reserved apricot halves.

■ To Serve: Place a ½ inch (1.5 cm) slice of the Long White Cloud on a plate. Drizzle 2 tablespoons (30 ml) of sauce on the side. Garnish with a small branch of holly (just don't eat the berries!).

### Helpful Hints and Observations

DRIED FRUIT - Look for brands or varieties without sulfites if possible.

THE YOGURT - Most frozen non-fat yogurt comes in tubs, so please scoop it out quickly while frozen and pack it down into the mold. Press down hard to pop any air bubbles (this will make it easier to slice) and pop it back into the deep freeze to get really hard. Of course, you could find a block of frozen yogurt that would save all the trouble!

### Unusual Ingredients

APRICOTS - Fresh, canned, or dried, this golden fruit offers a bonus: carotene. Studies continue to link carotene to cancer prevention. They also have lots of potassium and iron.

# NEW BOOK PUDDING

*The classic recipe for Old Book Pudding, from one of my old television shows, was a real nutritional "shocker"! This Minimax version brings you the same luscious flavor with a greatly diminished risk factor. But it's the "toothpaste pump" idea that makes it truly memorable - see for yourself!*

## Nutritional Profile

| PER SERVING | CLASSIC | MINIMAX |
|---|---|---|
| Calories | 865 | 300 |
| Fat (gm) | 76 | 7 |
| Calories From Fat | 79% | 20% |
| Cholesterol (mg) | 199 | 1 |
| Sodium (mg) | 131 | 240 |
| Fiber (gm) | 7 | 3 |

■ *Classic Compared – Old Book Pudding*

## Time Estimate

Hands On
Unsupervised

*Minutes* 10 20 30 40 50 60 70 80 90

## Cost Estimate

Low          Medium          Medium High          Celebration

*Serves 4*

## INGREDIENTS

¾ cup strained yogurt (177 ml) (recipe page 210)

2½ ounces dry coconut macaroons (71 gm), crumbled in a food processor

8 tablespoons raisin puree (120 ml) (see Helpful Hints)

4 drops almond extract

¼ teaspoon ground cardamom (1.25 ml)

2 tablespoons cocoa (30 ml)

1 tablespoon finely chopped almonds (15 ml)

6 egg whites

Pinch of salt

COCOA SAUCE

5 tablespoons water (75 ml)

4 tablespoons brown sugar (60 ml)

3 tablespoons cocoa (45 ml)

1 tablespoon arrowroot (15 ml)

GARNISH

Plain yogurt

Lime slices

Fresh mint leaves

## NOW COOK

■ In a large bowl, stir together the strained yogurt and macaroon crumbs. Add the raisin puree, almond extract, cardamom, cocoa and chopped almonds.

■ Beat the egg whites with a pinch of salt and a drop or two of water to help them whip and retain volume.

■ Gently fold a third of the egg whites into the yogurt mixture, then fold in the rest.

■ Put the mixture into a round mold (such as a recycled, 1 inch (2.5 cm) diameter toothpaste pump, see Helpful Hints) and freeze until solid - about 2 hours.

■ To Make the Cocoa Sauce: Pour the water into a small saucepan. Over medium heat, add the brown sugar and cocoa and stir until dissolved.

■ Take out a tablespoon (15 ml) of the cocoa sauce and mix with the arrowroot to form a paste. Remove the saucepan from the heat, add the arrowroot paste, return to the heat, and stir until thickened.

■ To Serve: Remove the pudding from the mold and slice into ½ inch (1.5 cm) pieces. Pour enough cocoa sauce to just cover a small plate. Spoon a little plain yogurt into a piping bag. Pipe thin, straight lines across the cocoa sauce, about 1 inch (2.5 cm) apart. Lightly drag a toothpick back and forth, at right angles to the yogurt lines, to make a "feathered" design. Lay New Book Pudding slices on top and garnish with the fresh lime slices and mint leaves.

## Helpful Hints and Observations

RAISIN PUREE - Put ½ cup (118 ml) raisins in ½ cup (118 ml) hot water, let sit for 30 minutes, then place in a food processor or blender and whiz until smooth.

TOOTHPASTE PUMP MOLD - To make this innovative pudding mold, it's most helpful if you wait until the toothpaste pump is empty! Then saw off the "delivery end" and wash well. The plunger end can be pushed down to expose the iced pudding so that it can be cut off in neat disks.

## Unusual Ingredients

MACAROONS - Fresh from the oven, these cookies are chewy, coconut confections. You'll find them at many bakeries or pre-packaged at the grocery store. Please note that we need them completely dry for New Book Pudding. If they aren't dry enough to crumble, you can bake them in a 200°F (95°C) oven.

COCOA POWDER - I want you to imagine for a moment, a tall, brown tree that blooms in red flowers all year long. The flowers ripen into yellowish fruit. Cut the fruit open and there are the seeds that are harvested to produce chocolate and all its products. The seeds are roasted, cracked to remove their hard shell, and then ground into a thick paste called chocolate liquor. When the cocoa butter is pressed out of the chocolate liquor, you are left with cocoa powder. Keep cocoa powder in a cool, dry place in a tightly closed container. It will probably last about six months as long as no moisture is allowed to make it lumpy or discolored.

# STEAMED MARMALADE PUDDING

$\mathcal{I}$ created this dish in 1987 on a visit to Scotland. It went down very well but has since been through several revisions to reduce the fat levels, and, as a result, the calories. It still has lots of appeal for a cold, blustery winter's day ... or even a hot summer's eve with the air conditioning set very low!

I always serve this at the table and cut it into four handsome wedges, or eight, if your meal has been substantial. The sauce should bring you rave reviews!

## Nutritional Profile

| PER SERVING | CLASSIC | MINIMAX |
|---|---|---|
| Calories | 523 | 241 |
| Fat (gm) | 38 | 9 |
| Calories From Fat | 65% | 34% |
| Cholesterol (mg) | 254 | 27 |
| Sodium (mg) | 213 | 196 |
| Fiber (gm) | 5 | 3 |

■ *Classic Compared – Steamed Fruit Suet Pudding*

## Time Estimate

| Hands On | | | | | | | | | |
|---|---|---|---|---|---|---|---|---|---|
| Unsupervised | | | | | | | | | |
| *Minutes* | 10 | 20 | 30 | 40 | 50 | 60 | 70 | 80 | 90 |

## Cost Estimate

| Low | Medium | Medium High | Celebration |
|---|---|---|---|

*Serves 8*

## INGREDIENTS

PUDDING

6 tablespoons (90 ml) + 1 teaspoon (5 ml) margarine

4 tablespoons Seville orange marmalade (60 ml)

¼ cup brown sugar (59 ml)

1 egg, lightly beaten

1 teaspoon vanilla (5 ml)

1¼ cups all-purpose flour (295 ml)

1½ teaspoons baking powder (7.5 ml)

¾ cup non-fat milk (177 ml)

½ cup unsweetened frozen raspberries (118 ml), unthawed

RASPBERRY AND ORANGE SAUCE

1 cup unsweetened frozen raspberries (236 ml), unthawed

¼ cup strained yogurt (59 ml) (recipe page 210)

¼ cup freshly squeezed orange juice (59 ml)

## PUDDING

■ Lightly grease a 6 cup (1.4 L) capacity pudding bowl with 1 teaspoon (5 ml) of the margarine.

■ Spoon the orange marmalade into the bottom of the bowl, smoothing it out evenly to cover about a third of the inner surface. This will eventually be the cap on the pudding.

■ In a mixer bowl, cream together the brown sugar and the remaining margarine.

■ Beat in the egg and vanilla.

■ Sift the flour and baking powder into another large bowl. Now combine this with the pudding mixture. Pour in a third of the milk, stir until completely combined, then repeat until all of the milk is added. Please don't overwork it. The fewer stirs, the better the eventual texture.

■ Carefully spoon a third of the pudding mixture on top of the marmalade and sprinkle about 8 raspberries on top of that. Repeat the layers, finishing with a layer of pudding mixture.

■ Cover the pudding with a sheet of greaseproof paper and a 14 inch (35 cm) square piece of cotton dishcloth. Place a rubber band over the lip of the bowl, so that it holds the layers tight, and, finally, secure this with a piece of string. Now bring the opposite corners of the dishcloth over the top of the bowl and tie them together. This creates a marvelous handle for fishing the pudding bowl out of the steamer.

■ Place the pudding bowl in a large pan of boiling water. The water should come half way up the sides of the pudding bowl.

■ Cover and steam gently over medium heat on top of the stove for 1½ hours. Keep the water at a gentle boil.

■ Let it set for 5 minutes before unmolding. To unmold, run a thin-bladed knife between the pudding and the bowl. Put a plate on the top, hold it firmly in place and turn the bowl upside down. The pudding should drop neatly onto plate.

## RASPBERRY AND ORANGE SAUCE

■ Push the raspberries through a fine sieve. Mix in the yogurt and orange juice and serve on the side.

## Helpful Hints and Observations

FRESH VS FROZEN RASPBERRIES - I've used frozen raspberries for two reasons. The best (non-sugared) frozen varieties in which each berry is individually frozen, are, in my opinion, better flavored than fringe season fresh. Let me hasten to add that prime season fresh berries cannot be beaten.

The second reason is that when added in their solid frozen form, they seem better able to retain their texture and flavor.

A THIRD AT A TIME - I always add the dry and moist ingredients alternately and a third at a time. It eliminates lumps and helps to keep the mixture light.

## Unusual Ingredients

SEVILLE ORANGE MARMALADE - In recorded time, there are three basic ways fruit has been cooked to help resist spoilage (and taste wonderful!): Preserves, which incorporate the whole fruit; Jams, in which the fruit is chopped; and Marmalades and Jellies, where small pieces of fruit, or the fruit's juice, are mixed into a sweet gel.

I recommend an imported Scottish Seville Orange Marmalade for this recipe. The Seville orange is a very sour Mediterranean orange that is considered the cream of the crop for marmalade. And then you'll have a few tablespoons left to serve with your toast at tea time.

# BLACKBERRY ZABAGLIONE

*𝒯his dessert has lived for years in my memory, regardless of how often I try to beat it into submission!*

*Italian in origin, it is said that the first zabaglione was invented by accident in the 17th century, by a chef who inadvertently poured wine into an egg custard. Well, in the 20th century, chefs purposely pour enough liquors into this dessert to create about a 40 percent alcohol content custard. For each egg yolk you add 1 ounce (28 gm) brandy and 1 ounce (28 gm) Marsala which, with the sugar, is like a superior egg nog.*

*But times have changed and now I've made a zabaglione that has a great new taste and color ... and doesn't haunt my dreams!*

## Nutritional Profile

| PER SERVING | CLASSIC | MINIMAX |
|---|---|---|
| Calories | 296 | 169 |
| Fat (gm) | 27 | 0 |
| Calories From Fat | 83% | 1% |
| Cholesterol (mg) | 294 | 0 |
| Sodium (mg) | 30 | 87 |
| Fiber (gm) | 0 | 3 |

■ *Classic Compared – Zabaglione*

## Time Estimate

| Hands On | | | | | | | | | |
|---|---|---|---|---|---|---|---|---|---|
| Unsupervised | | | | | | | | | |

*Minutes*    10   20   30   40   50   60   70   80   90

## Cost Estimate

| Low | Medium | Medium High | Celebration |
|---|---|---|---|

*Serves 6*

## INGREDIENTS

2½ cups frozen blackberries (590 ml), thawed

1½ cups de-alcoholized white wine (354 ml)

3 tablespoons real maple syrup (45 ml)

¼ teaspoon almond extract (1.25 ml)

¼ teaspoon vanilla (1.25 ml)

2 tablespoons cornstarch (30 ml) mixed with
¼ cup de-alcoholized white wine (59 ml)

1 cup water (236 ml)

1 cup egg substitute (236 ml), (I prefer
Fleischmann's Egg Beaters)

½ cup castor sugar (118 ml)

## FIRST PREPARE

■  Spoon 1½ cups (354 ml) of the blackberries into six (6 ounce or 170 gm) wine glasses. They should each be half full.

■  Push the remaining blackberries through a sieve to yield 8 tablespoons (120 ml) of puree.

## NOW COOK

■  In a saucepan, bring the de-alcoholized white wine to a boil. Add the maple syrup, almond extract and vanilla. Stir in the cornstarch paste, bring to a boil and stir.

■  In a medium sized saucepan, bring the water to a boil. Set a round copper bowl in the saucepan, giving a double-boiler effect and reduce the heat to a simmer. Now combine the egg substitute and castor sugar in the bowl and beat until the consistency is thick and creamy, like a frothy pudding.

■  Slowly whisk the syrup mixture into the sweetened egg substitute. Add 6 tablespoons (90 ml) of the blackberry puree and beat well over heat to combine.

■  Pour the custard over the blackberries in the wine glasses. Top with the remaining blackberry puree and serve hot. (Whole wheat cookies are entirely optional!)

## Helpful Hints and Observations

WHAT'S SO SPECIAL ABOUT COPPER? - See Helpful Hints, page 183.

## Unusual Ingredients

ALMOND EXTRACT - An extract with a murky past. You see, this delightful liquid flavoring is from the oil of the bitter almond (did you know there were two types of almonds: bitter and sweet?). And in its concentrated form, almond oil contains a poisonous substance, called prussic acid. But don't worry. When the oil is diluted with water and alcohol, it is transformed into this quite harmless baking ingredient.

BLACKBERRIES - If you have the opportunity, and it's a bright midsummer day, do put on a straw hat and wander down to your nearest blackberry patch and pluck plump, juicy berries straight off the brambles. Failing this you can also put on your straw hat and wander off to the nearest grocery store where frozen blackberries are readily available.

CASTOR SUGAR - Castor (also spelled caster) is basically just extra fine granulated sugar. You can find it labeled superfine in some markets. Since the grains are so small, they dissolve almost immediately when added to liquids. Castor sugar is a lovely ingredient for desserts where you want a very smooth texture. If you can't find castor sugar, regular granulated sugar will taste the same.

Castor is also the name given to a glass or silver shaker used to dispense fine sugar at the table. The dispenser has fine holes, hence the need for finely granulated sugar.

# CARROT CAKE

*𝒯his recipe is a perfect example of springboarding. It comes from an in-flight meal experience had by Chef David Burke of "The River Café" in New York City. He made changes to suit his special needs by making a hot, cream cheese souffle topping. I subsequently made my own changes and added a spiced, creamy apple butter topping.*

*I like to split the dish and serve half the cake hot with the topping and leave the rest of the cake for simple snacking. If you have 12 people to serve, just double the topping.*

## Nutritional Profile

| PER SERVING | CLASSIC | MINIMAX |
|---|---|---|
| Calories | 884 | 298 |
| Fat (gm) | 51 | 5 |
| Calories From Fat | 51% | 15% |
| Cholesterol (mg) | 305 | 36 |
| Sodium (mg) | 416 | 215 |
| Fiber (gm) | 3 | 4 |

■ *Classic Compared – Carrot Cake with Cream Cheese Souffle Topping*

## Time Estimate

| | | | | | | | | | |
|---|---|---|---|---|---|---|---|---|---|
| Hands On | | | | | | | | | |
| Unsupervised | | | | | | | | | |
| *Minutes* | 10 | 20 | 30 | 40 | 50 | 60 | 70 | 80 | 90 |

## Cost Estimate

| Low | Medium | Medium High | Celebration |
|---|---|---|---|

*Serves 12*

## INGREDIENTS

CAKE

½ cup raisins (118 ml), preferably flame seedless

1¾ cups all-purpose flour (413 ml)

⅔ cup whole wheat flour (157 ml)

2 teaspoons baking soda (10 ml)

1½ teaspoons cinnamon (7.5 ml)

1 tablespoon allspice (15 ml)

½ teaspoon freshly ground nutmeg (2.5 ml)

⅛ teaspoon freshly ground salt (.6 ml)

¾ cup firmly packed brown sugar (177 ml)

3 tablespoons extra light olive oil with a dash of sesame oil (45 ml)

2 eggs

⅔ cup buttermilk (157 ml)

2 teaspoons vanilla (10 ml)

1½ cups coarsely shredded carrot (590 ml)

1 (8 ounce) can crushed, unsweetened pineapple (227 gm)

TOPPING

½ cup apple butter (118 ml) (recipe page 169)

½ cup strained yogurt (118 ml) (recipe page 210)

2 tablespoons pure maple syrup (30 ml)

## FIRST PREPARE

■ Put the raisins in a small bowl, cover with water, and soak until soft and plump - about 10 to 15 minutes.

■ Preheat the oven to 350°F (180°C).

## NOW COOK

■ In a large bowl, combine the flours, baking soda, cinnamon, allspice, nutmeg and salt. Stir well and set aside.

■ In a large bowl, mix the brown sugar and oil. Add the eggs, one at a time, beating well with a wire whisk after each addition. Stir in the buttermilk and the vanilla.

■ Stir in the flour mixture. Add the carrots, raisins and pineapple.

■ Lightly grease an ovenproof skillet or round cake pan 11 inches (28 cm) in diameter. Pour in the batter and shake to distribute evenly. Place the skillet on the middle rack of the preheated oven and bake for 20 minutes. Turn out on a wire rack to cool.

■ The Topping: In a small bowl, mix the apple butter, strained yogurt and maple syrup.

■ Serve a wedge of the hot carrot cake with 3 tablespoons (45 ml) of the topping spooned over the top and garnish with a sprig of fresh mint.

## Helpful Hints and Observations

APPLE BUTTER - I like to think that my apple butter is the best (certainly from a Minimax point of view) but you can easily purchase it, ready-made, and cut out a great deal of cooking time. On the other hand, you can also make a large batch when Winesaps or Rome apples (and good friends) are in prime season! Apple butter freezes very well in good freezer bags.

# CHEESECAKE WITH FIGS

$\mathcal{W}$ell of course, when it comes right down to it, cheesecake is the number one, knock down, drag out, temptation. We all know it's loaded ... but what to do about it? Can anything compete? We've done our part but the real answer to the question is your own taste — combined with your own will to change! Have fun.

Any amount of fresh fruit served on the side is delicious. Fresh figs in season would be wonderful but for my taste, fresh kiwi fruit peeled and cut in half, lengthwise, is the perfect garnish.

## Nutritional Profile

| PER SERVING | CLASSIC | MINIMAX |
|---|---|---|
| Calories | 806 | 210 |
| Fat (gm) | 62 | 3 |
| Calories From Fat | 69% | 11% |
| Cholesterol (mg) | 290 | 28 |
| Sodium (mg) | 546 | 291 |
| Fiber (gm) | 0 | 4 |

■ *Classic Compared – New York Cheesecake*

## Time Estimate

| Hands On | |
| Unsupervised | |
| *Minutes* | 10  20  30  40  50  60  70  80  90 |

## Cost Estimate

| Low | Medium | Medium High | Celebration |
|---|---|---|---|

*Serves 16*

## INGREDIENTS

½ cup graham cracker crumbs (118 ml)

1¼ cups dried white figs (295 ml)

¼ cup water (59 ml)

2 envelopes unflavored gelatin

2 tablespoons freshly squeezed lemon juice (30 ml)

½ cup evaporated skim milk (118 ml)

1 whole egg

⅓ cup light brown sugar (78 ml)

2 cups low-fat cottage cheese (472 ml)

1 teaspoon vanilla extract (5 ml)

5 kiwi fruit, peeled and cut in half lengthwise

## FIRST PREPARE THE CRUST

■ Drop the crumbs and figs into a food processor. Blend until the ingredients are just sticking together. If you don't have an electronic assistant, you can chop the fruit to a pulp and stir the two together until moist and dough-like.

■ Press the mixture into the bottom, and halfway up the sides, of a lightly greased 9 inch (23 cm) springform pan. Keep a small bowl of cold water handy to keep your hands "non-stick".

## NOW PREPARE THE FILLING

■ Sprinkle the gelatin onto the water and stir gently. Add the lemon juice.

■ In a small saucepan, bring the milk to a boil, stirring constantly so that it doesn't stick to the bottom of the pan. Pour the milk into the softened gelatin.

■ Put the gelatin mixture into a blender. Add the egg, brown sugar, cottage cheese and vanilla. Blend until there are no lumps, yet the texture should look and feel somewhat "grainy."

■ Pour the filling into the crust. In order not to disturb the crust, you can pour it onto the rounded side of a wooden spoon held over the center of the crust.

■ Chill for 1-2 hours.

■ Garnish with the kiwi fruit.

## Helpful Hints and Observations

PRESSING IN THE CRUST - I've spent hours (in total) pressing crackers into pie dishes. Let's face it — it's a crummy job!! This recipe, which is entirely my own invention, makes the task almost easy, providing you keep a small bowl of cold water handy to keep your fingers too moist to stick.

THE CRUST ITSELF: FAT OR FRUIT? - Where some amount of fat is absolutely essential, it can be a good idea to also raise the amount of dietary fiber since some fibers help to reduce the cholesterol increasing properties of some fats. We moved away from the classic butter and the alternative margarine until we arrived at the high fiber fig as a crust binder and the kiwi fruit as a garnish. The nutritional numbers changed and the taste improved.

## Unusual Ingredients

FIGS - The early Egyptians heralded figs as a health tonic. The ancient Greeks celebrated figs as an antidote for all ailments. The first olympic athletes wore figs as medals of honor ... well, you might not go that far, but figs are certainly worth a spot in your larder. Figs have the highest dietary fiber content of any common fruit, nut, or vegetable, along with a great deal of calcium and potassium. A great snack idea perhaps, but watch the calories.

KIWI FRUIT - Who would have guessed that inside that egg-shaped, brown, furry object would be such a brilliantly green and tangy fruit? A great garnish for cheesecake, a lovely color to add to your fruit salads, do try kiwis in many dishes. A ripe kiwi should be firm, just giving a little when squeezed. They are available year round, and will keep for months in your refrigerator.

EVAPORATED SKIM MILK - When humans first started drinking milk back in the dim recesses of civilization, the most common milk of all was mare's milk. "The Mongols," wrote Marco Polo, "are accustomed to drink every kind of milk," but though they had flocks of sheep and goats, it was mare's milk they preferred. (They used sheep's milk, disdainfully, to caulk their tents.)

If you balk slightly at the idea of mare's milk, evaporated skim milk must seem quite mundane. It is produced when cow's milk is evaporated in a vacuum to reduce its water content by 40 to 50 percent. You can get it sweetened or unsweetened. It has the consistency of cream.

# MORAVIAN CAKE

$\mathcal{S}$nacking cake: it raises all kinds of visions of hospitality. A great cup of coffee and a hunk of spicy cake! I replaced the classic lard with a good margarine. Other than that, the original was such good news I left it alone!

The cake is naturally moist but should be stored in a tightly lidded cake tin or a large sealable plastic bag. With a good cup of coffee you'll have all you need for your next get together ... have fun!

## Nutritional Profile

| PER SERVING | CLASSIC | MINIMAX |
|---|---|---|
| Calories | 438 | 400 |
| Fat (gm) | 9 | 6 |
| Calories From Fat | 19% | 13% |
| Cholesterol (mg) | 8 | 0 |
| Sodium (mg) | 201 | 235 |
| Fiber (gm) | 4 | 4 |

■ *Classic Compared – Milkless, Eggless, Butterless Cake*

## Time Estimate

| | | | | | | | | | |
|---|---|---|---|---|---|---|---|---|---|
| Hands On | | | | | | | | | |
| Unsupervised | | | | | | | | | |
| *Minutes* | 10 | 20 | 30 | 40 | 50 | 60 | 70 | 80 | 90 |

## Cost Estimate

| Low | Medium | Medium High | Celebration |
|---|---|---|---|

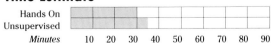

*Serves 8*

## INGREDIENTS

2 cups all-purpose flour (472 ml)

½ teaspoon baking powder (2.5 ml)

1 teaspoon baking soda (5 ml) combined with
1 tablespoon warm water (15 ml)

¼ cup sliced almonds (59 ml)

1 cup water (236 ml)

1 cup dark brown sugar (236 ml)

1½ cups seedless raisins (I prefer the "flame" variety) (354 ml)

⅓ cup margarine (78 ml)

1 teaspoon cinnamon* (5 ml)

⅓ teaspoon cloves* (1.7 ml)

¼ teaspoon nutmeg* (1.25 ml)

*If possible, freshly grind the spices. You can grind the cinnamon and cloves in a coffee grinder or a blender. You'll need 1 one inch (2.5 cm) stick of cinnamon and 6 cloves. The difference between these and the commercially ground produce is the fineness of the grind: I prefer roughly ground for this recipe.*

## NOW COOK

■ Preheat oven to 350°F (180°C).

■ In a large bowl, sift together the flour and baking powder. You now have self-rising flour! Make a well in the flour and stir in the baking soda mixture. Stir in the sliced almonds and set aside.

■ Pour the water into a high-sided saucepan on high heat. Mix in the brown sugar, raisins, margarine and spices. Bring to a boil.

■ Remove from the heat and pour into a bowl set in a larger bowl of ice water to cool the syrup.

■ Add the cooled, but still warm, syrup to the flour mixture all at once.

■ Pour the mixture into a 10 inch (25 cm) skillet and spread it evenly. Pop in the preheated oven and bake for 35 minutes or until the edges of the cake start to pull away from the sides of the pan. (Please be sure your skillet's handle is approved for 350°F (180°C) temperatures. Mine go up to 500°F (260°C) but be careful to drape a towel over it to remind yourself that it's hot!)

## Helpful Hints and Observations

GETTING A RISE WITHOUT AN EGG - If you are watching your egg yolk consumption, this cake is good news. It relies upon a combination of baking powder and baking soda for its texture. By adding the soda to the warm water and the powder to the flour, and then mixing them both together, you get the rise without the sometimes "metallic" soda taste. Of course, the spices also help to control this side effect.

BOILING THE SUGAR AND SPICE - Adding everything to cold water and then bringing it slowly to a boil really does help to infuse and combine all the flavors. You don't have to cool it quickly; it can be set aside to lose heat naturally. But if you are in the kind of hurry that faces me each day — the ice helps!

## Unusual Ingredients

FLAME RAISINS - Raisins are just dried grapes — and the most popular fruit in North America! The flame variety grape is a large, red grape that when dried, makes large, luscious raisins. I buy them in small plastic packages in the bulk food section of the supermarket. If you haven't seen them in your part of the world, ask the produce manager at your grocery to get them for you - they do listen! In a tightly closed container, kept in a cool place, raisins should last up to a year.

CLOVES - If you're strolling in Zanzibar (or even the Moluccas) one day, and note a tall, evergreen tree with smooth gray bark, and if you climb to the tip of one of its  branches to get a closer look at the buds of its purple-crimson flowers, you will be looking at the beginning of cloves. I say the beginning because the flower buds are picked and then dried to bring cloves to your kitchen.

# TADMILL MERINGUE GATEAU

$\mathcal{W}$hen one of my guests from the television studio
audience tasted this dish, she said, "I saw you make
it, but I can't believe it tastes so good!" Truly, the
original dessert from the Frogmill Inn was a luxuri-
ous-tasting confection: heaped full of whipped
French custard and drenched in creme de cacao
liqueur. But just as truly, this Minimax version has
its own moments of luxury.

Any meringue monster like this must really come
straight from the oven to the table. You can beat the
meringue itself in less than 5 minutes, so it's not too
much of a mid-dinner problem, providing everything
else is done ahead of time.

## Nutritional Profile

| PER SERVING | CLASSIC | MINIMAX |
|---|---|---|
| Calories | 427 | 215 |
| Fat (gm) | 11 | 2 |
| Calories From Fat | 24% | 10% |
| Cholesterol (mg) | 225 | 86 |
| Sodium (mg) | 162 | 126 |
| Fiber (gm) | 1 | 0.3 |

■ *Classic Compared – Frogmill Meringue Gateau*

## Time Estimate

| Hands On Unsupervised | | | | | | | | | |
|---|---|---|---|---|---|---|---|---|---|
| Minutes | 10 | 20 | 30 | 40 | 50 | 60 | 70 | 80 | 90 |

## Cost Estimate

| | | | |
|---|---|---|---|
| Low | Medium | Medium High | Celebration |

*Serves 10*

## INGREDIENTS

SPONGE CAKE

4 eggs
½ cup sugar (118 ml)
½ cup all-purpose flour (118 ml)
Pinch of freshly ground salt

PASTRY CREAM

1 cup strained yogurt (236 ml) (recipe page 210)
2 egg whites, beaten
2 tablespoons maple syrup (30 ml)
½ teaspoon almond extract (2.5 ml)
½ tablespoon slivered almonds (8 ml)

MERINGUE

5 egg whites
1 cup sugar (236 ml)
¼ teaspoon almond extract (1.25 ml)
Pinch of freshly ground salt

SAUCE

2 tablespoons maple syrup (30 ml)
2 tablespoons unsweetened cocoa powder (30 ml)
1 tablespoon water (15 ml)

## FIRST PREPARE

■  The Sponge Cake:  Preheat the oven to 375°F (190°C).  In a medium mixing bowl placed over a saucepan containing lukewarm water, beat together the eggs and sugar until slightly thickened and light yellow in color.  Fold in the flour and salt, gently and slowly, until it is incorporated.  Do not overbeat.

Pour the batter into a greased and floured 9 inch (23 cm) cake pan.  Tap the batter-filled pan on a hard surface to pop any air bubbles.  Bake in the preheated oven for 25 minutes, or until a toothpick inserted in the center comes out clean.

When the cake is done, let it rest 5 minutes, then remove it from the pan and cool on a rack.

When the cake is completely cool, cut it horizontally into 2 layers.

■  The Pastry Cream:  Mix the strained yogurt, egg whites, maple syrup, almond extract and almonds together.

■  The Meringue:  Make sure your bowl and beater are free of any fat residue of any kind or your egg whites will not stiffen properly.

Beat the egg whites, adding a pinch of salt and a drop of water.  This will enhance the stiffening process.  Start at a low speed and gradually increase to a higher speed.  This will keep lightness in the finished meringue.  Slowly stir in the sugar and almond extract.  Beat until very stiff, or the meringue just holds to an upside down spoon.  Be careful here because you can overbeat.

■  The Sauce:  In a small saucepan over medium heat, stir together the maple syrup, cocoa powder and water.

## NOW ASSEMBLE

■  Place the bottom layer of the sponge cake on an oven-proof serving plate.  Drizzle the cocoa sauce on top and let it soak in.

■  Spoon the pastry cream over the soaked sponge cake layer.  Gently cover it with the other cake layer.  Spoon the meringue over the top, spreading it completely down the sides.  Make a nice design by dabbing the meringue with the back of a spoon to form small, graceful peaks.

■  Pop the completed meringue into a 500°F (260°C) oven for just 2 minutes, until toasted just golden brown.

### Helpful Hints and Observations

A REVOLUTIONARY DESSERT - Every step in this recipe is a major change from the original.  Just one glance at the nutritional analysis will give you the idea.

I'm always sorry that restaurants don't try harder to make more desserts that are both visual celebrations and responsible offerings.  If you like this recipe, why not make a copy and deliver it to your favorite establishment?  Who knows ... we could start a revolution together!

### Unusual Ingredients

EGG WHITES - What is this substance that transforms into glorious meringue?  Mostly protein and water.  Kept in a covered container and refrigerated, egg whites can be stored for about 4 days, or frozen for up to 6 months.  (I can't think why you'd want to freeze egg whites, but there you go!)  What about the leftover yolks?  I recommend giving them to the pet dog.  Dogs don't seem to have the same cholesterol problem as humans.

COCOA POWDER - See Unusual Ingredients, page 189.

# CHAMPORODI GUAVA

*This is a triumph of mind over coconut matter, possibly the most delicious milk pudding in the entire world. I invented it as a creative alternative to the classic coconut and chocolate chip rice dish that is a breakfast favorite in the Philippines.*

## Nutritional Profile

| PER SERVING | CLASSIC | MINIMAX |
|---|---|---|
| Calories | 433 | 235 |
| Fat (gm) | 31 | .2 |
| Calories From Fat | 64% | 1% |
| Cholesterol (mg) | 9 | 1 |
| Sodium (mg) | 318 | 21 |
| Fiber (gm) | 2 | 1 |

■ *Classic Compared – Champorodi*

## Time Estimate

| | | | | | | | | |
|---|---|---|---|---|---|---|---|---|
Hands On
Unsupervised
*Minutes*  10  20  30  40  50  60  70  80  90

## Cost Estimate

| Low | Medium | Medium High | Celebration |
|---|---|---|---|

*Serves 4*

## INGREDIENTS

1 whole fresh coconut
2 ½ cups skim milk (590 ml)
1 cup uncooked short grain Pearl rice (236 ml)
1 tablespoon brown sugar (15 ml)

SAUCE
1 (12 ounce) can Guava nectar (340 gm)
1 tablespoon arrowroot (15 ml) mixed with
1 tablespoon water (15 ml)

## FIRST PREPARE

■ Pierce the eyes of the coconut with a skewer and drain, saving the coconut juice. Bake the emptied coconut in a 400°F (205°C) oven for 20 minutes. This makes it easy to peel away the outer husk and the inner skin. Hit the coconut firmly with a hammer or mallet to crack it. Remove the coconut meat from the shell and peel off the inner skin. Place the coconut meat in a food processor and process until shredded.

## NOW COOK

■ Combine 2 cups (472 ml) of the skim milk, reserved coconut juice and shredded coconut in a saucepan. Bring to a boil, then remove from the heat and allow the flavor to infuse for 20 minutes. Strain the infusion through muslin, squeezing out every last drop. Discard the fiber and cool the liquid until the heavier coconut "cream" floats to the surface. Put the rice in a baking dish. Remove ½ cup (118 ml) of the top surface coconut cream and set aside. Replace the cream with ½ cup (118 ml) skim milk, and pour this over the rice. Cover and bake at 350°F (180°C) for 40 minutes.

■ The Sauce: In a saucepan, bring guava nectar to a boil and reduce by half. Remove the saucepan from the heat, stir in the arrowroot paste, return to the heat and stir until thickened. Set aside. When the rice has finished baking, stir in the brown sugar and the reserved coconut cream.

■ Champorodi Guava can be served hot from the oven or chilled in small molds. To chill, fill 4 small (4 ounce or 113 ml) molds or timbales with the baked rice and set in the refrigerator to cool and set. Hot or cold, coat the servings with pink guava sauce — it is wonderfully delicious.

## Helpful Hints and Observations

COCONUT MILK - I must admit to being a coconut devotee. Now, how can this be, since most of us are clearly aware that this hairy masterpiece is actually crawling with saturated fat? It could actually be less dangerous to be hit by one than to eat it! Truthfully, the oil is highly saturated but that doesn't mean that the milk/cream is too - especially when we prepare it ourselves and it's used with moderation. Just glance at the nutrition analysis for a moment and you'll see that our dessert has only .2 grams of fat for each serving — only 1 percent of the total calories from fat. At that rate, the saturated nature of the fat doesn't really matter. So, coconut lovers of the world, take heart - by the time you've labored to remove the flesh you'll probably have worked off the calories!

SKIM MILK - There is a constant problem when heating any skim milk ... it catches easily and can burn before it boils. This is because there is no fat to grease the pan and protect the milk proteins. So? Well, watch it when bringing skim milk to the boil. Use a non-stick pan, a low to medium heat, and keep stirring from time to time with a flat ended spurtle or spatula.

## Unusual Ingredients

GUAVA NECTAR - The sweet juice from the small, fragrant, tropical guava. Originally from Mexico and Central America, guava is now harvested in New Zealand, Florida, Hawaii and South America. Guavas are about 4 inches (10 cm) long and oval shaped; they have a skin that turns from green to yellow; the flesh can be white, pink or red. Select guavas that are firm but slightly soft to the touch. Canned guava nectar is available at most supermarkets.

COCONUTS - One of the world's oldest food plants. Originating in Polynesia and southern Asia, there are over 29 billion nuts produced each year. Coconuts are in season between October and December; available year round on a limited basis. Don't be afraid to shake them while shopping. They should be full of juice and feel heavy.

# CAPIROTADA

*It's hard to believe that green peppers and onions can be part of a dessert, but here is a classic - this time served up without its incredibly high sugar content. This Mexican dish is often served during Lent, but frankly it doesn't seem to represent sacrifice! It has a wonderfully complex taste that doesn't need any whipped cream or ice cream or custard. I've added a very sharp non-fat yogurt sauce that balances well with the sweet bread pudding - you'll only need a wee drop!*

*Although every nation has its own bread pudding recipe, this one definitely takes the prize for tasteful originality. Nothing other than the sharp side sauce is needed, but you could use bright Mexican-style dishes for serving.*

## Nutritional Profile

| PER SERVING | CLASSIC | MINIMAX |
|---|---|---|
| Calories | 822 | 314 |
| Fat (gm) | 25 | 8 |
| Calories From Fat | 27% | 23% |
| Cholesterol (mg) | 37 | 3 |
| Sodium (mg) | 735 | 90 |
| Fiber (gm) | 8 | 4 |

■ *Classic Compared – Capirotada*

## Time Estimate

| Hands On | | | | | | | | |
|---|---|---|---|---|---|---|---|---|
| Unsupervised | | | | | | | | |

*Minutes*  10  20  30  40  50  60  70  80  90

## Cost Estimate

| Low | Medium | Medium High | Celebration |
|---|---|---|---|

*Serves 8*

## INGREDIENTS

PUDDING

1 cup low-fat cottage cheese (236 ml) (use lowest fat content available, but do not use "no-fat" cottage cheese)

¾ cup Minimax Seed Mixture (177 ml) (see Unusual Ingredients), coarsely cracked in an electric coffee grinder

1 cup raisins (236 ml)

2 apples (Rome apples are preferred when available)

2 lemon wedges

1 small uncut loaf of whole wheat bread

1 medium tomato, sliced

SYRUP

¼ cup seeded and chopped green pepper (59 ml)

¼ cup chopped onion (59 ml)

½ cup fresh chopped cilantro (118 ml)

½ teaspoon grated orange peel (2.5 ml)

½ teaspoon grated cinnamon stick (2.5 ml)

4 cups water (944 ml)

1 cup brown sugar (236 ml)

3 whole cloves

LEMON YOGURT SAUCE

Juice and grated rind of 1 lemon

2 cups non-fat plain yogurt (472 ml)

Honey to taste

## FIRST PREPARE THE PUDDING INGREDIENTS

■ Mix the cottage cheese, ½ cup (118 ml) of the seed mixture and raisins. Set aside.

■ Wash, core and thinly slice the apples. Put them into cold water with the lemon wedges to prevent browning.

■ Cut the bread into ½ inch (1.5 cm) cubes and toast 10 minutes in 350°F (180°C) oven.

## NOW COOK

■ Put all the ingredients for the syrup in a saucepan and cook for 30 minutes. Strain.

■ Layer half the bread cubes, cottage cheese mixture and apples in an 8 cup (1.8 liter) baking dish, finishing with a layer of bread. Scatter the tomatoes and remaining seed mix on top.

■ Carefully pour the syrup over the Capirotada. Let the bread cubes soak up syrup from underneath. Don't drown them from the top.

■ Bake at 350°F (180°C) for 1 hour. The Capirotada should be crisp on top, bubbling around the edges.

■ Combine the ingredients for the lemon yogurt sauce and serve it on the side! Wait until your taste buds have a go at it! It's a marvelous thing when a nuance of green pepper comes through!

## Helpful Hints and Observations

TEXTURE - This seems as good an opportunity as I will get to tell you about the importance of texture in an overall "soft" dish like this. Think for a moment about your breakfast cereal choices: is crispness a factor for you? Do you like potato chips that crunch? This is texture at work in harmony with its sound as you chew! I've added seeds and nuts to this dish not to get a crackle going but to give some sharp, pointed relief to the otherwise plain "landscape"! The seeds and nuts are only just broken by the small grinder. This allows for both texture and better assimilation of their nutrients. If left whole, they could whistle straight through without so much as passing the time of day with your ileum (small intestine).

ADDING THE SYRUP - You will note I've cautioned you to add the syrup so that the bread soaks it up from below. This is done to help the surface to crisp without burning and becoming caramelized.

## Unusual Ingredients

MINIMAX SEED MIX - A very nutritious way of adding crunch to a meal. It's quite tasty and high in protein. Combine equal measures of sunflower seeds, unhulled sesame seeds, green pumpkin seeds and flaked almonds. Combine with half measure of flax seeds. Seeds and nuts can be purchased in a variety of packages and a variety of processing. The more processed, the higher the price and lower the nutritional value. Choose nuts and seeds that are firm and smooth. If they are in the shell they should be heavy for their size, indicating a meatier nut. Always avoid nuts and seeds with mold, even if it seems the mold wipes away easily. Because nuts and seeds have a high oil content, light will turn them rancid. To avoid this, store in tightly covered dark glass or plastic jars.

GREEN PEPPERS - Wonderfully versatile and a great source of Vitamin C, Potassium and Calcium. Select firm, smooth-skinned peppers.

# CREPES SUZETTE TAKE II

The original Crepes Suzette was made as a prop in a Paris stage show. I have always believed it to be "No, No, Nanette," but I haven't been able to confirm this ...

I named this version "Take II," because of its obvious changes. It will, none the less, win you a standing ovation!

You can make the crepes before dinner and cover them with a towel. You can also make the sauce and then add the crepes to warm up and finish - a classic dessert without fuss!

## Nutritional Profile

| PER SERVING | CLASSIC | MINIMAX |
|---|---|---|
| Calories | 475 | 331 |
| Fat (gm) | 26 | 7 |
| Calories From Fat | 49% | 18% |
| Cholesterol (mg) | 260 | 111 |
| Sodium (mg) | 161 | 63 |
| Fiber (gm) | 1 | 4 |

■ *Classic Compared – Crepes Suzette*

## Time Estimate

| Hands On Unsupervised | | | | | | | | | |
|---|---|---|---|---|---|---|---|---|---|
| *Minutes* | 10 | 20 | 30 | 40 | 50 | 60 | 70 | 80 | 90 |

## Cost Estimate

| Low | Medium | Medium High | Celebration |
|---|---|---|---|

*Serves 4*

## INGREDIENTS

CREPE BATTER

1 whole egg

1 egg yolk

1 cup 2% milk (236 ml)

1 cup all-purpose flour (236 ml)

½ teaspoon vanilla (2.5 ml)

Grated rind of 1 lemon

1 teaspoon extra light olive oil with a dash of sesame oil (5 ml)

THE SYRUP

1 teaspoon extra light olive oil with a dash of sesame oil (5 ml)

1 tablespoon orange zest (15 ml)

½ cup de-alcoholized white wine (118 ml)

1 cup freshly squeezed orange juice (236 ml)

2 tablespoons freshly squeezed lemon juice (30 ml)

2 tablespoons brown sugar (30 ml)

1 tablespoon cornstarch (15 ml) mixed with 2 tablespoons strained yogurt (30 ml) (recipe page 210)

4 oranges, divided into segments

1 teaspoon fresh chopped mint (5 ml)

## FIRST PREPARE

■ The Crepe Batter: In a small bowl, mix the egg, egg yolk and milk. In another bowl, sift the flour and make a well in the center. Pour the egg mixture into the well and gradually stir together until the flour is fully incorporated. Add the vanilla and the grated lemon rind. Set aside in a cool place and let rest for 30 minutes.

## NOW COOK

■ The Crepes: Heat the oil in an 8 inch (20 cm) saute pan, then pour it into the crepe batter. This makes the crepes self-releasing. Pour ¼ cup (59 ml) of the batter into the pan and swirl to make a round thin crepe. Toss so that the crepe becomes slightly brown - approximately 1 minute on each side. Place the cooked crepes on a plate and set aside, covered with a damp towel.

■ The Syrup: Heat the oil in a 10 inch (25 cm) skillet. Add the orange zest and cook to extract the volatile oils - about 2 minutes. Add the wine and reduce until it is like a syrup, dark in color but not burnt.

■ Add ¼ cup (59 ml) of the orange juice, 1 tablespoon (15 ml) at a time to keep the dark color. Slowly add the remaining orange juice, the lemon juice and brown sugar. Stir until dissolved.

■ Strain the syrup, removing the zest. Return the syrup to the skillet. Slowly stir in the corn-starch paste. Bring to a boil and stir until the syrup is well combined and slightly thickened.

■ Place one cooked crepe into the syrup and coat well. Using a spoon and fork, fold the crepe in half and in half again, so the crepe is now in the shape of a triangle. Move the triangle crepe to the side of the pan. Repeat the coating and folding process with the rest of the crepes. Spoon the segmented oranges and the mint into the syrup with the crepes.

■ To Serve: Place the crepes on a warm plate and spoon the orange segments with syrup over the top.

## Unusual Ingredients

ORANGES AND LEMONS - Such a common commodity in our produce aisle, we forget the intensity that citrus fruits can add to our cooking. Low in calories, high in Vitamin C, fresh and sweet, try experimenting with orange and lemon juice in other dishes (Scallops and Shrimp Vincent is a good example, see page 46). All citrus fruits are ripened on the tree and ready to eat when you see them in the grocery. Select citrus fruit with firm, thin skin, that feel heavy in your hand.

# TRIFLE WITH CRYSTALLIZED VIOLETS

*This is no "mere trifle": it is actually one of the best known of English desserts. Even the Italians call it Zuppa Inglese, or English Soup - doubtless because of the addition of sherry in the classic version.*

*I made this dessert as one large bowl-full for at least 6 people. You may wish to assemble it and fill several small dessert cups.*

*Your guests will never miss the traditional whipped cream when you dazzle them with crystallized violets scattered enchantingly over the top. You can find these in many cooking stores, or make your own!*

## Nutritional Profile

| PER SERVING | CLASSIC | MINIMAX |
|---|---|---|
| Calories | 634 | 434 |
| Fat (gm) | 21 | 4 |
| Calories From Fat | 30% | 9% |
| Cholesterol (mg) | 196 | 143 |
| Sodium (mg) | 202 | 119 |
| Fiber (gm) | 9 | 6 |

■ *Classic Compared – Trifle*

## Time Estimate

| Hands On | | | | | | | | | |
|---|---|---|---|---|---|---|---|---|---|
| Unsupervised | | | | 2 Hours | | | | | |
| Minutes | 10 | 20 | 30 | 40 | 50 | 60 | 70 | 80 | 90 |

## Cost Estimate

| | | | |
|---|---|---|---|
| Low | Medium | Medium High | Celebration |

*Serves 6*

## INGREDIENTS

SPONGE CAKE

4 eggs

¾ cup sugar (177 ml)

1 cup all-purpose flour (236 ml), sifted

JELLY

4 cups fresh raspberries (944 ml) (or frozen
berries with no added sugar or syrup)

3 cups cold water (708 ml)

2 tablespoons brown sugar (30 ml)

2 packages unflavored gelatin softened in ½ cup
water (118 ml) for 5 minutes

CUSTARD

2 cups non-fat milk (472 ml)

1 vanilla bean (or 1 teaspoon (5 ml) vanilla extract)

2 tablespoons cornstarch (30 ml)

2 tablespoons liquid egg substitute (30 ml)

3 tablespoons honey (45 ml) Fireweed Honey if
possible

2 packages unflavored gelatin softened in ½ cup
water (118 ml) for 5 minutes

## FOR THE SPONGE CAKE

■ Beat the eggs and sugar together in a large
bowl over warm water until the volume has
doubled. Stir in the flour until fully incorporated.
Pour into a greased and floured 9 inch (23 cm)
cake pan. Tap the pan on the counter to release
any trapped bubbles. Bake in a pre-heated 375°F
(190°C) oven for 25 minutes. Turn out to cool on
a rack, then cut into 1 inch (2.5 cm) cubes.

## FOR THE JELLY

■ In a medium saucepan combine 3 cups (708 ml)
of the raspberries with the water and brown sugar.
Heat to a boil. Pour the contents through a sieve,
catching the raspberry liquid in a bowl. Now
capture the last essence of raspberry flavor by
gently pressing the raspberries in the sieve to
extract the juice. BE GENTLE. You don't want
seeds in the raspberry juice. While the juice is
still warm, stir in the softened gelatin mixture.

■ Put the sponge cake pieces and the remaining
cup (236 ml) of raspberries into your best clear
bowl and cover with the warm raspberry juice.
Press the sponge cake into the juice so that each
piece is soaked. Put a plate on top to keep the cake
submerged in the juice. Pop this into the refrigerator to cool and set.

## FOR THE CUSTARD

■ In a large saucepan, heat the non-fat milk and
the vanilla bean pod (or vanilla extract). Bring
the heat up and scald the milk.

■ In a small bowl, whisk together the egg substitute, honey and cornstarch. Tip this mixture into
the scalded milk, bring just to a boil and stir until
thickened. Add the softened gelatin to the custard.
This gives it more "holding power." Let it cool.

## TO ASSEMBLE THE TRIFLE

■ Take the cooled sponge cake out of the
refrigerator. Pour the custard on top. Cover with
plastic wrap and pop the trifle back into the
refrigerator until set, approximately 30 minutes.

## Helpful Hints and Observations

CRYSTALLIZED VIOLETS

½ cup superfine sugar (118 ml)

4 drops peppermint extract

2 egg whites

Large fresh violet blossoms: about 20 blossoms

Very small clean paint brush

Preheat the oven to 180°F (82°C), and line a
baking sheet with foil. In a small bowl, rub the
sugar and peppermint together with your thumb
and forefinger. Whip the egg whites to stiff peaks.
Paint each violet on both sides with a thin layer
of egg white.

Dip the painted violets into the bowl of sugar
and place them carefully on the lined baking sheet.
When all the violets are painted, place them in
the pre-heated oven for 1 hour. Leave the door
slightly ajar to prevent any accumulation of
moisture. Remove carefully and cool completely
before using. Store the crystallized violets in an
airtight jar in a cool, dry place.

## Unusual Ingredients

VANILLA BEANS - These "beans" are actually the
pod fruit of a vine that is a member of the orchid
family. They are native to Central America and
used by the Aztecs in drink and food. There are
three grades of vanilla: fine, woody and vanillons.
Fine vanilla beans are very black and eight to ten
inches long (20 to 25 cm). Often, fine vanilla will
have small crystals of sugar; they are actually
drops of vanilline and are a sign of highest quality.
Vanilla beans can be used up to ten times. After
each use, place a notch in one side and keep
buried in a jar of sugar.

# STOCKS & STANDARDS

## BEEF OR VEAL STOCK

1 pound defatted beef or veal bones (450 gm)

1 teaspoon extra light olive oil with a dash of sesame oil (5 ml)

1 onion, chopped

½ cup celery tops (118 ml)

1 cup chopped carrots (236 ml)

1 bay leaf

2 sprigs thyme

4 sprigs parsley

6 peppercorns

2 cloves

■ Preheat the oven to 375°F (190°C).

■ Place the beef or veal bones in a roasting pan and cook for 25 minutes or until nicely browned. This produces a richer flavor and deeper color.

■ Saute the vegetables in the olive oil, add the bones and the rest of the ingredients. Now add enough water to cover the ingredients completely. Maintain this water level by adding more as needed.

■ Bring to a boil, removing any foam which rises.

■ Lower heat and simmer 8-10 hours.

■ Strain. Set the amount necessary for this recipe aside and refrigerate or freeze the remaining portion.

## CHICKEN OR TURKEY STOCK

1 pound chicken or turkey bones (450 gm)

1 teaspoon extra light olive oil with a dash of sesame oil (5 ml)

1 onion, chopped

½ cup celery tops (118 ml)

1 cup chopped carrots (236 ml)

1 bay leaf

2 sprigs thyme

4 sprigs parsley

6 peppercorns

2 cloves

■ Saute the vegetables in olive oil to release their flavor.

■ Add the chicken or turkey bones to cover with water.

■ Add seasonings and bring to a boil, removing any foam which rises.

■ Lower heat and simmer 4-5 hours.

■ Strain. Set the amount necessary for this recipe aside and refrigerate or freeze the remaining portion.

## FISH OR SHRIMP STOCK

1 pound fish bones (no heads) or shrimp shells (450 gm)

1 teaspoon extra light olive oil with a dash of sesame oil (5 ml)

1 onion, chopped

½ cup celery tops (118 ml)

2 sprigs thyme

1 bay leaf

6 peppercorns

2 cloves

■ Gently fry the onion, celery, thyme and bay leaf. Cook until onions are translucent and flavors are released, being careful not to brown. This will ensure a light colored stock.

■ Add the fish bones or shrimp shells and cover with water.

■ Add peppercorns and cloves.

■ Bring to a boil, then simmer for 25 minutes.

■ Strain through a fine mesh sieve. This will keep up to a week in the refrigerator and 6 months in the freezer.

## STRAINED YOGURT

■ Put plain, non-fat yogurt (with no gelatin added) into a coffee filter, within a strainer.

■ Place the strainer over a bowl and let stand 5 hours or refrigerate overnight. The whey drains out, leaving you with a thick, creamy yogurt cheese - an invaluable ingredient for many recipes!

## BOUQUET GARNI

■ To make a bouquet garni, cut a 4 inch (10 cm) square piece of muslin or cheesecloth, put the ingredients in the center and tie the four corners securely to form a tight pouch. Hit the bouquet garni several times with a mallet or the back of a knife to bruise the herbs and spices, helping them release their volatile oils.

# Index